# Interviewing in educational research

**Routledge Education Books**

Advisory editor: John Eggleston
Professor of Education
University of Warwick

# Interviewing in educational research

Janet Powney
*and*
Mike Watts

**Routledge & Kegan Paul**
London

First published in 1987 by
Routledge & Kegan Paul Ltd
11 New Fetter Lane, London EC4P 4EE

Set in 10/11 Monophoto Times
and printed in Great Britain
by Butler & Tanner Ltd
Frome and London

© *Janet Powney and Mike Watts 1987*

*British Library Cataloguing in Publication Data*

*Interviewing in educational research*
  *(Routledge educational books)*
  *1. Education—Research   2. Interviewing*
  *I. Powney, Janet*
  *370'.7'83     LB1028*

*ISBN 0–7102–0623–2 (p)*

# Contents

# Preface

This book is based on the belief that 'the interview' is not just another data collecting method. There seems to be a temptation to think of interviews rather like thermometers – they can be conveniently inserted almost anywhere within the body of the research and simply read off to provide a series of trustworthy observations. Continuing this analogy, there seems to be an assumption that there is a fairly high correlation between those observations and the general state of the research, so that the act of data collection ceases to be of interest and therefore ceases to be discussed and debated. That is, people's interview responses are unproblematic, they represent firm data, and the interview method can be used to directly determine the state of the interviewee(s) without undue worry. Furthermore, the mechanics of operation are so straightforward that the tyro can easily be tutored or can operate competently self-taught.

Interviews, necessarily of course, involve people talking and listening to people. People are delightfully varied in their abilities and willingness to talk, or listen, to provide accurate information, abide by what they have previously said or thought, said they thought or thought they said. The research interview, then, is a very particular kind of data collection method and deserves due caution and expertise in use.

We see research interviews as conversational encounters to a purpose. We have chosen to see that purpose extending in time well before – and certainly well after the actual encounter, so that the interview session itself is seen as only one facet of the whole process of interviewing. Other aspects consist of planning, organisation, recording, transcribing, analysis and reporting. We have attempted to focus on each of these in turn and to consider both the formalised and the pragmatic issues involved. To assist us in retaining pragmatism, and to illustrate some of that variety of context and richness

*Preface*

of detail, we have recruited six colleagues to present case studies of their work. They have written to a fairly loose brief and have tried to do the impossible – to give enough background information to make their interview style meaningful, to give enough detail of actual practice to make their procedures clear, and to stay within 2,000 words. The cases represent a cross-section of approaches and educational settings. We have used them liberally throughout as both exemplars and cockshies in order to highlight the many complexities involved.

Our intention has been to write a cross between a 'user's guide' and a 'reader'. We hope there is enough guide to be useful to a range of users, and enough reader to tackle some of the more taxing concerns. We continue to conduct educational research and to sharpen our interest and own practice in interviewing. In setting out recommendations for others it is always a salutary exercise to re-examine one's personal performance, note disparities, indiscretions and rank failures, and to develop remedies. Interviewing, as a systematic art, needs constant practice and appraisal.

We would acknowledge our debts to those with whom we have worked. We are grateful to our six contributors for their efforts and hope they approve of the final product. We owe much to the comments made by colleagues at various conferences and seminars when we have tried out our ideas. We thank our respective households for their support and patience in encouraging us to make time to meet, talk and write. We are indebted to our colleagues at work for their tolerance of our preoccupation with interviewing. We thank, too, Hilda Hirst for her diligent transcribing and Sylvia Barnes for her rapid and careful typing.

# Chapter 1

# Setting the scene

## Introduction

This book is about interviewing as a recognised method of gathering information in the social sciences – within which we include the study of education and educational research. We shall not be referring to other uses of interviews, for example for selection or diagnosis, although many of the skills used in that kind of interviewing often have general application.

Within the book we try to present a mixture of discussion and practical advice. Much of the discussion concerns ways of categorising interviews, issues of ethics and morals, and theoretical implications of various approaches. The practical advice stems from our own numerous efforts to conduct interviews, and the good advice we have received from colleagues as they have done the same. We highlight some of these in a series of case studies.

Throughout, we try to promote interviewing as a cyclic and interactive process although, for the sake of clarity, we have dealt with the various aspects in separate chapters. We have a strong sense of not wanting the book to be too linear, so that the reader might start with our case study examples, the theoretical discussions or the more practical chapters. Some of these chapters are intended to be reasonably free standing. Even within chapters we move between the discursive and pragmatic, between practice and theory, in our attempts to emphasise their interdependence. We discuss the interviewing process in some fine detail and examine a wide variety of approaches since each feature – from defining the research project to the evaluation of the interview reports – has pros and cons. We have tried, where possible, to present each approach with some advantages and disadvantages so that readers can 'shop' for appropriate methods for their own research tasks.

However, the other aspect of the book is to illustrate the common features of interviewing. The most important is that of establishing the research framework. Sometimes this follows a traditional format of setting out hypotheses and testing these by collecting data. Conversely, it might be a more flexible framework where broad questions are defined and tentative hypotheses grow from data. In our view, all interviews must be considered and conducted against some theoretical framework, whether this is a traditional or more loosely framed exercise. Other parts of the interviewing process should then follow consistently. Identifying and approaching interviewees, and obtaining, analysing and reporting their comments and answers, should be congruent with the underlying principles of the research.

## The changing use of interviewing in educational research

Interviewing in educational research merits further study, partly because of the considerable growth in educational research during the past few years and partly because of the general lack of attention given to interviewing as a method. Although the development of interviewing owes much to large-scale survey research, with its quantitative emphasis, changes in educational research have made interviewing a widely used research tool. Two of the most important of these changes have been in the use of more varied methods and in the tremendous increase in small-scale educational research.

Research has no status unless the methods and findings are open to public scrutiny and debate. If interviewing is to be treated as a serious research method, it must be conducted and reported as rigorously as any other method. This is not to say that all interviews have to follow an exact and predetermined format designed to glean respondents' knowledge, attitudes or beliefs. We will demonstrate very different, but quite valid interpretations of what it means to interview. Interviewing is a particularly useful way to gather people's views as one formulates research hypotheses. Piaget says that the interviewer is normally setting up hypotheses during the interview: before, during, and after, these are equally legitimate provided all relevant circumstances are made explicit and available for scrutiny by fellow professionals and others – like the interviewees, for example.

Regrettably, many established educational research studies have paid little attention to the preparation, conduct and reporting of interviews and might even be called into question for this cavalier approach. Our aim is to encourage a more rigorous approach to interviewing in educational research.

2

*Definition of educational research*

The systematic, empirical and critical inquiry into matters which directly or indirectly concern the learning and teaching of children and adults.

This is the definition of educational research we are using in this book. It is empirical in the sense of being observed reality, whether that reality is an experimentally contrived or controlled one, or whether it is careful observation of some aspect of people's everyday experience. The inquiry is not random, but systematically related to hypotheses or propositions being held and developed by the researcher or derived from the empirical data assembled. In natural science and in normative methods in the social sciences, observations confirm or reject previously stated hypotheses. Inductive reasoning used in interpretive approaches in the social sciences allows propositions or hypotheses to emerge from careful observations. These hypotheses can be subsequently considered in the light of further observation or even re-examination of the research data.

*Changing perceptions of what is 'research'*

Interpretive approaches have been important with the growth in the number of small-scale educational research studies. The newer element in small-scale studies is practitioners having the 'temerity' to investigate their own actions. Disenchanted with the lack of applicability of most formal educational research to the day-to-day problems of the classroom (Bassey 1981), teachers are making systematic inquiries into their own practice with a view to improving it. This movement owes much to the pioneering work of Lawrence Stenhouse and colleagues at the Centre of Applied Research in Education, work that has been gradually developed by teacher training institutions especially in the public sector. School-focused in-service courses such as the B.Ed. and M.Ed., established as long ago as 1973 and 1975 respectively at North East London Polytechnic, and in many other institutions since, require teachers to examine their own practices. When these early courses were validated by the Council for National Academic Awards, the validation panels discouraged the use of the word 'research' for such inquiries. Nowadays, teachers as researchers are commonplace and can provide a reasonably sized readership for up to-date research handbooks for teachers doing research (see Walker 1985; Nixon 1981). Moreover, the movement has stimulated such diverse activities that Wilf Carr (1985) has sufficient material to attempt distinctions between different kinds of school-based, action research, most of it carried out by teachers. Correspondingly, there has been an increase in the use of qualitative methods in which interviewing is a major component. Needless to say, interviewing as part of an action research programme has its problems. These are explored in the chapter on theoretical issues – especially in relation to working with a peer group and also in a situation where the interviewer is well known to the interviewee(s) and relationships continue after the interview.

## Critiques of interviewing

Increased use of interviewing should have led to more critical appraisal of, and improvements in, methodology. In the UK, since the 1950s, survey research has been regarded as increasingly useful in assisting social policy, such as describing and explaining social conditions. Interviewing has been a key tool in this development. Hoinville, however, (1983) suggests that the way projects have been funded has generally discouraged methodological investigation into the survey process. Financial support has concentrated instead on the instruments of measurement. The areas that have been investigated are those likely to appeal to statistical analyses, such as interviewer bias, interviewer error, interviewer variability. The trend has been towards improving standardisation.

Similarly, methodological critiques of interviewing are difficult to find in the educational literature, whereas abstracts on quantitative approaches such as sampling and statistical analyses are common in the British Education Index. For example, of all the critiques of *15,000 Hours* (Rutter *et al.* 1979) published by the University of Exeter (Wragg 1979) and the University of London (Tizard *et al.* 1980), only the one in the latter by Michael Young comments on interviewing. Rutter and his team collected complementary data from their own observations and from questionnaires, but interviewing provided a useful and sometimes necessary contribution to the study, especially to the section on school processes. Unfortunately, the information about the interviews is very limited. There is no interview schedule or list of topics for any group being interviewed, although it is usually possible to glean the gist of the interview from working carefully through the presentation of results. (In contrast the full questionnaire is included as an appendix.) Nor is there any indication of the techniques used by the interviewers or how the data was recorded and subsequently analysed. Three researchers conducted the interviews, but the book ignores details of their previous interviewing experience, how they collaborated on the project, and what each of them told the interviewees about the research. It was apparent that the research team did not see interviewing as problematic, although there were questions on decision making, joint planning and professionalism – for example, questions about a teacher's punctuality could be regarded as a sensitive issue. The Rutter study is only one of the many important educational research projects we could have chosen to illustrate gaps characteristic of reports of research using interviews. We suggest that a less casual approach to reporting interviewing is necessary.

## Some general approaches to interviewing

Interviewing has many styles. Many factors influence the style to be used, or indeed, whether interviewing is the most appropriate source of data collection. In Chapter 2 we attempt a simple typology based on the interviewer–interviewee relationship. We also consider definitions of interviews as special kinds of conversations.

Individual interviews, using closely structured questionnaires, persist as a means of collecting information about people's knowledge, beliefs and attitudes. Questionnaires are not the only practical framework. Sufficient interesting alternatives now exist to encourage the educational researcher to choose the most appropriate form of interviewing. Each method has its own assumptions. Consider an interview where the respondent is limited to answering questions posed by the interviewer. Contrast the assumptions behind this with an ethnographic situation, which blurs the roles of researcher and participant, interviewer and respondent. 'Interviewees' inform the observer about things they think are important, rather than allow the interviewer to determine everything that should be discussed. We make a basic and possibly simplistic distinction in Chapter 2 between 'informant' and 'respondent' styles of interviewing.

Brown and Sime (1981), for example, believe that individuals should be given the opportunity to relate their personal record of an event and its context. This they term an 'account interview'. Other examples introduced in Chapter 2 include group interviews using one or two group leaders, or moderators, 'double' interviews taking place consecutively with two related interviewees. (See Case Study 1 in Chapter 4.) Telephone interviews have been developed by some researchers, although these have not been used extensively in education as yet. Some educational researchers have been more creative in collaborative interviewing and in using such things as photographs (see Di Bentley's study in Chapter 4, Case Study 4, for instance) or shared events as the basis for an interview. Adelman and Walker (1975), for example, used synchronised audio tape and photography as a basis for subsequent 'triangulation'. Similarly, other researchers such as Dave Ebbutt (see Case Study 5 in Chapter 4), and Logan (1984) have gone far beyond a simple interrogative approach. In both projects, the interviewers have discussed their perceptions of the group interviews with the participating teenagers, giving them the opportunity to clarify, contradict, disclaim etc. The interview data was not just collected by the researchers. It was negotiated with the participants. There are many other such examples of negotiated data in the literature.

In Chapter 2 we consider how interviews might profitably be classified or whether indeed it is more useful to look at interviewing as a process, with interviews as special kinds of conversations. The tremendous increase of small-scale research – especially as part of the teacher-researcher movement – has had a corresponding increase in the number of interviews carried out under the banner of educational research.

To the uninitiated, interviewing is only as difficult as having a conversation. Indeed, in many examples quoted in this book the conversational element is foremost. Burgess (1983), for example, uses series of 'conversations' in his ethnographic study of Bishop McGregor school and emphasises (1985b) the sterility of interviews conducted and reported as though in a vacuum. He also notes the problems of distinguishing conversations from some kinds of interviews. One distinction, we try to bring out in our discussion of various kinds of interviews in Chapter 2, is the extent to which the 'conversation' is directed, led or followed by the interviewer. At what point does the conversation become an interview? We suggest it is when the conversation is

> initiated by the interviewer for the specific purpose of obtaining research relevant information and focused by him on content specified by research objectives of systematic descriptions, prediction or explanation.

This definition of an interview, ascribed to Cannel and Kahn, by Cohen and Manion (1981) allows for the most, or least, structured examples. It is the explicit intentions and actions of the researcher, or interviewer, which converts 'a chat' between two or more people into a 'study' of phenomena. Often the conversion is subtly presented

6

by an interviewer, who is personally unobtrusive but still elicits the information relevant to the research. In his case study in Chapter 4, Norman Evans describes how he listened to 160 teachers and their 60 tutors in conversations which we would consider were really interviews. In other examples quoted in Chapter 2, there is a fixed stimulus such as slides or photographs. The different processes involved in interviewing are elaborated subsequently by the implications for the role of interviewers and interviewees in Chapter 3, with more examples in the case studies in the following chapter.

Chapter 4 is the centrepiece of the book. We have six very useful accounts of interviewing in various contexts, and by various methods. Throughout the chapters we draw very heavily on what our contributors say – theirs are the examples of practice that enliven the points we want to make.

## Interviewers–interviewees

It should already be apparent that we think interviewing can be a daunting task. In Chapter 3, we consider in some detail who the interviewers and interviewees are in educational research and some of the effects of their relative status.

Clearly, the essential ingredient of all interviews is talk. Data is gathered through direct oral interaction. As with all such interaction, it makes a difference who says what, who is asking the questions, how they ask them and what they make of the answers. For example, a teacher carrying out an inquiry into an aspect of his or her own school will have separate but related roles as colleague, researcher and interviewer, roles which might impinge on and interact with each other.

A major difficulty for educational researchers on small or non-existent budgets (and that's most of us) is that our interviewers tend to be untrained: and many have limited interviewing, educational or other relevant experience. Often they are researchers or research students undertaking their own interviews. They may be research assistants taken on just for the project. Furthermore, even with fairly large-scale projects, the interviewer is in many cases, intimately involved with the development of the research, possibly contributing to the hypotheses and research design as well as carrying out interviews. In this sense, interviewers are closer to ethnographers than to survey researchers, who employ professional interviewers with roles normally limited to conducting, and possibly writing up, the interview. Usually, they are not concerned with planning or analysis.

7

Occasionally, organisations will use an experienced interviewer as a consultant at the preliminary phase of an exploratory project, as in Jill Keegan's case study in Chapter 4.

There has always been small-scale research inquiry, especially by post-graduate students. Regrettably, they often have little opportunity to practise interviewing. Their training is often 'on the job' while doing their first interviews – which are still expected to be valid! Lack of expertise has often been overlooked by their academic supervisors, perhaps because they, too, may also have very limited interviewing experience or because they see interviewing as generally unproblematic.

Most people *can* become competent interviewers. In Chapter 3, we consider the characteristics of 'good' interviewers. Zweig (quoted in Logan 1984) says that an interviewer needs 'to have a certain understanding of himself' (p. 19) and a broad range of experience to be able to appreciate and empathise with the ambivalent concerns of interviewees.

Survey researchers have long been aware of the problems of interviewer bias, of error and of other factors in the interviewing situation likely to affect the data collected and reported. Sophisticated techniques using trained interviewers have been developed by the professional agencies to tackle these problems. Academics have notably lagged behind these developments, perhaps because professional researchers have emphasised techniques more than theoretical issues. The 1980s have brought a resurgence of interest in research methodology and detailed technologies. Academic researchers are beginning to appreciate that even in interviewing it is necessary to consider theory and practice as interwoven. The detailed practical implementation of theoretical ideas can reflect or contradict those very ideas. Brenner (1981a) has gone so far as to offer a framework for evaluating the adequacy of interaction in a research interview based on 'task rules' for the conduct of the interview. We set these out in more detail in Chapter 3.

Since interviews involve at least two people, the latter part of that chapter is devoted to interviewees. Everyone has been, and may still be, involved directly or indirectly in education. Therefore everyone is potentially an interviewee in an educational research project. Indeed our case studies provide an indicative range of potential contributors: parents, teachers, head teachers and deputy heads, lecturers, teacher-students, adolescents out of school, and pupils of various ages in school. Educational research often involves children as interviewees and later we take special account of what is involved in this social interaction.

Anyone who agrees to be interviewed takes risks. For example, they may expose their ignorance, prejudice, apathy or intolerance. Interviewees are especially vulnerable in small-scale research when the participants already know each other. In Chapter 3 we also consider potential conflict, or confusion, between the roles of an interviewee and normal professional roles.

*Our case studies*

Many researcher-interviewers may never have seen an interview schedule – few are published in research reports, whereas questionnaires are usually included fully as an appendix. For this reason, in Chapter 4, we have chosen a range of case studies to illustrate widely differing structures for asking questions. All the studies are related to education, although two involve interviews outside educational institutions. In a third, Norman Evans interviews tutors and teacher-students in polytechnics and colleges. Figure 4.1, at the beginning of Chapter 4, summarises the methodology characteristic of each case study. The examples include individual and group interviews carried out by professional and non-professional interviewers, working with a wide range of interviewees in research projects of different scope and purpose. Whilst neither we, nor the authors of the case studies, would argue that there is no scope for improvement, certainly we feel the selection is interesting and provocative. The case studies should enable the reader to explore variety in interviewing processes and to consider what common elements might exist across apparently diverse approaches.

*Guidelines for interviewing*

It would seem that educational researchers from quite different disciplines and points of view have found that interviewing in one form or another offers a very flexible and accessible research tool. We argue, throughout this book, that it is not a tool to be used complacently. Interviewing is beguiling in its simplicity; anyone, it would seem, can ask a few questions to get someone else's point of view. We would argue it is only as easy as writing a book – most of us have basic literacy skills but few attain literary art. The ability to interview effectively cannot be taken for granted. The interviewer needs careful preparation, and practice to develop social and recording skills, and the ability to analyse and evaluate the data collected.

These skills are not innate but need to be acquired, explored and practised.

> Each interview is new and one cannot rely on either previous assumptions or one's complacency due to experience. (Logan 1984, p. 24)

Whilst not offering a comprehensive manual, in Chapter 5 we attempt some guidelines for using the limited time of an interview to best effect. These are concerned with translating the broad questions of a research project into a plan for interviewing. Thorough preparation should include all the elements of interviewing, even the initial contact and practice in methods of recording and analysis. We also discuss the language and behaviour deployed by the interviewer, ways of asking questions and getting out of the door at the end of the interview.

## Analysis

Each stage of the interviewing process is important. In Chapter 6, we consider perhaps the most daunting task – making sense of all the material collected in the interviews.

An interview is a co-operative venture but the reconstruction of what occurs is usually seen as the analyst's sole prerogative. The basis for analysis is seldom made explicit and yet the grounds on which some data is omitted, some included, not only reflect the theoretical predispositions of the researcher. They also convince the reader whether the research story is true or false. Analysed data should represent as faithfully as possible, responses made during the interview – though we also assume that fidelity is in the eyes of the beholder. Social survey reports will only normally use responses made to structured questions, whereas ethnographers seek information gleaned from a variety of sources. Whatever the approach, the basis of the analysis should be made as explicit as possible. Yet whilst the analysis has to be authentic, able to be substantiated by an explicit database, it is not simply descriptive. Analysis also involves interpretation and is thus a creative process, with the analyst as an accountable god. For example, Whyte's 'Streetcorner Society' style of presentation (1981) makes very compelling reading with, in one part, Chick Morelli telling his story in the first person and only occasionally prompted by a question from Whyte. The reader needs to keep in mind, however, that this was a re-creation by Whyte. He

had not tape recorded his informant. In fact there is no clear indication of how his interviews were noted; some incidents were mem-
orised and then written either as soon as possible after the event, or
by dashing to the men's room at intervals to make notes.

Part of the creative process in analysis, is to impose a structure on
the accumulated material. Hull (1984) considers this to be an 'exact
art', comparable to literary analysis. Another inevitable part of
analysis is the filtering of data through the analyst's own perspectives,
attitudes and language. Judgements are made at every point as to
what material is relevant, and what irrelevant, to the research project.
Hull raises interesting questions about what is 'relevant', especially
among the interviewer's 'black market' of observations. Deliberate
selection is necessary at all stages – sampling, observation, field
notes. In turn the researcher, the interviewee and the interviewer have
each discarded possible data and elected to retain other information.
Much material is therefore lost. The analyst is faced with a cumulative database of filtered information which (s)he will rearrange,
disregarding some further data in the process. Di Bentley's case
study highlights another kind of data-loss, from the very process of
recording the interview.

In survey research, a series of interviews is almost always completed before any analysis is attempted. Ethnographers, on the other
hand, seldom work in such discrete stages. They are more likely to
have a rolling plan, with feedback from one stage of activity into
another. Thus the ethnographer moves constantly between selecting
a problem, collecting cultural data, analysing cultural data, formulating ethnographic hypotheses and writing ethnography. This
involves continual rethinking. Ethnography thus uses a different kind
of paradigm from the research which involves a fixed order of events –
the stereotypical 'select problem, formulate hypotheses, collect data,
analyse data, write up results'.

Another important point to note is that language differences
between informant and interviewer have many consequences beyond
what is, or is not, 'translated' for analysis. To paraphrase Spradley
(1979), every ethnographic description is a translation which
resembles more or less closely the concepts of informants. He suggests that, at one extreme, descriptions are almost totally based on
the language and the culture of the outsider (the researcher in social
survey work); whilst at the other end of the spectrum, life histories
and ethnographic novels are very close to the insider's point of view,
largely using the informant's own language. Most social science
descriptions show that researchers *are* outsiders. The informant's
point of view, is analysed according to the interviewer's concepts,

rather than those used by informants themselves. Ethnographers, on the other hand, attempt to allow their analyses to be structured.

> As a translation, ethnographic descriptions should flow from the concepts and meanings native to that scene rather than the concepts developed by the ethnographer (Spradley 1979, p. 24)

He goes on to demonstrate domain, taxonomic and componential analyses, all of which will help in the discovery of cultural themes. In Chapter 6, we discuss more elementary levels of analysis but readers requiring more depth for ethnographic analysis are recommended to Spradley's text.

Other areas covered in Chapter 6 include the identity of the analyst. Is (s)he the same person who did the interviews or someone else? How is interview data related to other sources of information? Davies and Kelly (1976), for instance, found they need not waste their data collected from participant observation when they were compelled to shift to focused interviewing. They were able to relate the interview data back to earlier observational data. They also considered this combination added an important time dimension to their analysis.

Whether or not the analyst has access to single or multiple supplies of data; whether the analysis is, as we suggest in Chapter 6, 'between' or 'within' interviews – the reader should be convinced that discussions, interpretations, conclusions and any implications drawn have a firm foundation.

## *Reporting*

In reading a research report we want to believe the researcher's story. We want to feel confident that the results obtained are reasonable in the circumstances and that, therefore, the conclusions and implications that have been drawn can be justified as a basis for debate. This means that there should be no parts of the interview process where it is uncertain what has been done. Such strictures apply to data collected as part of the verification of theory generated by logical deductions from prior assumptions. They apply equally forcibly to 'data generated by the research act' which provides the basis for theory. The 'grounded theory' of Glaser and Strauss (1968) for example, should not have to depend on unspecified sources of information. Whatever the style of research, elegance and good experimental design alone cannot compensate for a full description of the researcher's quest for meaningful verbal relationships and their consequences for action. In Chapter 7 on reporting interviews, we discuss some of these difficulties. We offer a checklist which we feel would elicit sufficient information for a readership to feel confident about what had occurred in a single or series of interviews.

## Some issues and implications

Interviewing is a tool to find out about people. The narrowest scope is in the highly structured interview to identify people's attitudes towards specific items. At the other extreme, interviewing contributes towards data collected from a number of different sources in an attempt to describe a culture. 'Culture' in this sense is the acquired knowledge that people use to interpret their experience and generate social behaviour. For example, one way of finding out about school assembly would be to interview the headteacher. The case study from Steven Eales illustrates a fuller approach, and its costs in time. Ethnographers avoid the automatic imposition of a researcher's theories on the people being studied.

> Before you impose your theories on the people you study, find out how those people define the world. (Spradley 1979, p. 11.)

Logan (1984) suggests that we should delay developing our theories of social meaning until after analysing the patterns found in informants' actions and the meaning in their statements. The patterns are based on what people say and do. Too often, educational researchers use pupil data, for example, to fit pre-existing categories and theories. For instance, Logan's own work with youngsters was conceived around old notions about transition from school to work, notions about motivation and disaffection. He suggests that from 'Hollinghead to Willis' the spectre of social class has been used in research design and forecloses on the existence of equally significant explanations which might have emerged from the data.

The ethnographer's life is itself not unproblematic. There is, for example, the moral question raised by the discreet methods used. Whilst not unduly disrupting the events and interactions being observed, ethnographers do inevitably invade privacy and do so in ways which are inexplicit but pervasive. Issues such as these and the conflict situations that a non-judgemental interviewer might face are some of the issues we have selected for discussion in Chapter 8.

Yet another is language. Some of the mysteries of language, especially those of talking, are contained in the relationships between statements, beliefs and actions. For the behaviourist, all interviews, all accounts of what people say gain meaning only when related to actions – be they contradictory or confirmatory. For instance: is prejudice congruent with discriminatory acts? Does opinion relate to actual choice? Do expressed motives match observed actions? Or, for that matter, can an observer impugn appropriate motives to be confirmed by interview?

Perhaps the converse is also true – that all actions can only be understood through a discussion of an actor's motives. For example in a radio broadcast, 'The World at One' (BBC, 9 November 1984), two accounts are presented of the same violent action during the then ongoing coal industry dispute (not exact quotes):

(a) from a police spokesman: 'officers only put on riot gear when attacked by ball bearings from catapaults':
(b) from local union official, 'it was really quite merry, quite peaceful, until the police put on their riot gear'.

Both could be seen to be accurate from limited perspectives; but should we once take descriptions of beliefs, attitudes or events out of an interviewee's perspective, we then have to reconsider carefully our own notions about 'truth' and the level(s) of truth accessible (or possible) to an interviewer.

The term 'language' of course, means much more than the actual words being tape recorded during an interview. Language pervades all stages of a project, providing the researcher with a framework for expressing the original ideas and a tool for collecting and analysing another person's opinions. Sometimes a framework can restrict, giving certain cues to an interviewee about the interviewer's values and personal philosophy. Sometimes language can block understanding between people, especially when they do not share common vocabulary or meanings. As researchers, we need to sort out how general constraints on the use of language in interviewing, apply to our own situations whether using highly structured questionnaires or more 'informant' directed approaches. Language, though, is not only a means of communicating ideas. It is also the tool for an individual to construct her, or his, own reality. An interviewer's own linguistic framework is used to ask questions but in doing so, it also imposes a frame of reference on to the whole interview situation. In listening to interviewees, the interviewer needs to hear via the same linguistic and social framework to make sense of what is being said. Without that language, we cannot understand another culture whether this be in another country, or the culture of an unfamiliar group in our own society.

> Because it involves a complex speech event, ethnographic interviewing requires practice to acquire the necessary skills. (Spradley 1979, p. 68)

Researchers should report this 'complex speech event' so that the reader can follow and believe the research report. Moreover, 'language' includes paralinguistic and extra linguistic expressions, for example, the body language that features in Di Bentley's case study (Case Study 4), and in the 'Conversation with an interviewer', both in Chapter 4. One problem is the way interpretation can be changed in making (necessary) translations from a spoken 'language' to the public written form of research reports. We raise these problems later in reference to analysis and feel they are important enough to reconsider as a main issue in Chapter 8.

Each interview is a record of a social interaction. As such there is a tension between the communications regarded by social scientists as valid and reliable and yet which retain the essential elements of two people talking to each other. Both are necessary and both require empathy and a shared language for the participants.

*Summary*

Interviewing methods may be derived from a variety of sources but certain characteristics are common to all approaches to interviewing used in educational research. Some characteristics are only relevant to particular kinds of interview. It is our intention to identify common, and more idiosyncratic factors with the aim of encouraging more sensitive and effective use of interviewing as a technique in educational research.

# Chapter 2

# Different ways of collecting talk

*Introduction*

This chapter is about forging distinctions. In the first part we consider what we think to be an important distinction between two major styles of interviewing. We trace this distinction through three separate strands which, over time, have shaped interviewing as we know it today. These historical antecedents have given way to a multiplicity of methodological variations. We look at some of these variations and consider pragmatic issues involved in each.

From our reading of the literature it is clear there is no single definition of what exactly constitutes an interview. People often assume when they mention interviews that readers will understand exactly what was taking place as if there were some consensus view. In Chapter 4 we illustrate the opposite, and show practical examples of the great variation in types of interviewing.

In trying to identify a variety of approaches it is sometimes useful to describe types of interviewing as lying on a series of dimensions or continua. For example, if interviewing is thought of as a means of collecting talk, then it is perhaps important to remember that talk is dynamic – a quality it loses as soon as it is collected in any way. It is somewhat, as Whitehurst (1979) observes,

> like catching rain in a bucket for later display. What you end up with is water, which is only a little like rain.

Some methods of interviewing are better at encapsulating this dynamic quality than others, and one possible way of differentiating between methods might be to grade them according to some 'dynamic factor'. Another possibility is that methods could be ranged according to whether they are attempting to capture people's spon-

16

taneous self-expression, or whether they resemble more a kind of remorseless, impersonal interrogation. Needless to say, different interview types have different assumptions underpinning them. These assumptions may be about the nature of the information required, the psychological model of human beings, or the philosophy of the researcher who chooses the method.

## Two main interview styles

There have been a number of attempts to categorise approaches to interviewing. For example, in the many research reports that have been written there is talk of 'structured' and 'unstructured', 'focused' and 'unfocused', 'limited' and 'in-depth' interviews, and so on. We have chosen to characterise interviewing in just two main ways. In making that choice, we might not be doing full justice to the complexity of interviewing as a process. There is always a sense in which any seemingly neat division into two distinctive camps gives the impression of clarity and simplicity. We do not imagine that all interviewing can be tidily allocated into either one of our two types. Rather, we see these as just two fruitful ways of sorting ideas. We call them respectively 'respondent interviews' and 'informant interviews'. There is no suggestion that many of the terms to be used in these discussions have yet achieved consensus status. The best that can be done is to abstract from common usage the most likely meanings and then to try to specify what we mean by them and how they are to be used in this context.

The major distinction between our two approaches is in where lies the locus of control for what happens throughout the interviewing process. That is, in what happens both before, during and after the actual interviewing sessions, given the sort of sequence of processes that we have already mentioned above.

## Respondent interviews

The main characteristic of this style of interviewing is that the interviewer retains control throughout the whole process. That is, the locus of control remains with the interviewer at all stages. All interviews are structured in some way – if only minimally so. They are structured, in our view, primarily by the intentions of the researcher. A tightly structured interview commonly refers to that type of interview which follows a fairly clear and well-maintained schedule, or pre-organised plan. A loosely structured interview, on the other hand, implies a general set of ideas to which the interviewer would

17

like some responses at some point in the session, though the order and exact wording are not important.

There are two important parts to respondent interviews. Firstly, they carry the connotation that there are a set of questions that are to be answered, even if they are not in a prescribed order, so that the interviewer can arrive at some point at the major issues involved. Secondly, and more importantly, it is the interviewer's 'issues' that matter. The purpose of the interview is to satisfy the researcher's questions; it is he or she who overtly directs the proceedings.

*Informant interviews*
In this approach to interviewing the goal is to gain some insight into the perceptions of a particular person (or persons) within a situation. Again the agenda might be tightly or loosely structured, but in this case it is primarily the interviewee who imposes it. This kind of interviewing is sometimes called 'unstructured', when what is actually meant is that it is unstructured from the interviewer's point of view.

Again, there are two parts to this. There are some people who adopt this sort of method because, as McDonald and Sanger (1982) suggest:

> they don't know what line of questioning they will pursue until they have a chance to see what kind of information is available. 'Unstructured' in this sense means no more than tactical opportunism.

Secondly, there are those for whom unstructured implies a relinquishing of some major aspects of control in the interview session. In this sense the interviewer is attempting to help the interviewee express his or her *own* concerns and interests without feeling unduly hampered. Such an interview is seen as an invitation to a person to explore certain issues, to impose their *own* structure on the session, in collaboration with an interviewer. This is the sort of approach adopted by Norman Evans in Case Study 3, in Chapter 4. In his view it is 'patently unsatisfactory for the resulting evidence not to include items which were significant for the interviewee'. For him, structuring the interview is one way of reducing the deficit between what the interviewee said and what they *wanted* to say.

Who controls the interviewing itself is, of course, only one part of the whole process. The important feature of respondent interviews is in their purpose and procedural organisation. That is, the interviewee is present in order for the interviewer to ask questions, or explore issues, and to receive responses even to very open and facilitative questions. It is the interviewer who constructs the agenda which, at some later stage, will be used to direct the analysis, the interpretation of data and possibly the reporting. As convention has it, in respondent interviews the data is being collected overtly, almost formally, with all the problems that that raises. It is being collected more subtly – or perhaps more nonchalantly – in informant ones.

## The development of interviewing

We see these two main approaches to interviewing in educational research as derived from three fundamentally different sources. These are:

- survey research pioneered by Booth in the 1880s
- the clinical interview typified by Piaget in education and Freud in personality development
- ethnomethodological approaches which owe much to the related techniques developed in anthropology.

### Survey research

Survey research started with the early inquiries of Booth and later Rowntree into the conditions of the poor in Britain. Stimulated by philanthropy and funded by charity, they were a mixture, as Marsh (1982) calls them, of investigative journalism and statistical inquiry. Little progress was made until 1937 when Charles Madge and Tom Harrison founded Mass Observation. It was one of the first organisations to use systematic methods to study people's beliefs and behaviour. The founders studied contemporary communities at first by adapting techniques from social anthropology and particularly from the anthropologist Malinowski.

Initially, data was collected from a national panel of informants and from intensive studies undertaken by full-time observers. Mass Observation subsequently depended more on orthodox interviews and questionnaires, though, according to Madge (1953), they still used participant observation sporadically. Throughout this early period there was little stimulus to improve methods. It was only after the Second World War that Britain followed the trend that had been marked in the United States of government money being spent on the *methodology* of survey research, including aspects of interviewing.

19

the general picture of pre-Second World War survey research in Britain is one of limited application, limited methodological development and a limited organisational structure for conduct of surveys. (Hoinville 1983)

Survey researchers (according to Brenner 1981a) treat all responses as if they are answers to factual questions and therefore, in principle at least, able to be corroborated from other sources. Researchers have been persistently reluctant to recognise the difficulty of gaining accurate data from interviews or at least of taking notice of those difficulties that cannot be resolved. We demonstrate in Chapter 3 that bias exists both in interviewers and interviewees. Brenner suggests that most survey researchers actually ignore the known sources of bias. They consider data collection by means of the research interview as:

unproblematic ... adequate measurement is simply assumed.

It is the recognition of the limitations of this 'interviews as facts' approach, that has encouraged the use of other approaches to interviewing. Such methods recognise that working with people is problematic and does not produce tidy results. Methods such as those we list below acknowledge the problems openly.

*Clinical interviews*
In contrast to methods where hypotheses are confirmed by evidence collated from large-scale surveys, Piaget developed the use of clinical interviews. He used these, backed up by observation, primarily with children in order to generate hypotheses about intellectual development, indeed as a base for his theories of genetic epistemology. As early as 1928–29, Piaget interviewed children to glean their beliefs and explanations for everyday phenomena. Flavell (1963) argues that Piaget's studies have the formal properties of 'experiments proper' in the sense that the behaviour being studied is elicited from the start by some stimulus provided by the experimenter. Where this stimulus is oral it might be more appropriate to rename the experiment as an interview. In this we would include both inquiry into remote events, as in *The Child's Conception of the World* (1929), or with questions and answers relating to some concrete events which the child is witnessing, as in *The Child's Conception of Physical Causality* (1930). Flavell claims that Piaget's studies of cognitive development 'almost always include some verbal, interview-like component wherever questioning is feasible' (p. 27).

The precise nature of such interviews is determined by the child, since the child's answers determine the next experimenter/interviewer's question. An interesting comparison can be made between these and contemporary diagnostic and therapeutic interviews. Some of the case study interviews we have included in Chapter 4, especially the group interviews used as exploratory studies in the project on Parents' Needs and the depth interviews in Julia Field's study, might be considered as a development of the Piagetian model.

In addition to the normal difficulties experienced by interviewers, there are extra problems when working with children. Some of these are described, for example, by Eales in his case study. Others might be of over- or under-estimating the child's intellectual level by rash interpretation of what the child has said or done, or premature intervention or leading by the interviewer.

It is so hard not to talk too much when questioning a child, especially for a pedagogue ... The good experimenter (we might say interviewer) must in fact unite two often incompatible qualities; he must know how to observe, that is to say let the child talk freely, without ever checking or side tracking his utterance, and at the same time he must be constantly alert for something definitive: at every moment he must have some working hypothesis, some theory, true or false, which he is seeking to check. (Piaget 1929, pp. 8–10.)

Piaget argued that only by letting the other person determine the content and direction of the conversation, can an interviewer approach real understanding. The clinical interview was the nearest he could get to spontaneous speech relevant to the interests of the interviewer. Thus Piaget's small-scale, depth interviews, presents an alternative to the survey inquiries – for which the sampling procedures and the questionnaire design were considered the most important determinants of quality.

### Recent qualitative approaches

For many years, Piaget was criticised for his lack of quantitative data and rigour in comparison with current standardised procedures. Over the last twenty years various alternatives to experimental and quasi-experimental research models in the social sciences have been developed.

Qualitative methods developed by anthropologists and ethnologists have been adapted for the social sciences, including educational research. New emphasis has been given to analysing an individual's reactions within the normal context in which they might occur. This avoids reducing the complex responses or behaviour of an individual to a single number in a maze of statistical calculations. The focus becomes the detail and quality of an individual or small group's experience rather than the number of people who responded in a particular way. Piaget bridged this change. Although he contrived situations he used them to concentrate on how children perceived various aspects of their world. He did not assume they shared his – the interviewer's – perspectives or even the same framework of thought. In this sense, he shared ethnographers' attempts to understand a culture by examining it through the eyes of individuals sharing that culture.

The term 'ethnography' as used by anthropologists means studying a culture by living as a member of the group being studied. Interviewing would be just one of the field methods being used, alongside observations, working out genealogies and relationships, and analysis of written documents where these were available. Ethnographers engaged in educational research focus on subcultures in a community such as a school, a class, a club. They try to learn from the people in the group how they think, and feel, and how their behaviour fits in with the normal expectations of their group. Ethnographers become participant observers in the group they are studying.

Ethnography has increased since the 1960s and it would be interesting to speculate on the reasons for this. Certainly workers in this country owe a debt to Harrison and Madge for their early work. Mass Observation had participant observers based in families in Lancashire and London as, in a more dramatic way, Malinowski had isolated himself from other Europeans and immersed himself in the life of the village he was studying in the Western Pacific. Tom Harrison, supported participation as a matter of principle:

> If results are to be 'realistic', investigators must penetrate and *live* in the communities they study. A major factor hindering field work has been the separation – in physical and psychological terms – between the sociologist and his subject-matter. (Quoted in Madge 1953)

One of the earliest participant observation studies using anthropological techniques was Whyte's pioneering inquiry into the social structure of an Italian slum in North Boston in the United States in the late 1930s. Whyte moved into the locality and participated in a sufficient range of activities to be accepted by the community so that he could observe a full range of circumstances and relationships. He interviewed people, he knew and who knew him, about events they had both witnessed. The interviews were not providing discrete data so much as helping Whyte make sense of puzzling information. In this sense, ethnographers use interviews to enhance insight into a 'total situation'. The interview is the personal record of an event by the individual experiencing it, told from that person's point of view. The account interview, as Brown and Sime (1981) call it, is the context in which the story is related. It is interesting to note that other researchers are intimately concerned with the large parts – if not the total situation. Jill Keegan, in Case Study 2, for example, is keenly interested in people's 'scripts' as she calls them. She makes the point that as much time should be spent trying to contextualise the interview as is spent on actually doing it. Ours is a very brief look at the historical antecedents to latterday interviewing. These three strands, survey interviews, ethnographic research, being bridged by clinical methodologies, are not the only influences that have been felt over time. We do see them, however, as being formative in the ways that interviewing styles have developed. We pick up some of the theoretical implications of what we have said later in Chapter 8.

## Other typologies

Our earlier distinction between 'informant' and 'respondent' is perhaps too ambitious in many cases. Not all interviews will fit into it tidily. We think it is worth retaining since, in essence, it concerns whether or not categories of response have been established by the researcher before the interviewing takes place. There is a sense in which this must always be the case – that the researcher has explicit (or somewhat implicit) theoretical conceptions of the outcomes otherwise he or she would not embark on the research in the first place.

Cockburn (1980) makes a somewhat similar distinction in approaches to research, which he calls 'sociological' and 'phenomenographical'. Sociological interviewers, in his typology, are people who see themselves distanced from the phenomenon under scrutiny, from the main issues of the interview. They hold apart from the actions of others in the belief that their analysis will gain in objectivity, and therefore in credibility. They are trying to match the actions of others against some established pattern. The priority in their use of interview material lies with the *researcher*'s interests and concerns.

On the other hand, phenomenographic interviewers see themselves as outside a particular system trying to look in. They are not part of

23

the system, but are tapping the perceptions of 'insiders' in order to be able to work out how the system functions. Cockburn says:

> ... in this phenomenological way, case studies can be made on interview-based fieldwork. The interviewer in this sense is a collector of specimens and the analysis is retrospective. The researcher brackets whilst in the field and relaxes bracketing after. Fieldwork is evocative of data and parsimonious of structure.

This distinction relates to the kind of view the researcher has of the research activity itself. At one end of Cockburn's dimension is the interviewer who is trying to wrest some information from the interviewee, whilst at the other end is, perhaps, a worried and anxious person who is trying to seek help from an interested and attentive interviewer. For example, someone interested in the television viewing habits of adolescents might be seen as the first case, whilst a school counsellor might be seen as the other.

There are, of course, many other terms in use that could be used to differentiate between interviews. We have already made the point that we see no one approach as inherently better than any of the others. They have all been developed and used with particular needs in mind. For example, there are both virtues and drawbacks to the informant approach. Having no pre-ordered, sharply worded list of questions allows the interviewer to shape the interview as it happens, in response to the sorts of things being said. However, as Simons (1981) points out, this relies a great deal upon the personal skills and judgement of the interviewer and so it is therefore very much open to manipulation and distortion. An important issue that stands behind any interview is the ethical stance of the researcher and the philosophical underpinnings of the research methodology. To share those assumptions with the interviewee, to negotiate their acceptance, is often made easier by having a prepared list of questions.

### Other types of interviews

The philosophy behind the use of the interview is important, but is only one part of the considerations to bear in mind when thinking of interviews. Here we list some others and relate them to our two main types of interview. These are what we have come to call the 'sensitive variables' of interviewing (Powney and Watts, 1984). We return to this notion in Chapter 7 on reporting interviews.

*Number of interviewees*

There are two aspects concerning the number of people that are involved in the interviewing. The first is the overall sample size, the second the number of people present being interviewed at any one time. The sample size is determined by the intended research design and the available funding: sometimes it is in the thousands, sometimes a sample of one. The larger the number, the more likely it is that a respondent approach is adopted. Survey research interviews are sometimes conducted with samples of thousands of individuals. In such cases, the interviews are likely to be conducted independently by many interviewers and so the questions are standardised and tightly controlled to allow uniformity. Julia Field's work (Case Study 1) is a good example of this approach. All prompts and supplementary questions are provided, as are the range of answers that can be dealt with. If the needs of the research design are such as to require this level of information, then an informant approach would not be suitable. A large sample is not the only reason for using respondent interviews, they have often been used, too, with small samples. However, the converse is not always the case – informant interviews are often used with small samples but not with large, often because of the expense involved.

The number of people present is also a factor to be considered. By far the greatest number of interviews reported are one to one, although there are examples of one interviewer to two interviewees, and one to many. One-to-one interviews have a number of advantages. They are easier to manage; issues can be kept relatively confidential; analysis is more straightforward in that only one person's set of responses are gathered at any one time, and so on. Group interviews also have their advantages in that they can allow a discussion to be developed so that a wide range of responses can be collected. This is the type of approach described by Dave Ebbutt in Case Study 5, where groups of up to 15 youngsters are interviewed at one time. Such interviews are useful, for example, where a group of people have been working together for some time or common purpose, or where it is seen as important that everyone concerned is aware of what others in the group are saying. Walker (1985) suggests that group interviews are the main tool of the ethnographer, though – as Jill Keegan's study illustrates – they can often be used as exploratory or feasibility studies prior to more substantial research. They are, however, sometimes difficult to manage if some record is required of individual's responses. A single tape recorder in the centre of a group of people might capture all that is said but it is then also often difficult to separate comments and attribute them to particular individuals. Clearly, the more people involved, the more difficult this becomes without, say, video taping the proceedings. This in turn involves its own advantages and disadvantages. It is worth noting that Jill manages to tackle some of these problems by having two interviewers present with the group. It is effective provided that the situation does not overwhelm the interviewees – as Dave Ebbutt suggests might have been the case in his study.

Case Study 1 is also interesting in that it uses 'paired' interviews. Only one interviewee is present being interviewed at any one time, however it is particularly important for the research that each teenager interview is followed at some time with an interview with one of their parents. Interviews coupled in this way allow for specific kinds of analyses to be undertaken.

*Interviews which complement other data collection methods*
Interviews may not be the only source of data within a particular research design. In some cases they may be the main source, supplemented with observational field notes, questionnaires, repertory grids and so on. In other cases it may be the interviews that supplement some other main source. Learners might be set written tests, for instance, which – after an initial analysis – are followed by interviews with a selected subset, for further data. Engle-Clough's (1984) work in science education is an interesting example of this. In some cases the interview is part of a fixed sequence of activities. It is used in some instances in order to pilot issues as a pre-test for a main survey. Pilot interviews can give some indication of the range of responses to be expected and therefore are an attempt to validate possible survey questions. For example, research conducted by Marketing Direction Ltd (1984) for the Electricity Council concerned the uptake by teachers of the range of educational materials produced by the 'Understanding Electricity' service. This is an instance of two-phase research with the interviewing seen as the qualitative first pilot stage, to be followed by a (quantitative) questionnaire second stage. Both group and individual interviews were used, with one aim being to 'help design a questionnaire for quantitative evaluation' of the service being provided.

In other cases the interviews might come after some initial field work, say some participant observation to clarify puzzling events or to capture opinions after the event. Whyte (1981), for example, used formal interviews with individuals on their own when he needed to sort out confusing or conflicting information arising from previous discussions and observations.

Davies and Kelly (1976) also used interviews after some preliminary participant observation, but in their case it was more by necessity than by choice. When some young people in a Manchester City Project were shown a preliminary report (well-praised by academics and social workers) they felt quite alienated from the research. As Davies and Kelly say

> They had no idea that they were revealing so much when they sat talking to a friendly young person in the project premises.

The researchers then relinquished participant observation in favour of interviews and reported renewed co-operation from the young people – 'they preferred being interviewed to being observed'.

Denicolo (1984) has used interviews with teachers in conjunction with classroom observations, repertory grids, open-ended questionnaires and workshops. The central issue within her work is both teacher and pupil use of metaphor and analogy in A level chemistry. She suggests that multi-faceted data collection allows a picture to be drawn of the complexities that characterise teachers' and students' actions within a classroom setting.

*Methods of recording*
The two most common methods of recording interviews are by field notes and by audio tape recording. Again, both have their advantages and disadvantages. Full note taking is difficult at the speed of normal discourse, it can intrude upon the interviewer's concentration and upon the flow of an interviewee's responses and – perhaps more seriously – leads to the collection of only a small fraction of the data possible to accrue from an interaction. For example, much anacolutha and paralinguistic information is lost. However, paper and pen are portable, more fail-safe than other technologies, they dispense with lengthy and costly transcriptions and are, in some cases, less intrusive than tape recorders or video cameras. A person in authority, for instance, may reject the notion of being tape recorded and yet readily accept conventional note taking in an interview.

Video taping interviews is growing in popularity as the technology becomes more available, portable and easily used. Gilbert and Pope (1983), for instance, video taped youngsters as they articulated their ideas on the concept of energy in school science. This study is interesting on two counts. Firstly, although the youngsters were aware of the cameras and microphones, these were operated remotely by technicians in a viewing gallery above the participants. The room was a sizeable classroom and cameras could focus both upon a group of youngsters sitting at a table and upon the pictures which were the focus of the discussion. Secondly, the students were interviewed as groups of three or four. The interviewer introduced the pictures and initiated responses concerning energy until a point when discussion began to get going. The youngsters were then left to continue on their own, effectively interviewing themselves for the remainder of the time. At the end of that period (between 20 and 40 minutes) a second interviewer joined them to gather immediate reactions to the experience and to engage them in a 'debriefing' interview (Watts and Powney, 1985). We comment further on these aspects in Chapter 6 where we try to establish some guidelines for good practice.

*Different focus interviews*
Unlike Cohen and Manion's (1985) use of the term 'focus' discussed earlier, we use it here to indicate any substantive task, stimulus, point of interest or control in which the interviewee is engaged during the interview. For example, the focus might be a questionnaire as in Julia Field's work (Case Study 1) or a set of slides as in Di Bentley's interviews (Case Study 4). In some cases, needless to say, it may be simply the questions posed between interviewer and interviewee. Listed below are just some of the many commonly used methods.
*Stimulated recall*    In the work mentioned above (Watts and Powney, 1985) the focus of the debriefing interview was the video recording of the initial interview. The interviewee was asked to take control of the video playback equipment and to stop the video tape at any point she thought was significant or needing of comment. This is an example of stimulated recall interviews. Steven Eales' case study, too, (Case Study 6) has elements of stimulated recall where, during interviews, youngsters are guided through and asked to comment upon a school assembly which has been conducted previously by the deputy head. This is similar to work by Hodgson (1984) where university lectures were video recorded and extracts played back to individual students within 24 hours. Some eight or so extracts were replayed and the students then asked to recall their thoughts or feelings at the time of the extract. Their comments were themselves recorded and used to analyse both their attitudes towards lecturing as a teaching method and their own approaches to learning within lectures. Hodgson notes that stimulated recall techniques were originally developed by Bloom (1953), who says

> The basic idea underlying the method of stimulated recall is that a subject may be enabled to relive an original situation with vividness and accuracy if he is presented with a large number of cues or stimuli which occurred during the original stimuli.

28

Bentley and Watts (1986) use a similar approach when they interview about 70 youngsters about their impressions of some science education television programmes they have just watched. Young sters, and their teachers, are asked to recall various aspects of the programme and comment on its visual effectiveness.

*Pictures* There is a long tradition of using pictures in social and psychological research, far too many for us to do other than cite a few examples. Cortazzi and Roote (1975), for instance, used a method called 'illuminative incident analysis', developed primarily to explore the thoughts and feelings of members of teams working in health and social services. It is based upon the idea that team development can be encouraged by a frank exchange of ideas and feelings about experiences involving the team as they have worked together. Cortazzi and Roote used illustrations of incidents drawn by team members. They argue that there is often considerable emotion connected with such incidents and that the drawings help to clarify the position of each team member.

Swift, Watts and Pope (1983) report that, for them, pictures provide an excellent facility for focusing attention, stimulating recollection of experiential details, refining and directing previous statements, allowing protracted and varied discussions, and exploring the extent to which the meanings received by the interviewer are similar to those of the interviewee. They consider two particular pictorial interview methods – the 'interview-about-instances method' (Gilbert, Watts and Osborne 1985) and 'responding-with-pictures'. In the first, the interviewee is asked to respond to, and comment upon, pictures provided by the interviewer – in this case pictures characterising aspects of scientific concepts. In the second the interviewees draw pictures of their own which in some ways captured elements of what they themselves wanted to convey. In this sense, Di Bentley's work in Case Study 4 is similar to the first in that she provides the series of slides to which the students are asked to respond. In Ryder's (1978) work, in contrast, he asks youngsters to recreate diagrams they have seen on a television news bulletin – that is, to respond during the interview with drawings of their own, depicting how they think a nuclear reactor works. In a slightly more unorthodox way, Thomas Fox (1981) attempted to capture descriptions of classroom practices by recording graphically pictorial representations of certain intended statements – using coloured pens and overhead projector transparencies. He says:

Words were still a major source of information, meaning, description, and disagreement – but they were portrayed and aggregated in a graphic rather than a literate style. Contradictions, ambiguities and misunderstandings about what was done in a school programme became graphically apparent as the interviews were taking place.

Photographs, too, have been a common focus for interviews. Holland (1981), for example, reports a study consisting of an extended interview based on a set of 24 colour photographs of easily recognisable food items. Her interest focuses in particular on the types of principles which a group of 8-year-old children spontaneously and commonly use to classify familiar materials.

*Repertory grids*   The grid techniques that stem from George Kelly's (1955) work, some of which we have already mentioned, have been well-documented in a wide range of texts. Pope and Keen (1981), for example, provide an excellent review in terms of grids in educational use. There is no such thing, they say, as 'The Grid' – there are numerous variations on a theme. Grids are essentially numerical approaches to investigating people's constructs about other people, objects or even abstract ideas. A construct is a dimension which involves the way in which two elements are similar and yet which contrast with a third. This dimensionality allows the researcher to extract matrices of inter-relationships between constructs and between elements.

*Concept maps*   Novak and Gowin (1984) describe concept maps as 'intentions to represent meaningful relationships between concepts in the form of propositions'. Their educational benefits lie in helping to make clear to both students and teachers key ideas within their subject area. It is a technique, the authors say, for externalising understandings about concepts, relationships and meanings within a domain of activity. In this sense, the interviews that use concept maps as a focus are primarily diagnostic of learners' knowledge and reasoning strategies. An interview might begin with the learner being asked simply to list a number of key words they associate with a particular topic. These can be added to at any point as the map develops. They are asked to construct a map by joining the key words together with propositional relationships such as 'is a', 'produces', 'leads to', or 'therefore needs'. Most questions are for explanation of particular connections or for clarity of meaning for particular terms used. They may be open-ended: 'Please tell me about this (word) (link) (statement)'; or closed around some specific detail.

Interviewing of this kind should not be 'Socratic teaching', the authors warn. Teachers as interviewers too often want to steer learners towards a particular understanding – a temptation they must resist. The goals of the interview are to allow the learner opportunity to explore and make explicit their own understandings, for the interviewer to gain some appreciation of these and for the learner to teach the teacher-interviewer (cf. Piaget). More recently Johnson (1983) interviewed a young girl, Karen, about her knowledge and understanding about 'sums' in maths. Johnson says

> During the interviews the child tried to teach me her point of view. The dialogue would continue until the child was satisfied that I had learnt what she herself knew. My notes made on paper and my post-interview summaries were inspected by the child, to test if I had hold of the right end of the arithmetic stick.

*Apparatus*   We have spent quite some time discussing Piaget's interviews and interviewing style. Beyond the philosophy of his approach lies the actual practice he used. This was frequently to focus the interview upon some apparatus or experiment and to ask questions concerning youngsters' understanding of that. It is an approach that has produced a range of variations, often in the context of science education research. Osborne and Freyberg (1985) give a review of this body of research. Other aspects of Piagetian interviewing are considered in Donaldson (1980). The Assessment of Performance Unit (DES 1984), for example, enter into what is essentially an apparatus-based interview when they assess youngsters' abilities at practical scientific problem solving.

*Telephone interviews*   Telephone interviewing is not common in this country, though perhaps it is becoming more so, and is not well-documented at all in educational research. We include it here to provide some sense of completeness. It is becoming more established in market research and a very useful summary and discussion is given by Sykes and Hoinville (1985). Some of the advantages that telephone interviewing provides are seen to be the ease of access to interviewees that might otherwise be difficult to achieve. People who are not easy to contact – either because of very busy schedules, for example, or who are deterred by face-to-face contact, might more easily be reached by telephone. Offset against this are such things as the limitations of the channels of communication. As Sykes and Hoinville say:

> communication between respondent and interviewer is limited to verbal and paralinguistic utterances with neither person able to see the facial expressions, gestures and other non-verbal messages conveyed by the other.

31

Other drawbacks include the possibility of the interviewee giving short, non-committal responses, the difficulty of using visual tasks, of providing encouragement, of deciding whether the interviewee understands the question, or of accessing sensitive, or affective information.

There are many other kinds of focus for interviews and all we have hoped for here is to give some flavour of the variety that abounds.

# Chapter 3

# Interviewers and interviewees

*The interviewer*

The outcome of an interview or series of interviews is dependent on the participants – the interviewer(s) and the interviewee(s) – and is a summary of their interaction. However each interview does not start with an empty slate. Before the first question has been put, the participants have coloured the slate with their histories and their expectations. In this chapter, we examine the main characteristics of 'an interviewer' and 'an interviewee'.

*Importance of the interviewer*
Educational research reports usually give scant attention to the style, characteristics, status and bias of an interviewer although these may be crucial factors in the quality and reliability of the information collected. Perhaps reporting interviewer characteristics is simply seen as unimportant in a research report. Even if interviewers may not be taken for granted, reports might involve personalised details not normally regarded as scientific and therefore detracting from the methodology as a research tool. Many research reports are written by people who have themselves done the interviewing which may make it difficult or apparently unnecessary to pursue rigorous appraisal of their interviewing skills and what they bring to an interview.

*Who are the interviewers in educational research?*
There is no single model of educational research and interviewers have different degrees of intellectual and emotional commitment to the project they are working on. We have made pragmatic distinctions below but a single interviewer may come into more than

one category, by, for example, designing the research project and analysing the interviews.

(a) *Professional interviewers* such as those used in Julia Field's work with adolescents and their families are traditionally the least involved. By professional, we mean those who earn their living by interviewing. It is usually assumed that as professionals, the interviewers will have no vested interests in the outcome of the research. Certainly one expects the less committed to ask questions dispassionately but then they may also miss relevant points because they are uninvolved. Their strength is experience and professional skills in drawing out interviewees, in knowing where to pursue points, and where to keep a receptive silence.

Being professional does not necessarily mean lack of commitment. Many professionals are engaged in the development of projects, using interviews for exploratory work as Jill Keegan did in interviewing parents about schools. This engagement becomes commitment and may make it harder for the interviewers to distance themselves from both the informants and the research team than in interviewing where they remain detached from the project.

(b) *Interviewer as research designer.* In small-scale educational research, researchers often carry out their own interviews. Besides the difficulty mentioned elsewhere that they may not be very experienced or competent interviewers, there is the added problem of their commitment to the outcome of the project.

(c) *Interviewer as analyst.* There is a difference between analysing the report of an interview carried out by someone else and analysing one's own interviews. Charles Hull (1984) considers that an interviewer has a 'black market' of impressions, nuance, extra clues that are not available to anyone except the participants in the interview. What the interviewer chooses to report from that interview can only be very limited in comparison to the wealth of detail in the interviewer's head. Most researchers treat such information as irrelevant. Researchers who conduct their own interviews usually analyse them – Norman Evans and Steven Eales being two examples in our case studies.

(d) *Interviewer in ethnographic research trying to merge with the culture under observation.* In this situation, interviews may not be formalised since the participants meet informally as part of the research design. There are many variations of ethnographic interview, and often the interviewers are well known to their informants, as with Steve Eales (see Case Study 6), who was a teacher in the school where he conducted interviews of staff and pupils.

(e) *Other non-professional interviewers.* In collaborative work, there could be situations where individuals contribute their interviewing skills without being substantially involved in the design or analysis of the research. In a collaborative survey of teachers' perceived needs in their teaching of literacy, some of the institutions involved also made use of extra interviewers (LITRIP 1985). There are also instances of children being used as interviewers (Woods 1979; Pollard 1985). Pollard considered his child interviewers had the trust of the other children and very privileged access to certain information. In themselves they also became extra-informative.

The categories (a) – (e) above demonstrate that interviewers coming from different sources have variable levels of commitment. Another consideration is an interviewer's bias or even self-interest.

*Interviewer bias*
Interviewers, being human, have their own perspectives and biases which may not be made explicit and in some cases the interviewers might ignore or deny their bias. Perhaps a 'personal perspective' is a less accusing term than bias but it is inevitable that the interviewer's perspective is also limited by knowledge and experience as is the interviewee's.

In an interview, like any other instance of social interaction, both individuals influence each other. As such, every interview is a unique interaction however closely the interviewer tries to obey the 'rules' and 'standardise' the interview. The basic sources of interviewer bias clearly acknowledged in the social sciences are:

(a) *The background characteristics of the interviewer* e.g. age, education, socio-economic status, race, religion, sex. Some of these, like age or race, will be apparent to the group being interviewed and will have their own effect. Others such as education or religion may be wrongly assumed by the interviewees.

Sue Scott's experiences during her study of the context and process of post-graduate research in the social sciences led her to conclude that interviewing is seen as a fairly low-status activity. This caused her problems partly because she felt interviewing was not 'proper' academic work. She found she was patronised by many male interviewees but ruefully admitted that people were more willing to talk to her informally as a woman. We pick up this point again later from the interviewees' perspective.

(b) *Psychological factors* such as the perceptions, attitudes, expectations and motives of the interviewer. For example, as part of

35

the self-fulfilling prophecy a respondent's answer may reflect the expectations of the interviewer. Unintentionally interviewers may give clues to their own attitudes and values and even to the kinds of answers they would like to receive from their interviewees.

(c) *Behavioural factors* related to any inadequate conduct of the interview e.g. incorrect reading, recording or probing of the questions. These are largely dependent on the skill and reliability of the interviewer as we discuss below. Early studies which monitored professional interviewers' behaviour identified cheating in the sense of deliberately inventing replies at the end of a long series stretching from carelessness, through omissions, bias and prompting, to cheating. Durant (1946) found it was not the length or even the complexity of questions, so much as lack of interesting material which encourages an interviewer to skip through proceedings, becoming more 'creative' to speed up the process. Bias has been found to be much more difficult to eradicate than cheating. In analysing election results of 1945, Durant found that 3 out of the 200 interviewers were clearly biased. He quotes one Labour interviewer working in a constituency where Labour was known to be weak, claiming that 90 per cent of her interviewees were going to vote Labour. Similarly, Conservative interviewers working in constituencies where Labour candidates had won, had found more Conservative contacts than the actual election results warranted. Bias was most marked where interviews were completed in small communities. There, respondents were already likely to be known to some extent. Bias almost disappeared in large urban communities. Durant concludes from this that bias arises from the circumstances in which interviewing is done and not from the deliberate slant of the interviewer.

Sheatsley (1949) found interviewers were not put off by lengthy sub-questions. One might expect that if an interviewer knows that a 'Yes' means she will have to follow up with a lot of sub-questions, she may skip that extra work by (unconsciously) encouraging the interviewee to say 'No' or 'Don't know'. Sheatsley's sample of interviewers proved to be more conscientious than this. Nevertheless bias did emerge as interviewers elicited more answers from respondents; the answers tended to be in line with the interviewer's own attitudes. Interviewers didn't avoid questions but 'encouraged' them in their own direction.

We are not suggesting that educational interviewers are either cheating or demonstrating undue bias. We are underlining the point that interviewing is as complex as any other social interaction. All in all, we can't avoid interviewer bias: '*To want to interview without interviewer influence is a contradiction in terms*' (Brenner 1981a, p. 122.)

To complicate matters even further, interviewers and all their quirks are perceived differently by each interviewee. Several interviewers working on the same project do not automatically share the same perspectives and even if they did, their presentations or styles of interview will incur different perceptions and reactions from the people being interviewed. We sense the danger of losing our grasp of the reality of an interview in the complexity of the relationship networks and Laingian knots, so let us assume we can put aside bias for the present.

*The quality of the data collected will depend on the skill of the interviewer:*

> No amount of sophisticated scale-building or statistical analysis can rescue a research project in which the conceptualisation and instrumentation have been built on poorly conducted exploratory interviews . . . . When taken seriously, interviewing is a task of daunting complexity (OU DE304 3.1.)

It is almost as complex as teaching but requires different skills, although careful listening is an asset to interviewers and teachers alike.

Interviewers must also remain vigilant. For example, it is tempting to develop 'a set', an expectation of the main issues which will be raised. The first interviews are fresh, the interviewer provoked by the new material. After several, maybe as many as 10 or 20, expectations of getting a different perspective have faded and the presentation of the interviewer may even diminish the chances of the interviewee saying anything different from the previous contributors – or at least the chances of the interviewer recognising original ideas have diminished. This is not laziness or even incompetence but a result of the interviewer's endeavour to build a coherent and total pattern from the responses to the main issues relevant to the inquiry. The interviewer may only hear responses compatible with the picture which is taking shape.

Certainly interviewing skills matter if the researcher wants to avoid unnecessary loss of adequate answers. As an aid to new interviewers, we have set out guidelines in Chapter 6. These can only be of limited use since the most important skills are developed through practice and careful evaluation of one's own technique.

It behoves the researcher – where this is a different person – to note interviewers' reports. Years ago, Sheatsley (1949) advocated the use of interviewer report forms on which interviewers could record their reactions not just to individual questions or interviews but to an assignment generally. In 'Conversation with an Interviewer' in Case Study 2 in this book, Jill Keegan makes it clear that researchers miss important information if they ignore interviewers' reports. Such reports can identify interest level, difficulty/ease in giving or replying to particular questions. It is not merely the length, wording or potential ambiguity of questions, although these are important in interviewers' reports. It is also the public and individual interest in the subject-matter, accessibility of informants, the number of interviews and even the weather or season. Educational researchers familiarly find it difficult to collect data in the middle of Christmas festivities – carol concerts, nativity play, school parties or in the summer season of field trips, sports days and examinations.

One of the essential skills of interviewing must be questioning ability. Brenner (1981) demonstrated the difficulty of this, in his analysis of how accurately experienced interviewers followed precise instructions. He looked at the interaction between interviewers and respondents participating in a survey directed by a social scientist at the University of Wales and concerned with mobility in a South Wales valley area. From the 60 taped interviews that he analysed, only two-thirds of all questions were asked as required. Even these experienced interviewers broke a basic rule and significantly altered the wording of the question at the interview. Consequently the answers recorded in an apparently standardised interview were in fact responses to different and not, as the analyst might assume, the same questions.

*Interviewer reliability*
Inconsistency in framing questions raises issues of interviewer reliability not just between interviewers but even for one interviewer on different occasions or during the interaction of some interviewers with specific questions and with some respondents. Experienced interviewers have a repertoire of styles but to increase reliability for a set of interviews, the interviewer should consistently use just one acceptable repertoire of techniques. In this way Brenner argues, she will be aiming to achieve a reliable and precise stimulus to which respondents may fulfil their role. This is treating interviewer and interviewees as mechanistic in the most structured interview situation. But how much more variety and potential misconception might there be in unstructured interviews.

We are especially concerned by the large numbers of untrained and inexperienced interviewers engaged in educational projects. Many of them may not appreciate the difference between a probe and a prompt, where to use a checklist, where to keep silent. Where several interviewers are used, the number of potential inaccuracies increases or at least becomes more noticeable in the interview record. They need to agree and monitor consistency in approach to each interview. The survey literature is full of evidence to show how the personality, bias and preconceptions of interviewers inevitably affect the conduct and reporting of an interview. There is no reason to assume that less structured interviews avoid interviewer intrusions although these can, if noted clearly, provide important insights.

*Researcher/interviewer*
Intrusions of a slightly different kind may occur when the interviewer is also the researcher as is the case with much small scale educational research. One might argue the dangers of self fulfilling prophecies where interviewers are research students, research assistants or even the professor herself and are intimately involved in the research design.

The researcher's role should be made explicit whichever methodological approach is used.

> in evaluating the products of covert research we cannot afford to ignore the researcher: we must know the role he played, how he played it and how others reacted to him. (OU DE304, p. 102, 2.13.)

Whyte made this responsibility explicit for ethnomethodologists:

> If ... the researcher is living for an extended period in the community he is studying, his personal life is inextricably mixed with his research. A real explanation then of how the research was done necessarily involves a rather personal account of how the researcher lived during the period of study. (Whyte 1981 p. 279).

Interestingly, Whyte didn't make this information available in his first edition (1943) but 12 years later in the 1955 edition of *Street Corner Society.*

As we said in our introductory chapter, one of the most common elements of the self-fulfilling prophecy is that educational researchers use pupil data to fit their own pre-existing categories and theories. Logan (1984) argues that as interviewers, we need 'constant self monitoring to reveal to what extent we are still guilty of importing into and imposing our categories on to interviewees' (p. 24).

Researchers are constantly being faced with choices each of which will limit the data they are collecting in one way or another. Sometimes this must produce conflict whether or not such methodological anxiety is recognised in the research report. For example one might argue that all research should take account of the impact of the personal characteristics and idiosyncrasies of the researcher on the findings. Yet ethnographers try to reduce their impact on the situation and get 'normal' reactions that might be incurred by an outside interviewer.

*Confidence in the interviewer*
Interviewees need to trust the person interviewing them. Many people believe that the confidential information collected by an interviewer gives him or her considerable power. Effective and trustful interviewing depends on how the social situation is defined. Whilst most of this trust depends on personality, some of it also depends on the story of the interviewer, who s(he) seems to be, where from, and the reasons for asking the questions. Initially, it was assumed by the villagers being interviewed by the anthropologist, Berreman, that he had been sent by the government. Similarly, people developed their own explanations about Whyte's place in their community – they decided that he was writing a book about them, which was only part of the truth since he was trying to analyse the social structure of an Italian slum in North Boston.

It is remarkable that so many ethnographers and other interviewers are accepted by people willing to share some of the most personal details of their lives. Whilst most of us would be flattered by the undivided attention of an interviewer, there also comes a point where we consider this outsider as too intrusive. We are likely to go further in our confidences when we trust the interviewer or observer not to betray confidences. We are also likely to be more forthcoming when we think that our information is going to make an improvement in human lives, in education in general if not in our own classroom or school. Having accepted an interviewer or observer, cognitive dissonance ensures that unless something catastrophic happens, an informant continues to be co-operative. To change would reduce or threaten one's self-respect or standing in the eyes of the interviewer/observer or in the view of someone else the respondent considers important. In North Boston, locals were willing to explain Whyte's presence as he was sponsored by 'Doc', a fairly reticent, but well-known and respected leader in the community.

Known, or expected, alignments or loyalties are crucial to the way in which an interviewer is perceived. Whyte felt it necessary to enlist as a voluntary helper in the campaign for state senator. This was a carefully made decision as he wished to extend his research to understanding local politics. At the same time, he did not want to antagonise his existing friendship/informant groups and prejudice his ongoing research.

An interviewer needs to establish good rapport with respondents but this does not entail identifying completely with them. People did not expect Whyte to be just like them; indeed they were quite shocked when he swore in the way the locals did. They were interested and pleased to find him different. Adelman (1985) canvasses against unnecessary deceit, arguing it is only when a researcher is accepted as a competent member by a community that participant observers are really 'culturally immersed'.

Logan (1984) actually discussed this problem with his informants during a study on the transition from school to work. Interviewees were actually aware of the signals being given by the interviewer's clothes, hair style, accent etc. and would label interviewers in such a way that it would affect what was said. For example:

> Well if you turned up in hippy gear I'd feel, 'Oh look at him, he's trying to be in with the kiddywinks', sort of thing. (17-year-old in FE College.)

Whereas the interviewer who wears a formal suit would be clearly identified as being different and according to the same informant:

> Well, it's better than, sort of what could well be a cover-up, if you see what I mean ... sorry about that. (pp. 22–3.)

## The interviewer's personality and involvement

An additional problem for participant observers is where involvement in a community is likely to distort relationships with informants. Whyte found it difficult when a 'friend' wanted to borrow money. Whyte eventually refused.

Paying attention to technique in interviewing is necessary but not sufficient for a really skilled interviewer. There is the added and vital ingredient of the interviewer's own personality which Zweig gave pre-eminence:

> the art of interviewing is personal in its character, as the basic tool of the interviewer is in fact his own personality. (Quoted in Logan 1984, p. 19.)

Zweig therefore suggests the interviewer needs to have a certain self-understanding and range of experience to be able to appreciate and empathise with the ambivalent concerns of the interviewee. This ties in with the importance of putting each comment into context which can best be done by an interviewer who is close to the informant's understanding. Interviewers who have a narrow range of experience would find this difficult and be more inclined to make abstract comments.

There is another decision here for the interviewer, as empathy brings its own difficulties, like how far the interviewer should or should not get into the other person's problems. A useful strategy might be, as Logan claims, to democratise interviews which might otherwise be threatening to the interviewees. In these cases the interviewers would share and relate their own biographies. They would indicate how, for example, they share experiences, attitudes or tastes with the informants in order for the latter to be more trusting. This can backfire if the authority relationship is unequal. Other critics would argue that it is bringing too much of the interviewer's bias into the open. It would certainly break conventions of professional interviewing and at least two of Brenner's (1981) interviewing rules for survey research interviews. These 11 basic task rules are aimed at reaching a consistent approach by an interviewer on each occasion and as far as possible, consistency between interviewers in structured situations. According to Brenner,

The interviewer must:

- read the questions as they are worded in the questionnaire
- ask every question that applies to the respondent
- use prompt cards and other instruments when required
- only probe non-directively
- make sure she has correctly understood an answer and that it is adequate
- not answer for the respondent
- not give directive information
- not seek or give unrelated information
- repeat a question or other action when requested by the respondent
- when asked for clarification, give it nondirectively
- act nondirectively to obtain an adequate answer where it is inadequate

By bringing in the interviewer's personal viewpoint, the respondent is not only distracted but may be in danger either of being acquiescent or of being prey to a self-fulfilling prophecy and giving the kind of information that coincides with what the interviewer apparently wants.

Another danger that experienced interviewers appreciate is that respondents may become dependent even during a fairly brief interviewing session especially where the topic is one which highlights a major unresolved situation for the interviewee. Questions focusing on the long-term unemployed, coping with chronically sick relatives, educating severely handicapped children, surviving changing emphases in educational policies, describing one's teaching career, could be sensitive issues for interviewees. The interviewer may be one of the few well-informed people who has sympathetically listened and apparently understood the difficulties of the interviewee. This same interviewer now has to leave the situation without offering advice or hope for very immediate improvement. Professional interviewers learn quickly about the necessity to maintain distance but sometimes it is difficult not to feel responsible for, and often upset by, interviewees' problems.

Perhaps these last few points suggest the interviewer is in a superior position to the person being interviewed. This is certainly not the case. The relationship is asymmetrical. The interviewer initiates and to a greater or lesser extent determines the direction of the interview. This is one aspect of the asymmetry in the relationship. The interviewer will also hold confidential information which will enhance his or her power position after the interview. In the end, however, the interviewee holds the ultimate sanction: the power to refuse to continue with the interview. The interview is only compelling for the interviewer who is responsible for maintaining the informant's interest, thus gaining the maximum amount of information relevant to the inquiry. But interviewees are not necessarily passive creatures waiting merely for an interviewer's prompt. They have their own perspectives.

*Who are the interviewees?*
Education is one of the few areas where it can almost be guaranteed that people over the age of 5 have experience and some knowledge. Our involvement in education is lifelong, whether as pupil, parent, voter, ratepayer or voluntary or paid employee contributing directly to educational services. Consequently, we all have opinions and perspectives of potential interest to educational researchers. Even the small range of case studies included in this book has drawn on a wide range of interviewees – junior and secondary age pupils, parents, teachers, deputy and head teachers, and lecturers. Add to this list governors, employers and local authority staff and there are few people omitted from being quite directly concerned with education.

## Some definitions

At this point it is probably useful to distinguish different terms for interviewees and for the assumptions behind those terms. The principal distinction we made in Chapter 2, is between *respondents* who answer specific questions posed by an interviewer and *informants* who give information about their culture or situation, in their own language either in response to a very general query from the researcher or unsolicited and gleaned from the 'interviewer's' observations. Having made these distinctions, we shall continue to use the term 'interviewee' for general purposes and 'informant' or 'respondent' where we judge either as clearly applicable.

Spradley (1979) argues that ethnographers try to understand an informant's point of view and thus use informants differently from those researchers who treat people as respondents, subjects or actors. Spradley may be underestimating the sensitivity of much positivistic inquiry. Good interviewers always try to see things from the respondent's point of view. The differences may be more about whose frame of reference the data should fit – the researcher's or the interviewer's. *Subjects* and *respondents* are used to test the researcher's hypotheses. It is even possible to observe people in their natural setting but they are mere actors if they are objects described in the concepts and language of the researcher. To put it at its most negative, respondents may be relegated to being data-giving machines.

Part of the research deal is that people learn to be good respondents. Interviewers are frequently asked: 'What do you want me to say?' almost as if there are fixed and correct answers.

Logan (1984) describes how two 15-year-old girls tried to repeat an interview they had with him when the tape recorder had unfortunately not been on. Though they were unsuccessful in conducting their own interview, they did 'have a model of an interview in their own heads'. They imitated the question-answer sequence, used posh voices and reflected the original interviewer's words and phrases.

## Vulnerability of the interviewee

An interview is a contrived social situation with an asymmetrical relationship between the interviewer and the interviewee. Both play out roles which are learned. To some extent, all interviews are seen as threatening by those being interviewed and one of the main skills of the interviewer is to gain their confidence and to establish a good relationship between the interviewer and the interviewee. The person being interviewed makes some kind of judgement about the interviewer and the kind of definition of themselves and their situation that they want to project. It is a decision as to which layer of truth they will make accessible to the interviewer. Goffman presented attempts to convey a desired impression as part of any social interaction and it is as well for interviewers to take account of the way each respondent tries to present a particular image. This was made clear to Lynn Davies (1985) by the teenage girls she was interviewing. They were concerned to know whether or not her husband would hear their tape recordings. The researcher interpreted this as an indication that the girls were more concerned what a man would think than herself. It is reasonable to assume that interviewees tailor their information, comments and opinions to their imagined audience.

As teacher Steve Eales points out in his report on interviewing his head and deputy head teachers, co-operation does not necessarily mean that suspicions are allayed. Interviewees are vulnerable to many pressures and the audience for the research may be a key factor in gaining co-operation and a relaxed interviewee. Mostly informants are worried if peers or their employer will have access to their comments from the interviewer, from someone else present at the interview or in subsequent publication. They are less worried by an academic audience (see the Eales study) or if they are confident of anonymity.

Vulnerability in an interview also comes from internal pressures. It is a situation in which it is very possible to lose face, to be confronted with one's own inconsistencies in beliefs and behaviour, to answer questions embarrassing in the way they slice through normal defences. An interviewer can highlight our ignorance. Therefore one of the main aims for the person being interviewed is to maintain self-esteem. There are strategies for doing this — ways of answering and not answering questions. Brenner (1981) shows how respondents maintain their self-esteem by their tendency to deny what they consider (or perhaps what they think the interviewer will consider) as undesirable traits and to admit to socially desirable ones. An interview could be analysed as the attempt by the interviewee to maintain a consistent story. In discussing interviews after they have taken place, interviewees have admitted 'lying' i.e. telling an untruth, grossly exaggerating or omitting information in such a way as to mislead the interviewer (Watts and Powney 1985). It then needed more 'lies' to maintain the story and the interviewee's credibility. It seems curious to go to such lengths rather than refuse to answer questions which are patently causing anxiety since the interviewee does not wish to answer truthfully. It seems that interviewees are not only unwilling to snub their questioners once the interview is under way, they also want the interviewer to like, or at least respect, them. Ethnographic methods were developed to record people's

responses in more natural settings without pressures to distort information deliberately to fit in with the researcher's predetermined
questions or the interviewee's assumptions about the inquiry.

*Status*
The key to the interviewee's level of knowledge to which an interviewer can gain access is relative status. Equal status has shared
meanings and assumptions. We would argue that a person only gives
such information in an interview as is compatible with the relative
status of interviewer and interviewee. This was neatly, if serendip-
itously, illustrated by Berreman (1962) carrying out an ethnographic study in and around a peasant village of the lower Hima-
layas in Northern India. His first assistant, a high-caste Hindu
Brahmin from the plains, became ill after some time on the project.
His place was taken by an older man who was a Muslim and
therefore, like the American researcher, regarded as untouchable by
the orthodox members of the village. This turned out to be an
unexpected advantage in giving the research team far greater access
to information. Previously, the high-caste villagers would not admit
to any beliefs or practices which would prejudice their status before
a high-caste Brahmin. The lower castes would in any case have been
very circumspect. It further transpired that the picture the Hindu
research assistant had transmitted to the foreign researchers was
consistent with maintaining the image of a good Hindu community.
Both the villagers and the research assistant were in unwitting col-
lusion in only revealing the layers of truth appropriate for an
outsider. The new Muslim assistant had no pre-commitment to the
society, had greater access to the lower castes and intervened less
between the researcher and his informants. Consequently Berreman
collected quite different information from informants. If this should
seem a remote example consider a case where data on the same
project is collected by a professor of education and young research
assistants or where informants are faced with an interviewer from
their own school, possibly their head teacher.

Changing the team of interviewers can alter the relative status of
all the participants in the interviews and with it the informants'
behaviour and the kind and quantity of information they are willing
to give. In Berreman's case, some low-caste people resented their
inferior position and were not committed to maintaining a unified
impression of the village. Consequently they were even willing to
reveal information embarrassing to the higher castes. This in itself
presents other problems for the interview analyst. If a respondent is
managing an impression of what he or she wants the interviewer to

believe is a reflection of the situation, that wilful impression is all the interviewer can feel confident about without cross checking with other interviews and observations.

Berreman's work showed that respondents react differently to different interviewers and in the presence of other people. A teacher, or pupil, will react differently in each other's presence than when alone with the interviewer.

Interviewees adopt what they think is the appropriate role, aided and abetted by the interviewer and they try to please by giving the kinds of information and replies that they believe the interviewer wants. Also informants will select information to give the ethnographer based on what they think he/she wants and already knows. Berreman for example got more information when his questions assumed polygamy existed among the hill people than when he tried to identify its existence in the first place. If he already knew about it, there was one less secret for the villagers to hide. This can rebound if an interviewer makes assumptions that meanings are shared when they aren't really.

Participants in Whyte's study made it clear to him in retrospective discussions (1981) that they had been alert to formal and informal situations in his research. For formal interviews, the respondent puts on a public image with tidy clothes, clean face etc. With informal interviews carried out as part of participant observation, the informant has no opportunity to put on and maintain the role associated with a public appearance. Hence a more vulnerable but possibly more forthcoming informant.

Effective interviewing depends on how the social situation is defined. The less a researcher defines the context of the inquiry and declines to offer a focus for the informant, the higher the risk of irrelevant material. Eales (Case Study 6) shared the approach of many exploratory studies in listing some general questions as the core of the interview but allowing the interviewees to digress and to redirect the interview somewhat. Informants are likely then to be more confident. People are very obliging, especially to the research community, and if the researchers don't define their position, then those they are working with will ascribe motives, interest areas etc. for them. Berreman's villagers ascribed various explanations and motives for his visits including missionary, government agent, tax inspector, land assessor and official collecting information for military service.

Subsequent information selected for the interviewer will be presented with this ascribed definition of the situation in mind. Eales considered that the timing of his interviews was important. They took place after a term of data collection in the school so everyone was aware of the investigation. The interviewees felt they were going to make a contribution to serious research. Incidentally, the timing also allowed the researcher to refine the issues he was interested in and ask more relevant questions.

### Children as interviewees

Educational researchers often want to interview children which may be quite difficult. All the general rules of good interviewing apply but some areas may be additionally sensitive.

In the previous section on interviewers we referred to the occasional use of children as interviewers but these were unusual cases. Whether or not the interviewers are teachers with the authority relationship this implies, they will normally be adults whom children will treat accordingly. They have spent the years since birth coming to grips with parental demands and all their school lives working out what teachers want and how to please them. An interviewer may be seen by children 'as a teacher in disguise, giving an oral examination' (Bell *et al.* 1981). In her case study, Di Bentley notes that children sometimes regarded her with extreme suspicion, 'as though I were a spy from the enemy camp wanting to know what they thought of the staff.'

Bell and colleagues evolved practical hints from their work with children of the same age group. They used the interview-about-instances approach and we have included most of their advice in the guidelines chapter. Essentially, it is based on general good practice in interviewing with special care with listening and clarification techniques, and avoidance of being identified with the teacher – not an easy task for teacher-researchers. The way of asking questions may be like a teacher, using school language rather than the children's idioms. Adults in an authority role may expect children to be obedient. Interviews with children should follow the courtesies of adult interviews. These include the careful attention to explanation and listening to responses in children's interviews and possible checking back with the children that the interviewer has 'got it right'.

It may be more difficult than with adult interviewees, to find children willing to assert their own views without being intimidated by their peer group, the interviewer or the situation. Another difficulty is young children tend to be more literal and may pay attention to unexpected details, disconcerting the interviewer who is using different logic or priorities. The researcher may also need to make special arrangements for access and conduct of interviews with children.

In spite of these difficulties, Eales still favours interviewing as the best method of data collection from children who have limited literacy skills. This may be unrecognised but equally true in interviewing adults unfamiliar with receiving and responding to inquiries in writing.

A salutary warning is given in the Open University text on research methods (OU DE304, 5.20/21) to interviewers working with children. They should expect that the information communication system which, if not unique to children, is certainly very efficient in schools, means that after very few interviews, the whole school has a version (garbled) of it. The Opies (1969) identified the incredible speed with which children's games and rhymes might be transmitted across the country. Similarly many teachers know how rumours, games or even new strategies on the microcomputer can spread throughout a school within a few days or even hours.

*Locating the best interviewees*
In small-scale educational research, the sample chosen for the particular information they are likely to provide may give undue pre-eminence to head teachers. As we said earlier, other interviewees might include teachers, pupils, parents, administrators or even 'members of the public'. Everyone has experienced some form of education and may feel more willing and able to particpate in educational inquiries more than other forms of research.

Given limitations of sample size, it is essential for interviewers to locate the best informants. Dean *et al.* (quoted in OU DE304, 7.12.) suggest that researchers should have two main criteria in finding the best informants:

- they should be especially sensitive to the area of concern
- they should be willing to inform

These two categories were expanded considerably both by Dean *et al.* and by Spradley (1979) who considered the minimum requirements for identifying the good informant for ethnographical studies as:

1   Thorough enculturation (the informant should not be new to the situation unless that is the focus of the study);
2   Current involvement. (We would add to this that the informants' status should be taken into account in analysing their contributions);
3   So that the researcher takes nothing for granted, the culture should be unfamiliar;

4   Informants who have adequate time;
5   Non-analytic informants i.e. who do not try to make analyses
    in the terms they believe the researcher may be using such as
    socio-economic status. (On the other hand some analysis may
    be very helpful if informants use their own 'folk theory'.
    Normally researchers do not want informants to be filtering
    information via categories they, rather than the researchers,
    believe to be appropriate.)

Most people find that strangers make better informants. This is
probably true of all kinds of interviewing but presents one of the
common problems for researchers in a small educational community.
Not only is there the difficulty of overcoming previous expectations
on the part of both interviewer and respondent, there is the frequent
dilemma of the researcher not being willing to ask apparently
obvious, but necessary, questions. Or respondents may not answer
fully because they believe, or know, that the researcher already
has the answer. For example, if a teacher is trying to trace a curriculum change in her school, she may be reluctant to ask colleagues
dates of specific initiatives since they are meant to be sharing that
common knowledge already.

## Interviewees have certain degrees of freedom

These may be exerted simply in an encounter with problems such as
the need to have a question repeated or clarified. In more extreme
cases the interviewee may be unwilling or unable to give adequate
information or indeed just refuse to answer. Much research assumes
that interviewees will fulfil the role marked out for them by the
researcher or interviewer. The stimulus-response model of interviewing outlined by Brenner for survey research, assumes that
respondents are willing and able to be faithful respondents who will,
to the best of their knowledge, give responses in accordance with
reality. To counteract this assumption, are well-researched aspects of
'undesirable' motivation in informants who have a tendency towards
'acquiescence' and 'need for approval'. People are not logical and
consistent, as researchers may have to assume. In some ways the
interviewee's situation is much more open than the interviewer's.
Sometimes interviewees settle their anxieties by adopting fixed strategies in answering questions so that the researcher may get a
response bias in terms of a person's apparent competence to answer
questions and willingness to answer.

Interviewees may see the interview as an opportunity to express
personal views on issues beyond the interview. They may even chal-

lenge the interviewer in ways that cannot be reciprocated without prejudicing the interviewee's position. The success of research interviews is dependent on interviewees' good will to maintain the necessary working consensus.

Brenner's attempts to describe in detail the interaction between respondent and interviewer and analyse it in terms of rule-keeping/breaking may provide a tool for understanding the interview as a social situation and improving questionnaire and interview design and practice.

In discussing interviewers earlier in this section, we referred to Zweig's ambivalent concerns of the interviewee. Most of us are ambivalent about certain topics but informants may also feel ambivalent about whether or not to reply, and whether or not to tell the (whole) truth. Unless they are like Logan's 16-year-old informant who, especially after a drink, could *really* talk to Logan:

> ... like sometimes I have problems talking to people, y'know, showing my true feeling but I can really talk because it brings out all like I was brought up and I had a lot of problems with people, being rejected and shit, so I got like defences – you're not really gettin' to know me y'know like drink takes that away, even though I don't want it now, it's still there – and that like rips all that down, so it's a lot easier to talk to people – there's nothing in the back of yer head that says ' ... shall I tell him this about ... ?' y'know – 'What'll happen will they still like me?' or something – just tell them what's on your mind, y'know. (Logan 1984, p. 28.)

We conclude this chapter by reiterating our belief that each interview is dependent on the skills of the interviewer and the willingness of the interviewee. The interview is just one incident of social interaction which depends on the co-operation of all participants. In the end the limitations on the information collected in an interview, are those imposed by the interviewee. They are the levels of truth that person is willing to disclose to that interviewer on that occasion.

# Chapter 4

# Examples of interviews in use

One way of impressing the use and potential of interviewing upon the new interviewer – or the reflective long-timer – is through examples. This chapter represents a central part of the book. In it we offer 6 case studies of interviews of various kinds and in a variety of situations. On the whole, the order in which the case studies are presented is a shading from professional researcher through to the school-based practitioner. The general characteristics of the studies are summarised in the table in Figure 4.1. They are:

1  Julia Field, 'Education in sex and personal relationships';
2  Jill Keegan, Janet Powney, 'Conversation with an interviewer: group interviews concerning parents' information needs about schools';
3  Norman Evans, 'Evaluating in-service work';
4  Di Bentley, 'Interviewing in the context of non-verbal research';
5  Dave Ebbutt, 'Pupils' perceptions of their science education 11–16';
6  Steven Eales, 'How pupils read school assemblies'.

In each case there are differing number of interviewees, in different contexts and being interviewed for different purposes.

The interviewers range in their experience of interviewing and in the approaches they have adopted. Julia Field describes survey research of about 200 'paired' interviews conducted by professional interviewers. The interviews are structured, pre-coded and contain a number of open-ended questions. One interesting feature of this case study is the approach adopted by the researchers in selecting their interviewers and interviewees.

Jill Keegan also describes professional interviewing, this time of group interviews – of 27 parents in 3 groups. Jill is herself a pro-

Figure 4.1

| Case studies | Title of project and sponsoring body | Researchers | Interviewers | Interviewees | Nature of interviews | Format for interviews |
|---|---|---|---|---|---|---|
| 1 | A Survey of Health and Sex Education, funded by Family Planning Association and Family Planning Information Service | Principal Researcher: Isobel Allen – Policy Studies Institute Project Director: Julia Field – Social and Community Planning Research | Professionals (16) | Teenagers and Parents 200 'pairs' | Individual interviews as part of full study which included desk research and other interviews | Structured; pre-coded; many open-ended questions |
| 2 | Parents' Information Needs About Schools, funded by National Consumer Council | Jill Keegan – Social and Community Planning Research | Professionals collaborating closely with researchers (1) | Parents – 3 groups equalling 27 people | Group discussions to form exploratory study for subsequent study/questionnaire | Discussion guide; list of questions |
| 3 | Preliminary Evaluation of the Inservice B.Ed., funded by Department of Education and Science | Norman Evans – Cambridge Institute of Education | Researcher-Interviewer (1) | H.E. Tutors – 1st Stage 63, 2nd Stage 63. BEd-Teacher-students 1st Stage 164, 2nd Stage 77. Interviewees in 6 institutions | Two rounds of conversations based on topics evinced from documentary evidence individual interviews | List of 47 statements/hypotheses as basis for conversations |
| 4 | Interviewing in the Context of Non Verbal Research – PhD Fieldwork | Di Bentley – Secondary Science Curriculum Review | Researcher-Interviewer (1) | 10–16 year olds 120 | Informal individual interviews | Unstructured but based on slide photographs and four major topics |
| 5 | Pupils' Perceptions of Their Science Education 11–16, funded by Secondary Science Curriculum Review | Dave Ebbutt, Mike Watts – Secondary Science Curriculum Review | Researcher-Interviewers (2) | 6th formers – 6 groups of 15 pupils each | Freewheeling discussions in groups | Loose schedule of questions |
| 4 | How Pupils Read School Assemblies, M.Ed Dissertation | Steven Eales – Deputy Head Se wyn Junior School | Teacher-Researcher-Interviewer (1) | Headteacher (twice); Deputy Head; Pupils in small groups | Linked with other data assembled through participant observation; interview paramount significance | Prepared questions; recording of an assembly |

fessional interviewer employed by an independent research institute, Social and Community Planning Research, and is usually in at the planning stages of projects. She normally works with the project leader, and sometimes the sponsor as well, before interviewing in depth or in groups. Such interviews might be exploratory, that is, intended as a preliminary stage of a more extended substantial project – as in this case, a precursor to a full-scale survey. Alternatively a series of depth interviews might be seen as the most appropriate method to collect people's views, for example the survey of parents of the mentally handicapped which is referred to in the case study. In this case study, however, we decided to turn the tables and report on Jill's work by interviewing her. The notion of 'interviewing the interviewers', all of them, was one that had entertained us for a while, though asking them to write their own accounts seemed – eventually – to be an easier (and safer) option. For a variety of reasons, it was not possible for Jill to write up her case study and so Janet took on the task of interviewing her and then reporting their discussion. Her study of parents' needs for information was commissioned by the National Consumer Council, and illustrates distinct features of interviewing not represented in our other case studies. Concerned as it is with group interviews, it involves amongst other things the procedures for recruiting groups from the general public and establishing rapport with a collection of people who have not met before, The questions were structured and the interviewer provided with a clear discussion guide.

In Case Study 3, Norman Evans describes interviews with 140 people which he himself conducted, with both tutors and teacher-students in institutes of higher education. He engaged in two rounds of conversations and used a list of statements, or categories, as a basis for each one. His list is provided as an appendix to his study. Di Bentley, as part of her doctoral research, discusses in Case Study 4 those aspects of interviewing within the context of her own work – non-verbal behaviour. She describes the non-verbal behaviour she engages in whilst interviewing individual pupils (a sample of 120) about their perceptions of teacher non-verbal behaviour. In Case Study 5, Dave Ebbutt returns to a description of group interviews, this time with sixth-formers about their recollections of experiences of science education. His work forms part of his strategy for evaluating the processes and products of a national science education curriculum project – the Secondary Science Curriculum Review. Six groups of sixth-formers, about 15 in each, using prepared questions.

Finally, in Case Study 6, Steven Eales, as part of an in-service M.Ed. course, employs interviews alongside participant observation and data collated from a range of documents. He uses both individual and group interviews with his colleagues and the junior pupils at the school where he is teaching.

We have asked each contributor to furnish some fairly common and basic bits of information so that their description allows us to draw out some implications for practices in interviewing. We have not expected that the detail provided is exhaustive, simply that it gives some fairly clear indication of the nature, shape and purpose of the interviewing that took place. Nor would we, or the authors of each study, expect that the interviews in each example have the same status. Some are more tentative and unpresupposing than others, their interest being precisely because they offer us the opportunity to explore some of the problems and rewards of interviewing. We have tried to collect a wide range of examples so as to draw out variety in the use of interviews, and to help us focus on their virtues and drawbacks. We very much hope they can be a useful resource for readers and for prospective interviewers.

**Case Study 1**

**Education in sex and personal relationships**

*Julia Field*

An interview survey of teenagers and parents carried out by Social and Community Planning Research (SCPR).

Project Director: Julia Field,
Principal Researcher: Isobel Allen, Policy Studies Institute.

The provision in schools of education about sex and reproduction has undoubtedly increased enormously in the past 10 years or so. There have also been significant changes in thinking about sex education on the part of educationalists and those involved in the provision of courses for secondary school students and for health care professionals in contact with young people. There has been a shift away from concentrating on human reproduction and methods of contraception towards a much wider programme concerned with personal relationships and preparation for parenthood. Courses in secondary schools are often firmly placed in a health education context, but may be found in almost any part of the school curriculum.

Practices vary widely partly in response to the type of lead given by different Education Authorities, and partly because of the traditional autonomy that individual schools have in setting their curricula.

Alongside many of the developments in schools there has been continuing pressure from groups and individuals, some claiming to speak for parents, some calling for restriction or abolition of sex education in schools and demanding the right for parents to withdraw their children from such lessons. Sex education in schools is sometimes alleged to encourage experimentation and promiscuity and is said to be the responsibility of parents. The pupils and parents, however, are the consumers of this education and their views should be heard and placed in context of recent educational developments. It is some while since their views have been systematically sought on any scale.

The main purpose of this study then was to draw together information on what is actually being taught, to examine the experience and views of both teenagers and their parents. As a result of detailed analysis of the present situation and possible future developments, it was hoped to make policy recommendations which could be of use to all those responsible for the education of young people, at all levels in our society. Funding for the study was jointly provided by the Family Planning Association and the Family Planning Information Service, which itself is supported by the Health Education Council and the FPA.

The full study involved the use of a variety of research techniques covering a range of sources of information: desk research (literature searches and reviews and analysis of published statistics), and exploratory and depth interviews (with teenagers, parents, Local Education Authority officers, school heads and teachers). The larger scale personal interview survey with around 200 teenagers and their parents largely utilised structured questionnaires and a combination of purposive and systematic sampling techniques. Fieldwork was carried out by interviewers drawn from SCPR's existing panel of trained and experienced interviewers, and by two non-SCPR freelance interviewers.

Responsibility for the overall design of the study and for analysis and reporting of the results rests with the principal researcher, Isobel Allen, at the Policy Studies Institute (PSI). SCPR's role was to provide consultancy on questionnaire design and layout and on sample design. Production of all fieldwork documents and selection of the sample as well as piloting and (most of) the field work were also carried out by the SCPR. The fieldwork was conducted between mid-February and mid-April 1985, and, at the time of writing, analysis of the results was in progress at PSI.

The questionnaire design went through many stages from consultation with 'experts' in the field about possible content, informal depth interviews with teenagers and parents, first drafts of the structured questionnaire, informal pre-piloting among teenage acquaintances of the researchers and other contacts and finally formal piloting. This took place in January 1985, using two trained SCPR interviewers and a sampling method analogous to that used for the main survey (though for reasons of time and cost the sampling procedure was not strictly adhered to). Interviewer briefing and debriefing sessions were held before and after the pilot fieldwork, after which final amendments to question wording and sequence, questionnaire length and layout were made.

Throughout it was the intention that, while the questionnaire should be fully structured (i.e. questions asked in predetermined sequence and using identical wording for each interview), a high proportion of questions would be open-ended – requiring the interviewer to write down verbatim responses and to probe for further information or elucidation of responses where necessary. This was in order that deeper insights into how people felt about sex education could be obtained than is the case when relying only on drier, if more statistically reliable numerical data. While open-ended material can be post-coded to a developed code frame it should be remembered that the derived numerical results are not particularly robust or reliable because the degree of freedom that interviewer, interviewee and coder have in dealing with such questions is much greater than when a set of predefined answer options is presented. The material can, however, provide a rich source of illustrative material to back up conclusions reached from the results of a survey. The questionnaires are too long to include in their entirety, but parts of the Teenagers' Questionnaire are included as an appendix to this case study. These extracts are intended to illustrate the format used in this survey, to show the kinds of instructions given to interviewers in asking questions, and to give examples of different kinds of question including fully structured and open-ended ones. The last page of the questionnaire requires the interviewer to give brief details of the cirumstances of the interview.

Of particular concern to the researchers in deciding on questionnaire content and style was that interviews should not amount to, or come across to respondents as an interrogation to test knowledge acquired in sex education lessons or as an investigation of the extent of sexual experience among teenagers. These were not within the aims of the survey and such testing would almost certainly have resulted in lower response rates.

On the factual side questions were aimed at discovering:

- what was being taught in school (the topics covered)
- when (in what years of primary or secondary school);
- in what context (in which part of the curriculum);
- by what methods (books, worksheets, film, outside speakers, class discussion etc.).

Most of this data could readily be collected using pre-coded response categories. Pupils' and parents' reactions and views about the above 'facts' were collected mainly through open-ended questions. The questionnaire for teenagers was developed first because of the need to pay particular attention to question wording in order to use language that would be readily understood and would convey relaxed, informal and unembarrassed an atmosphere as possible. While interviewers themselves would have prime responsibility for drawing out the shyer teenagers, it was important that the questions themselves should not hinder the establishment of rapport. This questionnaire could then readily be adapted for the parent version. Thelatter were asked in much less detail about what was being taught to their children and here it was certainly the intention to gauge the extent of parental involvement/knowledge about the child's curriculum. Otherwise, most questions were deliberately identical tothose asked of the teenagers. There were a few questions asked only of parents about, for example, whether the school had informed them about, or involved them in any way, in the sex education programme, and about their own sex experience when they were young.

The questionnaires were designed to result in interviews lasting, on average, an hour for teenagers and slightly less than that for parents. In practice this worked out as planned though the range of times taken was very wide. The target sample to be achieved was of teenagers aged 14, 15 and 16 to be paired with one parent of each teenager; approximately even numbers of mothers and fathers to be randomly selected when both parents were resident. The sample size was 200 pairs of interviews, that is, 400 individual interviews. Three cities or towns of different population sizes and in different parts of England were chosen. Sampling was conducted via electoral registers as a source of systematic random sampling of addresses. That is a system of selecting addresses from the electoral registers and getting interviewers to call at addresses to 'screen' for the presence of 14- to

16-year-olds. While this overcame all the problems associated with other sampling methods there were some difficulties:

- the cost of screening on top of the main interviewing costs which anyway generally form the largest item of costs in a survey;
- predicting, in advance, exactly how many addresses should be selected in order to yield the target number of interviews.

The cost of screening was kept to a minimum by using a technique known as focused enumeration, often employed in screening for minority groups. Addresses were selected from the electoral registers in blocks of six adjacent addresses. Interviewers call at two of the six addresses (the second and fifth listed) to inquire about the presence of the target group there and at the two addresses on either side. This represents a big time saving in

(a) getting from address to address and
(b) recalling at addresses where no-one was in at first (or subsequent) call.

The subject-matter of the survey is a difficult one in some respects. Unless carefully handled it could be seen by potential respondents as too personal and therefore intrusive and embarrassing, particularly for younger teenagers. Such factors can jeopardise response both in terms of willingness to participate and in terms of quality of response from those who do participate: honest, open and fully expressed opinions were obviously essential to the success of the survey. In addition, for any survey involving minors, formal parental permission must be sought to carry out the interview and beyond this, it is common courtesy to seek parental agreement to interview their children aged 16 or over who are still living at home. These factors might suggest that interviewing be confined to older teenagers. At the same time, accurate recall of what they have been taught and at what stage of their schooling will be short lived for many pupils. Their attitudes and reactions to the experience of school sex education also needs to be tapped at the time, or soon after the event if these are to be accurately reflected.

It was assumed that by age 14 most pupils would have received some sex education at school and would be of an age at which most parents would not object to the child being interviewed. Beyond 16, many would have left school and the impact of the sex education they had received there already overlaid by other learning and experiences. The range 14–16 within the sample would also allow for intra-year comparisons of results.

It was central to the survey that pairs of interviews be achieved so that differences and similarities in attitudes of children and parents could be examined in both cross-sectional and linked ways, and in particular that sub-groups of mothers/daughters, mothers/sons, fathers/daughters and fathers/sons could be examined.

The nature of the interview, with a large volume of verbatim recorded responses, dictated that the sample size should not be too large. This kind of qualitative data is time consuming and, therefore, costly to analyse in depth and returns (in the sense of additional ideas and information) fall off quite fast, that is, beyond around 60–80 interviews. The costs of fieldwork are also high, particularly where, as here, this includes screening a large number of addresses in order to locate eligible households. These considerations led to setting the target at 200 paired interviews split more or less evenly between three separate geographical areas.

Sixteen interviewers worked on the survey, 5 in each of the 3 areas plus one who took over from an interviewer who fell ill. Fourteen were regular interviewers for SCPR, 5 at supervisor level and all but 3 of the rest as part of the permanent panel. Interviewers are invited to join the panel after working for SCPR for some time and if they have a proven record of high standards of work in terms of accuracy, response levels, reliability and good relationships with respondents. All interviewers undergo a basic training with SCPR (whether or not they have worked as interviewers previously) and a rolling programme of refresher courses is also in operation.

The survey demanded a high level of interviewing skill because of the relatively sensitive subject-matter, the extensive open-ended questioning and the need to gain the co-operation and confidence of teenagers. All of the interviewers were women and they were chosen with great care. The choice of areas for the survey was influenced to some extent by the availability of enough interviewers of the high calibre needed.

Day-long project briefing conferences were held in each of the three cities, conducted by the SCPR researcher and attended by the principal researcher. After discussion of the sampling and screening procedures, the greater part of the day was spent in conducting a dummy interview with the researcher acting as respondent (using a pre-completed questionnaire). Interviewers took turns to ask 2 or 3 pages of questions with all interviewers recording responses. At the end of each turn there was discussion and instruction about particular questions and periodic checks on whether correct coding was being done. Interviewers were also provided with a full set of written instructions.

60

Before starting work interviewers reported in to local police stations to explain that they would be working in the area and what the survey was about. This is standard SCPR procedure which allows police to reassure any member of the public who may query with them the bona fides of the interviewer. All interviewers carry identity cards with their photograph on, to show to respondents. In contacting householders the survey purpose is explained verbally, but explanatory letters can also be shown if necessary. A copy of this letter (see Appendix to this case study) is in any case left with survey participants at the end of the interview along with a standard SCPR leaflet which briefly explains the work of the institute and the rights of the survey participants.

Overall, 338 households were found to be eligible, and paired interviews achieved with 205. A further 14 single interviews (10 with parents and 4 with teenagers) were carried out giving a total response of 65 per cent.

One major reason for non-response among eligible households was refusal by the parent. This was either on their own behalf or because they did not wish their child to be interviewed. Direct refusals from teenagers (only) added an extra few percentage points to the refusal rate, which was, as we had anticipated, relatively high at 29 per cent overall.

Response, as is usual, varies considerably from area to area and/or by interviewer but, without controlled experiments, it is not possible to disentangle both area and interviewer effects. In a couple of areas interviewers contacted the office to report their worries about the number of refusals they were getting (achieving high response rates is of great importance to most interviewers) and in one case the interviewer reported that she had a distinct impression that word had got round the area about the survey which led to refusals because of the amount of time it would take.

Over all the three areas the distribution of pairs was as follows:

| | |
|---|---|
| Mother and son | 29 per cent |
| Mother and daugher | 38 per cent |
| Father and son | 20 per cent |
| Father and daughter | 13 per cent |
| (Base: all paired interviews) (205) | |

SCPR's standard fieldwork quality control procedures were operated on this study, such as:

(a) All interviewers, however experienced, are accompanied by a

61

supervisor for a day's fieldwork about once every six months on a rotating basis.

(b) Supervisors re-call on some people who have been interviewed to check that they were indeed interviewed and that procedures were carried out correctly.

(c) The first few interviews sent in by each interviewer are subject to a thorough clerical edit and errors, omissions or other indications of poor interviewing (such as inadequate probing at open-ended questions) relayed back to the interviewer so that subsequent work can take account of remarks made.

(d) In addition all remaining interviews are subject to a more general clerical scrutiny before being passed over to the principal researcher, in this case at PSI – for coding and analysis.

**scpr**

**SOCIAL AND    COMMUNITY PLANNING RESEARCH**

Head Office
35 Northampton Square,
London, EC1V 0AX.
Telephone: 01-250 1866

P.816

February 1985

SURVEY OF HEALTH AND SEX EDUCATION

We are carrying out a survey among teenagers and their parents about what
teenagers get at school on health and sex education and personal development.
It is to find out what parents and teenagers think about what is being taught
and the way it is taught.

The survey is being carried out jointly by SCPR and the Policy Studies Institute
(PSI - see description overleaf). Everything you tell us will be treated in the
strictest confidence : no names appear on questionnaires and no individual
will be identifiable in any way in the report on the survey, which will be
published by PSI. Your address, among many others, was chosen in a random way
from the Electoral Registers.

The study is being funded by the Family Planning Association (FPA) and the Health
Education Council/FPA supported Family Planning Information Service. (The
Family Planning Information Service was set up by the Government to provide
information to the public and to professionals.) Consultation on this study
has taken place with the Department of Health and Social Security.

We will be most grateful for your co-operation in this study about a very
important part of education. It involves separate interviews with a teenager
and one of their parents, which can be arranged for a time that is convenient
to you. Our interviewer carries an identity card with her photograph on it,
which will be shown to you.

If you would like further information about the study please do not hesitate
to contact Julia Field at the above address.

Thank you for your help.

Yours sincerely

*Julia Field*

Julia Field
Research Director (SCPR)

*Isobel Allen*

Isobel Allen
Senior Research Fellow (PSI)

**Director** Roger Jowell. **Deputy Directors** Colin Airey, Barry Hedges. **Fieldwork Director** Jean Morton-Williams.
**Director, Survey Methods Centre** Martin Collins. **Director, Qualitative Research Unit** Jane Ritchie.
**Research Directors** Gillian Courtenay, Julia Field, Denise Lievesley, Patricia Prescott-Clarke, Douglas Wood.
**Data Processing Director** Stephen Elder.                    Registered as a Charity No 258538

*Examples of interviews in use*

Head Office: 35 Northampton Square London EC1V 0AX. Tel: 01-250 1866
Northern Field Office: Charazel House Gainford Darlington Co. Durham DL2 3EG. Tel: 0325 730 888

SOCIAL AND COMMUNITY PLANNING RESEARCH

| | | Col./<br>Code | Skip<br>to |
|---|---|---|---|

P.816                                           February 1985    (207)

SURVEY OF HEALTH AND SEX EDUCATION

III. TEENAGERS QUESTIONNAIRE

(201-03)     (204)              (205-06)

☐☐☐   ☐     ☐☐    02

Block No.   Address     AREA   OFFICE
             Digit      NUMBER  USE:
                             CARD

(ADDRESS SERIAL NUMBER)

TIME INTERVIEW STARTED _____

RING - FROM Q.2c of H/h Composition, CODE NUMBER OF TEENAGER ACTUALLY INTERVIEWED

| | |
|---|---|
| | 1 |
| | 2 |
| | 3 |
| | 4 |

---

**1.a)** RECORD SEX

(208)
Male — 1
Female — 2

**b)** Could you tell me how old you are?

(209)
14 — 1
15 — 2
16 — 3

**c)** And your date of birth

☐☐ ☐☐ 19 ☐☐
Day  Month    Year
(210-15)

---

**IF AGED 16** (OTHERS GO TO Q.3)

**2.a)** Are you...READ OUT

(216)
...still at school — 1 — Q.3
at a 6th form college — 2 ⎫
at another type of college — 3 ⎬ b)
working — 4 ⎫
on a Youth Training scheme — 5 ⎬
unemployed (looking for work) — 6 ⎬ Q.3
or doing something else? (STATE) — 7 ⎭

_____

IF 6TH FORM/OTHER COLLEGE

b) What is the name of the college? WRITE IN

(217-18)
☐☐

---

**ASK ALL**

**3.a)** Have you been at just one secondary school, or at more than one?

(219)
One — 1
MORE (ENTER HOW MANY)

IF MORE THAN ONE

b) In what year of secondary schooling did you (last) change schools?

During/at end of:-
(220)
1st year — 1
2nd year — 2
3rd year — 3
4th year — 4
5th year — 5

- 4 -

| | | Col./Code | Skip to |
|---|---|---|---|
| 8. | **ASK ALL**<br>We're interested to know how young people get to know about things like how their bodies work and sex and personal relationships. Can we talk about school first of all? | | |
| | Just thinking of <u>primary</u> school first - Did you ever have any lessons, films or discussions about any of these things - how your body works, sex or personal relationships at your primary school - either in the infants or the juniors? | (235) | |
| | Yes | 1 | |
| | No | 2 | |
| | Can't remember | 3 | |

| 9.a) | **ASK ALL:**<br>**SHOW CARD A**<br>Can I just check, did you have any lessons, films or discussions at all in primary school about...READ OUT<br>RING ONE CODE FOR EACH AT a) | |

| | a) | | | b) | | |
|---|---|---|---|---|---|---|
| | Yes | No | Can't remember | Age (ENTER) | | |
| ... Animal reproduction/animals being born? | 1 | 2 | 3 (236-8) | | | |
| Human reproduction? | 1 | 2 | 3 (239-41) | | | |
| Pregnancy & childbirth? | 1 | 2 | 3 (242-4) | | IF ALL CODED 2 GO TO Q.13 ON P.6 |
| Sexual intercourse? | 1 | 2 | 3 (245-7) | | |
| Changes in a girl's body as she grows up? | 1 | 2 | 3 (248-50) | | |
| Changes in a boy's body as he grows up? | 1 | 2 | 3 (251-3) | | |
| Family and parenthood? | 1 | 2 | 3 (254-6) | | |
| Personal relationships between male and female? | 1 | 2 | 3 (257-9) | | |
| Contraception/birth control? | 1 | 2 | 3 (260-2) | | |
| Not going with strangers? | 1 | 2 | 3 (263-5) | | |
| Anything else to do with how bodies work, sex and personal relationships (STATE) | 1 | 2 | 3 (266-8) | | |

| Had some sex education but can't remember what topics | 7 ----------------- c) |
| Can't remember at all whether had any sex education | 8 ----------------- Q.13 |

**FOR EACH 'YES' ASK**

b) How old were you when you had the lesson or discussion about_____(QUOTE)? ENTER (YOUNGEST) AGE IN COL. b)      (269)

**IF ANY 'YES' OR CODE 7 AT a)**

c) Altogether did you have just one lesson, film or discussion or more than one about these things?

| | | |
|---|---|---|
| | Just one | 1 |
| | More than one | 2 |
| | Don't know | 3 |

*Examples of interviews in use*

- 5 -

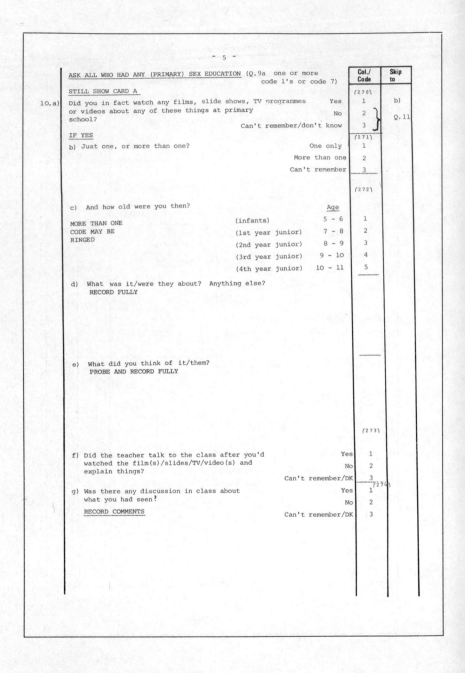

ASK ALL WHO HAD ANY (PRIMARY) SEX EDUCATION (Q.9a one or more
code 1's or code 7)

STILL SHOW CARD A

10.a) Did you in fact watch any films, slide shows, TV programmes
or videos about any of these things at primary
school?

| | | Col./ Code (270) | Skip to |
|---|---|---|---|
| Yes | | 1 | b) |
| No | | 2 | } Q.11 |
| Can't remember/don't know | | 3 | |

IF YES

b) Just one, or more than one?

| | Col./Code (271) |
|---|---|
| One only | 1 |
| More than one | 2 |
| Can't remember | 3 |

(272)

c) And how old were you then?

MORE THAN ONE
CODE MAY BE
RINGED

| | | Age | |
|---|---|---|---|
| (infants) | | 5 - 6 | 1 |
| (1st year junior) | | 7 - 8 | 2 |
| (2nd year junior) | | 8 - 9 | 3 |
| (3rd year junior) | | 9 - 10 | 4 |
| (4th year junior) | | 10 - 11 | 5 |

d) What was it/were they about? Anything else?
   RECORD FULLY

e) What did you think of it/them?
   PROBE AND RECORD FULLY

(273)

f) Did the teacher talk to the class after you'd
   watched the film(s)/slides/TV/video(s) and
   explain things?

| | |
|---|---|
| Yes | 1 |
| No | 2 |
| Can't remember/DK | 3 |

(274)

g) Was there any discussion in class about
   what you had seen?

   RECORD COMMENTS

| | |
|---|---|
| Yes | 1 |
| No | 2 |
| Can't remember/DK | 3 |

- 6 -

ASK ALL WHO HAD ANY (PRIMARY) SEX EDUCATION

| | | | Col./<br>Code | Skip<br>to |
|---|---|---|---|---|
| 11.a) | In your primary school did the teacher give you any work sheets when you learned about any of these subjects(I mean the subjects on Card A)? | | (275) | |
| | | Yes | 1 | b) |
| | | No | 2 | Q.12 |
| | | Can't remember/Don't know | 3 | |

IF YES

b) What about? Anything else?  RECORD VERBATIM

---

ASK ALL WHO HAD ANY (PRIMARY) SEX EDUCATION

| | | | (276) | |
|---|---|---|---|---|
| 12.a) | Did you use or look at, any books when you learned about any of these subjects? | Yes | 1 | b) |
| | | No | 2 | Q.13 |
| | | Can't remember/Don't know | 3 | |

IF YES

b)  What about? Anything else?  RECORD VERBATIM

---

ASK ALL

13.  Looking back  at your primary school(s) what do you think now about the education you had on these subjects (the subjects on card A)?
PROBE FULLY, RECORD VERBATIM (AND/OR RING CODE 7 IF APPROPRIATE)

| | | (277) | |
|---|---|---|---|
| | Didn't really have any education on these subjects | 7 | Q.15 |

*Examples of interviews in use*

| | | Col./Code | Skip to |
|---|---|---|---|

ASK ALL

16. Can we now talk about what you have learned about these things in <u>secondary</u> school (and at college).
SHOW CARD B

Did you have any lessons, films or discussions whether formal or informal, with any teachers about any of the things on this card, in any year at secondary school; what about...READ OUT

OFFICE USE (301-04)
S. NO CARD (305-06)
03

| | | Yes | No | Can't remember | | Col. |
|---|---|---|---|---|---|---|
| *NOT APPLICABLE | ...in the first year? | 1 | 2 | 3 | Not* applic- able | (307) |
| BECAUSE NOT REACHED THAT YEAR | second year? | 1 | 2 | 3 | | (308) |
| (YET) | third year? | 1 | 2 | 3 | | (309) |
| (IF RESP. STARTS GIVING | fourth year? | 1 | 2 | 3 | 4 | (310) |
| DETAILS EXPLAIN: I'll ask you about that in | fifth year? | 1 | 2 | 3 | 4 | (311) |
| more detail in a minute) | sixth year? (INCLUDE COLLEGE) | 1 | 2 | 3 | 4 | (312) |

INTERVIEWER ONLY

RESPONDENT SHOULD RETAIN CARDS B AND C THROUGHOUT Q's 17-30 , EACH OF WHICH DEALS WITH ONE TOPIC FROM CARD B.

FOR YOUR REFERENCE THE TOPICS ON CARD B ARE:

| | |
|---|---|
| Animal Reproduction | (Q.17) |
| Human Reproduction | (Q.18) |
| Sexual Intercourse | (Q.19) |
| Pregnancy and Childbirth | (Q.20) |
| Changes in a girl's body as she grows up | (Q.21) |
| Changes in a boy's body as he grows up | (Q.22) |
| Family and Parenthood | (Q.23) |
| Personal Relationships between male and female | (Q.24) |
| Guidelines on sexual behaviour | (Q.25) |
| Contraception and Birth Control | (Q.26) |
| Masturbation | (Q.27) |
| Venereal Disease | (Q.28) |
| Abortion | (Q.29) |
| Homosexuality and /or Lesbianism | (Q.30) |

- 9 -

| | | Col./<br>Code | Skip<br>to |
|---|---|---|---|

ASK ALL:  STILL SHOW CARD B

17.a)  Just to check, have you ever had any lessons, films or discussions
at all, in any year about <u>animal reproduction</u>?
N.B. INCLUDE (6TH FORM)COLLEGE

| | | Col./Code (313) | Skip to |
|---|---|---|---|
| | Yes | 1 | b |
| IF NO, PROBE BEFORE CODING:<br>Never? In any lesson at all? With any<br>teacher in any year? | NO (AFTER PROBE)<br>Can't remember | 2 ⎫<br>3 ⎭ | Q.18 |

IF YES:  SHOW CARD C

b) Which lessons or subjects was that in?  Any others?
CODE ALL SUBJECTS MENTIONED IN COL. b)

c) Are there any other subjects or lessons, which aren't on the
card, in which you have covered animal reproduction?

CODE YES OR NOT AT c); WRITE IN SUBJECTS IF YES

FOR EACH SUBJECT CODED OR ENTERED ASK:
d) In which year, or years, did you have lessons in_____ (QUOTE SUB-
JECT?)

| | b) Which<br>lesson(s)<br>subject(s) | d) Year<br>MORE THAN ONE CODE POSSIBLE | | | | | | | |
|---|---|---|---|---|---|---|---|---|---|
| | | 1st | 2nd | 3rd | 4th | 5th | 6th | DK | Col. |
| General Science | (314) 1 | 1 | 2 | 3 | 4 | 5 | 6 | 8 | (316) |
| Biology | 2 | 1 | 2 | 3 | 4 | 5 | 6 | 8 | (317) |
| RE/RK | 3 | 1 | 2 | 3 | 4 | 5 | 6 | 8 | (318) |
| English | 4 | 1 | 2 | 3 | 4 | 5 | 6 | 8 | (319) |
| Drama | 5 | 1 | 2 | 3 | 4 | 5 | 6 | 8 | (320) |
| PE | 6 | 1 | · 2 | 3 | 4 | 5 | 6 | 8 | (321) |
| Health Education | · 7 | 1 | 2 | 3 | 4 | · 5 | 6 | 8 | (322) |
| Home Economics | 8 | 1 | 2 | 3 | 4 | 5 | 6 | 8 | (323) |
| Form period/tutor group | 9 | 1 | 2 | 3 | 4 | 5 | 6 | 8 | (324) |
| Year Group | (315) 1 | 1 | 2 | 3 | 4 | 5 | 6 | 8 | (325) |
| General/Liberal Studies | 2 | 1 | 2 | 3 | 4 | 5 | 6 | 8 | (326) |
| Social Studies | 3 | 1 | 2 | 3 | 4 | 5 | 6 | 8 | (327) |
| Personal and social education | 4 | 1 | 2 | 3 | 4 | 5 | 6 | 8 | (328) |
| Child development/care | 5 | 1 | 2 | 3 | 4 | 5 | 6 | 8 | (329) |
| (c) Other(s)IF YES STATE | YES/NO | | | | | | | | |
| (i)_____ | 6  9 | 1 | 2 | 3 | 4 | 5 | 6 | 8 | (330) |
| (ii)_____ | 7 | 1 | 2 | 3 | 4 | 5 | 6 | 8 | (331) |
| (iii)_____ | 8 | 1 | 2 | 3 | 4 | 5 | 6 | 8 | (332) |

| FOR EACH YEAR CODED AT ALL AT d) | 1st | 2nd | 3rd | 4th | 5th | 6th | DK |
|---|---|---|---|---|---|---|---|
| e) In the____ (QUOTE YEAR) did you<br>have just one, or more than one,<br>lesson, film or discussion about<br>animal reproduction? | (333) | (334) | (335) | (336) | (337) | (338) | (339) |
| One only (or part of one) | 1 | 1 | 1 | 1 | 1 | 1 | 1 |
| More than one | 2 | 2 | 2 | 2 | 2 | 2 | 2 |
| Can't remember | 3 | 3 | 3 | 3 | 3 | 3 | 3 |

*Examples of interviews in use*

| | | Col./Code | Skip to |
|---|---|---|---|
| ASK ALL: STILL SHOW CARD B | | | |

18.a) Just to check, have you ever had any lessons, films or discussions at all, in any year about <u>human reproduction</u>?
N.B. INCLUDE (6TH FORM) COLLEGE

(340)

| | Col./Code | Skip to |
|---|---|---|
| Yes | 1 | b |
| IF NO, PROBE BEFORE CODING: NO (AFTER PROBE) | 2 ⎫ | |
| Never? In any lesson at all? With any teacher in any year? Can't remember | 3 ⎬ | Q.19 |

IF YES: SHOW CARD C

b) Which lessons or subjects was that in? Any others?
CODE ALL SUBJECTS MENTIONED IN COL. b)

c) Are there any other subjects or lessons, which aren't on the card, in which you have covered human reproduction?

CODE YES OR NOT AT c); WRITE IN SUBJECTS IF YES

FOR EACH SUBJECT CODED OR ENTERED ASK:
d) In which year, or years, did you have lessons in_____ (QUOTE SUBJECT?)

| | b) Which lesson(s) subject(s) | d) Year MORE THAN ONE CODE POSSIBLE | | | | | | | |
|---|---|---|---|---|---|---|---|---|---|
| | | 1st | 2nd | 3rd | 4th | 5th | 6th | DK | Col. |
| General Science | (341) 1 | 1 | 2 | 3 | 4 | 5 | 6 | 8 | (343) |
| Biology | 2 | 1 | 2 | 3 | 4 | 5 | 6 | 8 | (344) |
| RE/RK | 3 | 1 | 2 | 3 | 4 | 5 | 6 | 8 | (345) |
| English | 4 | 1 | 2 | 3 | 4 | 5 | 6 | 8 | (346) |
| Drama | 5 | 1 | 2 | 3 | 4 | 5 | 6 | 8 | (347) |
| PE | 6 | 1 | 2 | 3 | 4 | 5 | 6 | 8 | (348) |
| Health Education | 7 | 1 | 2 | 3 | 4 | · 5 | 6 | 8 | (349) |
| Home Economics | 8 | 1 | 2 | 3 | 4 | 5 | 6 | 8 | (350) |
| Form period/tutor group | 9 | 1 | 2 | 3 | 4 | 5 | 6 | 8 | (351) |
| Year Group | (342) 1 | 1 | 2 | 3 | 4 | 5 | 6 | 8 | (352) |
| General/Liberal Studies | 2 | 1 | 2 | 3 | 4 | 5 | 6 | 8 | (353) |
| Social Studies | 3 | 1 | 2 | 3 | 4 | 5 | 6 | 8 | (354) |
| Personal and social education | 4 | 1 | 2 | 3 | 4 | 5 | 6 | 8 | (355) |
| Child development/care | 5 | 1 | 2 | 3 | 4 | 5 | 6 | 8 | (356) |
| (c) Other(s) IF YES STATE YES/NO | | | | | | | | | |
| (i)_____ | 6  9 | 1 | 2 | 3 | 4 | 5 | 6 | 8 | (357) |
| (ii)_____ | 7 | 1 | 2 | 3 | 4 | 5 | 6 | 8 | (358) |
| (iii)_____ | 8 | 1 | 2 | 3 | 4 | 5 | 6 | 8 | (359) |

| FOR EACH YEAR CODED AT ALL AT d) | 1st | 2nd | 3rd | 4th | 5th | 6th | DK |
|---|---|---|---|---|---|---|---|
| e) In the_____ (QUOTE YEAR) did you have just one, or more than one, lesson, film or discussion about human reproduction? | (360) | (361) | (362) | (363) | (364) | (365) | (366) |
| One only (or part of one) | 1 | 1 | 1 | 1 | 1 | 1 | 1 |
| More than one | 2 | 2 | 2 | 2 | 2 | 2 | 2 |
| Can't remember | 3 | 3 | 3 | 3 | 3 | 3 | 3 |

- 27 -

| | | Col./<br>Code | Skip<br>to |
|---|---|---|---|
| | ASK ALL | | |
| 36 . | Now - in general - looking at all the sex education you've had<br>at secondary school (and college): | (863) | |
| a) | Did you always understand the <u>words</u> that the<br>teacher used to describe things? | | |
| | Yes (unqualified) | 1 | |
| | Most of them/most of the time | 2 | b) |
| | Not really/some of them | 3 | |
| | No (unqualified) | 4 | |
| | Has had no sex education yet<br>(i.e. Q.17a - Q.35a <u>all</u> coded 'NO/DK') | 7 | Q.41<br>(p.30) |
| | | | |
| b) | Do you think teachers should always use 'proper'<br>words or do you think it would help if they<br>sometimes used the words you or other young<br>people use? | (864) | |
| | Proper words | 1 | |
| | RECORD COMMENTS: | | |
| | Young people's words | 2 | |
| | Both | 3 | |
| | PROBE: Why? Why not? | | |
| | | | |
| 37.a) | Did you always understand the <u>diagrams</u> and <u>pictures</u> that<br>the teachers used? RECORD COMMENTS | (865) | |
| | Yes (unqualified) | 1 | |
| | Most of them/most of the time | 2 | |
| | Not really/some of them | 3 | |
| | No (unqualified) | 4 | |
| b) | Do you think diagrams and pictures are<br>useful ways of teaching things like this?<br>RECORD VERBATIM; PROBE: In what ways? | (866) | |
| | Why? Why not? | | |
| | Yes | 1 | |
| | Sometimes | 2 | |
| | No | 3 | |

**Case Study 2**

**Conversation with an interviewer: group interviews concerning parents'
information needs about schools**

*Jill Keegan and Janet Powney*

What follows is a summary of the research project and then the
central parts of a discussion between Janet and Jill. The conversation
is based upon the project but focuses primarily on the organisation
and conduct of the group interviews used. In this case the tables are
turned and Janet (interviewer) is interviewing Jill (interviewee).

*The project*

It is now widely accepted that children whose parents are 'involved'
with their education achieve better than children whose parents are
not involved. Access to information about, acquired knowledge and
understanding of a school is a prerequisite of involvement – however
that term may be interpreted.

Through the 1980 Education Act, Local Authorities must now
provide, by law, a considerable amount of information about each
individual school. Many of the requirements are aimed at helping
parents make an informed choice between schools, others towards
maintaining the flow of information once a child is attending a
particular school. The National Consumer Council (NCC) asked
Social and Community Planning Research (SCPR), an independent
research organisation, to carry out a small-scale exploratory study
to look at what parents themselves see as being their information
needs and whether they actually get what they want. The purpose of
this limited study was to provide a background paper for NCC
discussion on considering whether a piece of large-scale research on
this topic should be mounted.

Given the restricted budget, it was decided that group interviews
would give more perspectives than a few individual interviews. Three
group discussions, involving a total of 27 parents, were held – one
in Leeds, one in Ealing and one in rural Oxfordshire. Only one
representative of a family was invited. This was usually the parent
who took the most active role in home/school contact. Five men and
22 women attended.

The sample was recruited by a recruiting interviewer, a local person, briefed over the phone by the group interviewer and given notes on the kinds of people to be recruited and a little background to the project (see Recruitment Sheets in Appendix 2, Items 2.1, and 2.2). The recruiting interviewers contacted unknown households by knocking on the front door. Once contacts had agreed to participate, the recruiting interviewer left them with a brief formal letter, from Jill Keegan, explaining the project (see Appendix 2, Item 2.3). A person who agreed to be interviewed was used to contact another, thus 'snowballing' recruitment. A day or so prior to the discussion the recruiting interviewer would confirm that the person was still able to attend. This would also give them time to replace if necessary. The groups met in the recruiting interviewer's home and were paid a small attendance fee. The sessions were tape-recorded and subsequently the interviewer and one of the researchers listened to the tapes and discussed them prior to writing a report for NCC. With only three groups scheduled, it was decided with the agreement of the NCC to consider secondary schools only and to concentrate more on information needs once a child was in secondary school, rather than on information needs for making initial choice of school. All the topics covered in the discussions were approached through exploring the experiences of parents – what they did, and do, what the schools do for them, assessing the satisfactoriness of the actions, whether alternative approaches would be better and attempting to identify gaps in information provision. A 'guide' to topics to be covered in the course of the discussion was prepared in consultation with officers of NCC. A copy of the guide is also appended to this case study. (Item 2.4)

It is important to stress that group interviews are never intended to provide results that are representative of, or generalisable to, a population group as a whole. They are intended to indicate the possible range of experience and attitudes, but not to suggest numerical or proportional frequency of occurrence of particular experiences and attitudes. This caveat is particularly relevant here since funding meant that only three groups could be held. Given that LEA's vary considerably in their policies and modes of operation quite different issues could emerge from groups held in other areas.

*The conversation*

The conversation between Janet and Jill lasted almost two hours with much of it a broad discussion of interviewing and research methodologies. We have chosen extracts here which emphasise the group interviews and the problems and rewards of that particular methodology. Some of the transcript has been omitted and conflated; the extracts are quoted in sequence and verbatim. Where the questions have been rephrased for brevity and clarity this is indicated by (R). The conversation begins with a discussion of 'professional' versus 'non-professional' (amateur?) interviewers:

*Interviewer*:  Why do you think that it's not a good idea for researchers to do their own interviews? (R)
*Interviewee*:  I think in quite a number of cases they are almost too close to the subject. I mean this almost contradicts what I said (earlier in the transcript) about, you know, about being involved right at the word go. But if somebody who wasn't – o.k. if the researcher is also well-trained in techniques of interviewing, that's different. But if they are not they can so often think they have got the answer because they think 'That's it, that's what I'm looking for'. And if they'd gone back one stage farther they might have found it wasn't what they were looking for at all, or at least that wasn't the way the respondent was seeing it. It's always taking it that stage further that a professional interviewer knows how to do. And, if she is good, will do it and not leave when she thinks she has the answer, the answer she wants. And I think that's the problem with researchers. I mean J. (a senior researcher) had a very very good example of this when we were doing the mentally handicapped research. We were doing groups, and we had developed a system of doing groups together. It's a very good system of two people doing groups, it really is – and J. was in the middle of doing her part of it and somebody said to her – I've forgotten what it was – oh, I know, this woman said – 'But I couldn't let my daughter go, I just couldn't, I love her far too much', and so J. sort of nodded and smiled. And I said 'but that's not really an answer, you say you love her too much, why can't you let her go?' And she said 'Because if I did, I'd be like a ship without an anchor.' And the whole thing then, of her dependence on her daughter, which was amazing, the description which she then went on to give. . . . And J. said 'Never ever had thought of going further than that, because 'loved' seemed the answer'. And er, and it's that sort of thing that I think, you know, of when I say I think an *interviewer* would think 'that's not really an answer'. And that's where a researcher has to be careful.
*Interviewer*:  What's this two-person group interview? That's rather interesting.

*Interviewee*:   Yes it is, it's one we developed when we were helping DHSS to redesign forms, for finding out what the information needs are of the people getting forms from the DHSS. Then, we had an awful lot of forms to deal with and we decided the only way we could do it was for two of us to be there. We found it so took the pressure off the moderator, by having somebody else who was going to be able to sit there, pick on the points that were missed, that we found that we were really getting double the value from a group. And what looks on paper as a fairly expensive type of operation turned out to be well worth the extra expense. Because again, the person who wasn't actually doing it could see the person hesitating in the group who was longing to say something but really couldn't bring herself to, so she hadn't even got to beyond her eyes wanting to say something, but the other interviewer could see what was going on and just come in and say something.

*Interviewer*:   You think it's a good system?

*Interviewee*:   Yes, I mean, it really does work, and you really do get some amazing results from it.

*Interviewer*:   Would the group size make a difference? (R)

*Interviewee*:   No, no difference at all. Er, it so happens that the mentally handicapped group did turn out to be large groups because we recruited 12 in the hope of getting about 8, you know, as you do. But because of the very nature of the subject the people very much wanted to attend a group so we got twelve at the group. But those groups went on for three and a half hours. And I doubt it you could have done it, especially the stress and the tensions that were there in that group, I don't think one moderator could have coped with it. But two worked superbly.

*Interviewer*:   The term, 'moderator'?

*Interviewee*:   Yes rather than – I don't like the words 'group leader' – because I think the last thing you are doing is leading a group. I don't think you *should* be leading a group. In fact, if anything, you should be there to follow a group and therefore I would never use leader as a name. If I wanted to refer to things I would talk about 'group moderator'.

*Interviewer*:   If we turn to the NCC project, how did you get the groups started? (R)

*Interviewee*:   By getting them to relax and getting them – I think the important thing is, when they arrive, for them *not* to talk about what they have come to talk about. It's very difficult to keep them off the subject. It's very important because you haven't got the tape on – when one gem might be said. And so I deliberately steer them away from talking about it. It's very funny actually because it has finished up by getting me into quite a lot of trouble with interviewers who had done the recruiting for us. They referred to me as a prima donna, because they said 'She swans in, absolutely ignores the interviewer and just talks to the people who have come to the group'. And I said 'in a funny sort of way, that is a compliment'. I know it wasn't meant to be one, but I said that the important thing is making people see, you know, 'look we're here, we are a group of people meeting together to talk – I'm interested in you'. That's why I get things – like I pay them as soon as they arrive, get all that sort of thing out of the way. Make sure they have a cup of coffee and relax, start talking to each other so they to some extent start thinking of being a *group* from the moment they arrive ... as more people arrive coming into the group. So I would chat to them very casually for however long it takes for the group to arrive. I would then introduce myself, because at that stage I haven't even done that. I just say 'Hello, nice to see you, come and sit down, have a coffee'. I then introduce myself sort of formally then I tell them what I hope a group discussion is all about. I'd say, well, I'd usually say 'My name's Jill Keegan, I work for an organisation called "Social and Community Planning" which is an independent research institute. We are a non-profitmaking charitable trust and we do quite a lot of work for government departments, academic bodies and in this case for —; the important thing to tell you is that this is a *group* discussion. There are an awful lot of things I want to ask you but I don't want it to be a question and answer session. I want you to discuss it amongst yourselves – if you agree with the person who is saying something – say so – if you disagree – say that as well. Because that's what a discussion group is all about. I don't want you to feel that you have to talk to me the whole time, just talk to each other as you would normally'. And I say all that before I even mention a tape recorder – I mean the tape recorder is sitting there – then I say to them, you know 'With your permission I must ask you if I can tape it, purely for my benefit because I couldn't possibly sit and take notes if I was talking to you, is that all right with everybody?' And only once did somebody say no. And then you can switch on and do the introduction to the study itself which should be taped, because if you have misled them in any way on that introduction, it should be there for all to see, including the sponsor, that you have introduced it in the wrong way. So introduction is important.

*Interviewer*: And then what? (R)

*Interviewee*: And then I say, 'But er, before I start could I just ask you if you could tell me a little about yourselves, where you live and how many children you've got and whether you're married, single, widowed'. O.K. you've got it all on your contact sheet but, well you are interested in that for two reasons. One is for the purpose of them trying their voice out, which as you know doing depth interviewing is important. I think it's most important that everybody speaks once and hears the other people speaking. I hope then never again to have to go round the table. And so that way, apart from the poor woman or man who starts, you know, everybody else knows you are going to them next. And it gives them a chance to have to say something. It also gives you a chance to start what I mean when I talk about my script thing (discussed earlier in the transcript). 'Here's a woman with three children, she's got two, in this case at secondary school. I must remember that because when she talks about certain forms, or certain stages they are at, which child is she referring to.' So I might scribble an odd note to myself. And the other thing it is for the person who's transcribing the tapes they can recognise the voice, and if you are using stereo mikes, which I do, they can then always put 'female 1', '2', '3', '4', so you can always go back and you then have a script of one person recorded all along. So going round in that way makes it easier. That's how I would start and then I would hope my first question would be sufficiently arresting to get them talking. I think your first question is important to the group.

*Interviewer*: So how does the first question relate to your guide?

*Interviewee*: I always use the word 'we', I never say 'you' because I think again it's important it looks as though to some extent you are part of the group. 'We all know that now everybody here has got children at secondary schools and they started either last year or the year before (or whatever) – tell me did you feel you had any choice where – when you were first thinking about your child moving from primary to secondary school, did you feel you had any choice in the matter?' And then you sit there and wait.

*Interviewer*: And then things happen, it starts going? You are checking what you have got on the list roughly?

*Interviewee*: Yes.

*Interviewer*: And presumably also if you've been engaged in meetings with the researchers and the sponsors from the very beginning, you've got some priority in this, within these questions, about those things that you feel you must cover? (R)

77

*Interviewee*: That's right, yes. And I would say that if I haven't written the guide, or if the researcher and myself haven't written it together, if the researcher has just presented me with a guide, I always say to them 'O.K. which of those questions must be answered?' And I just put a star on my own guide – just makes sure. I think, as well, it's what you've also got to bear in mind with a group, how it sort of takes off and a lot of things come out at once. And you've got to decide in your own mind which lead you're going to follow up. And also whether you have the next point, or whichever point they have brought up as sufficiently well or whether you are going to go back to it. My instinct is to go back to points because you can usually come up with extras. But always making sure that the people know that you are going back to it. Indeed I say, you know, 'Mrs So and So was mentioning earlier that she found she'd absolutely no choice as far as school was concerned, but how about the rest of you? – did you feel you'd any choice at all or not?' or er, something like 'Yes, yes, I know, and I've recorded the fact, I know you've mentioned it, but I want to discuss it further as a group'. And again it's a case of teaching people their role within a group.

*Interviewer*: What would the pattern of questions and answers be?

*Interviewee*: Question, answer, question, answer, comment, comment, and then question and then comment, comment, comment, comment. And then perhaps if you are lucky, question from over here to over there. And then what can happen, of course, is question, answer, question and question. You know you start where the group leader starts. This is where I think the person you've got to watch within the group starts taking over. Where the dominant person starts.

*Interviewer*: Yes that's quite difficult isn't it in a group? On the one hand the dominant person is very helpful ... and on the other hand they can er ...

*Interviewee*: I've always thought how marvellous it would be if somebody could actually tape your thoughts. I mean it would fascinate me it really would. Because you've got to sort of decide: that person's useful, he's saying a lot of very useful things, that's why he's dominating because he knows a lot about the subject – well usually it is. I mean, if they are really useful how much more can I let them get away with it? Because I want that information, but how much am I going to risk losing the little lady sitting over here who is obviously intimidated by this man's knowledge? Already she feels her two-pennysworth is just not going to be

worth her saying. Which is going to be more important to get?
And it's very often a hard decision to make. I've had sometimes
to call their bluff, er the dominant person. I try and make the rest
of the group gang up against the dominant person in a case like
that. And I say 'Come on are we going to let him get away with
a thing like that sort of remark?' and hopefully, you know, sort
of let the group say 'Hey!'. You know, to see that I too know that
he's dominating and he's not going to dominate me, so why
should he dominate them? And mostly it works.

*Interviewer*:   But on the other hand you don't want at the same
time to antagonise him?

*Interviewee*:   Oh no, it's got to be a very careful tone of voice.

*Interviewer*:   Did you find that after starting the group off on
'Choosing a School' that people extended into other areas? (R)

*Interviewee*:   Yes, and I think it's important to keep a fairly tight
structure on this type of group because there's quite a lot that
you want. You want to know about the stages of choosing and
if they already go up to school. And if they say 'Mind you, now
that he's there he's absolutely fine and his teachers are marvellous
every time I go and see them', you know, I think 'Hey, just a
minute, that's much too far on'. So I will always sort of gently
take them back and make sure that they have finished that first
section before I move on to the second. I mean sometimes it's
taken out of your hands but I know, in this particular case I
knew, it was important to separate the actual choosing process
from what happens once they're at school. Because some of the
things they say can only really happen once they actually had got
to school and knew about it. You know, when I say 'Well what
did you know about this school?' 'Well you know the bullying is
absolutely dreadful' and all this sort of thing. 'Did you know
that when you were choosing the school or is that only since the
person's actually got to school?' And those sort of things. Again
it goes back to this role, you know, of sort of teaching. 'Come on
let's finish with this part and then we'll get on.' I know it makes
a mockery to some extent of what you'd call a 'group discussion'
because it's not quite as free flowing as it would appear when
you sort of start by saying 'I now want you to discuss'.

*Interviewer*:   Do you call yourself a moderator when you're
introducing yourself?

*Interviewee*:   I don't really call myself anything. If anyone says
'What are you here for?' I say 'I'm here to listen'. Very
deliberately. I don't even put 'researcher' on letters because, you
know, what are you going to research? Occasionally the project

79

director will sign the letters and put 'Project Director', or something like that and I, I always find that people seemed to be relieved that I'm not that person. As though they would have been expected to know far more. So I find it important.

*Interviewer*:   What about refusals, or non-answers in a group discussion? (R)

*Interviewee*:   I suppose the interesting thing there, about non-answers, were the people whose children had played truant. And their position, as to whether they were going to tell me about it or not, was interesting. Because a number *did* and – as soon as one mentioned it, somebody else came out with it – and it was almost by accident in the first place. Also one of them went so far as to say he'd got into trouble with shoplifting, and they'd been very helpful. And it's always interesting at what stage of the group that sort of thing comes out.

*Interviewer*:   But there wouldn't have been the same hesitation in an individual discussion?

*Interviewee*:   No, absolutely not. It's, er, and you can always tell then if a group is gelling as a group, if they feel they are ready to tell the group something like that.

**Case Study 2: Appendix**

*2.1 Guidelines for recruitment*

---

P.788                PARENTS INFORMATION NEEDS

### Project Instructions

Enclosed are the materials for recruiting and hosting the group discussion in your area.

| | | |
|---|---|---|
| Group 1 | Leeds | 16th January |
| Group 2 | Oxfordshire | 17th January |
| Group 3 | Ealing | 19th January |

Quota Sheet

Letters and invitation cards to be left with the people recruited.

Recruitment Data Sheets to be completed when someone is recruited.

* As mentioned on the Quota Sheet, I would like you to recruit 10 people per group, 5 of whom should be ABC1 and 5 C2DE.

* The sex of respondent is not important. The parent recruited should be the one who has most dealings with the school.

* At least 2 of your quota should have children who started secondary school last September.

* All parents should - in theory - have a choice of secondary schools in their area. Please try and recruit a group who have children at at least 2 different schools in your area.

* The discussion will centre around the amount of choice parents have when deciding on a school for their child and type of information they get - or would like to get - from these schools.

* Each group will start at 7.30 pm and will last about 1½ hours.

* I hope you will be able to act as hostess for your group, providing tea/coffee etc. if required to do so.

### Venue

Please refer to notes in yellow booklet provided. Do find one as quickly as possible so you can then start your recruitment.

Be sure to inform the police in the area you are working.

If you have any problems please phone me either at work, or home (01-995 6068).

Jill Keegan

# Examples of interviews in use

## 2.2 Recruitment Data Sheet

scpr

Head Office: 35 Northampton Square London EC1V 0AX. Tel: 01-250 1866
Northern Field Office: Charazel House Gainford Darlington Co. Durham DL2 3EG. Tel: 0325 730 888

SOCIAL AND        COMMUNITY PLANNING RESEARCH

P.788                    RECRUITMENT DATA SHEET GROUP

### Introduction

We are carrying out a study with parents of children at secondary school, about the
amount of choice, if any, parents had as to type of school their child attends.  Also
the kind of information the school gives to parents on all aspects of it's role.

### Explain about Group Discussion

* We are carrying out small group meetings in different parts of the country with
  parents of children at secondary school.

* The groups are being arranged by SCPR an independent research institute on behalf
  of the National Consumer Council who is sponsoring the research.

* The discussion should last about 1½ hours.

* £5 will be paid to each person attending to cover expenses.

  CHECK Quota Requirements.


### Classification Data of Respondent Recruited

Name:_____          Activity Status of Respondent

Address: _____          Activity Status of H/H

_____          Social Class        A  ☐

_____                              B  ☐

Tel. No: _____                              C1 ☐

                                                           C2 ☐
Age last birthday:_____
                                                           D  ☐
Household Composition:
No. in household aged   0 - 4  ☐                           E  ☐

                        5 -15  ☐        Child's starting date at school _____

                        16-65  ☐        No. of children at secondary school  ☐

                        65+    ☐        Name(s) of school(s) attended by child(ren):

Marital Status:     Married    ☐        _____ single sex     ☐
                                                                          ☐
        Widowed/Divorced/Sep.   ☐       _____ co-educational

                    Single     ☐        Date of recruitment:

                                        _____

                                                      Attended Group   ☐

                                                      Did not attend   ☐

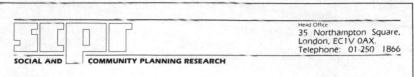

**SOCIAL AND** **COMMUNITY PLANNING RESEARCH**

Head Office
35 Northampton Square,
London, EC1V 0AX.
Telephone: 01-250 1866

P.788

### Parents Information Needs

We are carrying out a study with parents of children at secondary school, about the amount of choice, if any, parents had as to the type of secondary school their child now attends.

We are also interested in the kind of information schoools give to parents, and how they help them to keep in touch with their child's progress.

It is also hoped that parents may be able to suggest improvements they would like to see in these areas.

The study has been commissioned by the National Consumer Council and is being carried out by SCPR, an independent research institute.

We are carrying out a number of small group discussions with parents in different parts of the country on this subject. The discussion should last about 1½ hours. We will be paying each person who attends £5 to cover any expenses they may have, coffee will be served.

I look forward to meeting you.

Yours sincerely,

Jill Keegan

## 2.4 Group discussion guide

Head Office
35 Northampton Square,
London, EC1V 0AX.
Telephone: 01-250 1866

**SOCIAL AND COMMUNITY PLANNING RESEARCH**

P.788

Group discussion guide on parents information needs about schools

1. Choosing a school

   *Did parents feel they had any choice in school child now attends?

   *If choice - how to go about choosing. Does choice matter?

   *How do you know what a school has to offer?

   *Where do they get their information from about each school?

   *Do school give enough information

   *Is it easy to understand - should more be explained about teaching methods - subject choice, etc.

   *If school has problems due to socio-economic conditions should parents be told how school tackles these problems?

   *What is a good school - a bad school?

   *How do they get that reputation?

   *What things really worry parents when child transfers - bullying - settling in periods - attitudes of school to smoking - drugs, etc.

   *What information would you like to have that has not been mentioned already - academic results - career choices - equal opportunities e.g. computer studies - more oriental subjects?

   *How much did they in fact, make use of existing sources of information e.g. prospectuses - visits to school - academic reputation, disciplining and pastoral reputation - word of mouth - primary school advice - child's choice.

2. Once at secondary school

   *Do parents feel in touch with the school, and what goes on in school?

   *Do they want to be in touch; in what ways; is it easy or difficult?

   *Do they think it matters for parents to take an interest/participate?

   *How would they like to be kept informed, and about what, what do their children think about them taking an interest?

   *Last two visits to the school: what occasioned the visit, was it helpful, comfortable, a good or bad experience and in what ways?

   *How did they feel when they visited school?

   *What information/contact the school offers: formal (e.g. reports, open evenings, newsletters, events) less formal (e.g. PTA social events, access to teachers, methods of communication, homework, getting questions answered, understanding the curriculum and its organisation?

   *Should parents and school talk more about teenage problems and who should be responsible home or school?

   *How much use is made of what is offered, and why/why not?

Cont'd/...

**Director** Roger Jowell. **Deputy Directors** Colin Airey, Barry Hedges. **Fieldwork Director** Jean Morton-Williams.
**Director, Survey Methods Centre** Martin Collins. **Director, Qualitative Research Unit** Jane Ritchie.
**Research Directors** Gillian Courtenay, Julia Field, Denise Lievesley, Patricia Prescott-Clarke, Douglas Wood.
**Data Processing Director** Stephen Elder.                                           Registered as a Charity No 258538

- 2 -

3. Attitude to New Regulations on information to parents

   *Do they know what information a school must give by law?

   *Should these be changed - added to - what form of presentation would be best?

   *Should names of governors be made available - why?

   *Should school have to mention PTA or other parents organisation - why don't some schools do this now?

   *Should school have to give information on child's progress or lack of it in form of written reports or contact parent if there is problem with child?

   *Should school say how they can be contacted?

   *Should school give reason for certain rules - ask parents for their views on them?

   *Should school give more help in interpreting exam results - give more information about school achievements e.g. how many get jobs - how many go on to further study. What proportion learn to swim - training given in personal and life skills?

**Case Study 3**

**Evaluating in-service work**

*Norman Evans*

This piece is based on the Preliminary Evaluation of the In-Service B.Ed. Degree, which was a study funded by the Department of Education and Science at a cost of £36,000, and which lasted 32 months, from October 1977 to May 1980. The grant-holder was the Cambridge Institute of Education, where working facilities were provided.

The abstract of the research reads as follows:

With particular reference to further professional training review all full-time and part-time B.Ed. degree programmes, including bridging courses in England and Wales as courses available to experienced teachers, and give an account of them, noting especially the relationship between differing elements in these courses.

With that as one kind of evidence, consider the perceptions teacher-students and tutors have of these courses, the motives of teachers in following them and the evaluation of them by teacher-students, heads of schools and LEA's and the degree results achieved.

As such, it stood as a piece of policy-orientated research, essentially a short-term exercise. It was concerned with process; what actually happened, according to the people involved. It followed that qualitative rather than quantitative styles of inquiry seemed appropriate. And so it was that interviewing and case-study work became the order of the day.

I was faced with the problem of trying to make sense of 62 different validated programmes in which 6,740 teachers had enrolled as students. There were three sources of possible evidence. There was documentary evidence drawn from published information about courses, institutional papers about those courses, and of course, papers which told the story of validation. There was evidence which could be drawn from tutors teaching those courses. There was evidence which could be drawn from those studying the courses. The problem was to know how to obtain evidence from tutors and students to set alongside the evidence from documents. There was the predictable problem of the enormous gap which always gapes between what documents say will happen on a course and what actually happens. And there was the additional problem, also entirely predictable, that what tutors believed went on in a course was different from what students either experienced or thought they had experienced when asked about it. And vice versa. Listening to what tutors and teacher-students had to say about their courses seemed a good way to acquire the evidence.

Interviewing is one thing; having a conversation is another. Interviewing generally implies that the interviewer has a set of questions encompassing the general areas from which the information sought may emerge. There will be space for supplementaries prompted by remarks made by the interviewee, and maybe some hold-all section to cope with 'anything more you want to say about ..' But the overriding position is that the initiative rests with the interviewer, not the interviewee. Having a conversation implies nothing more than two or more people talking with one another. Now of course some conversations have a sharper focus than others. And some conversations are more like monologues. But for my purposes in the Preliminary Evaluation of the In-Service B.Ed., conversation seemed nearer than interview to describing accurately what was going on between me and some 160 serving teachers who were students, and their 60 tutors whom I tried to listen to. But what kind of framework would best provide for the talking and listening?

To hold these three sources of evidence in some steady relationship and provide a framework for this talking and listening, I tried to establish a common denominator. Using documentary evidence from the survey of the 62 degree programmes, I worked out a set of categories about the In-Service B.Ed. This set was tried out on two colleges as pilot studies and then revised to take account of what the teacher/students and tutors in these two institutions had made of them. Then I selected from the 62 different degree programmes 5 that I thought representative.

The survey revealed two poles of provision. At one end stood a degree offered to experienced teachers which was the same as that which had been offered to initial training students, and which was validated by a university. At the other end stood a degree specifically designed for serving teachers and sharply differentiated from a pre-service course as an explicitly professional degree for experienced practitioners. This was validated by the Council for National Academic Awards. These programmes were selected as two of the case studies.

In between these two poles 3 other programmes were chosen as case studies, as offering different variants of either the first or the second programmes already identified. First there was a CNAA-validated degree, designed as a professional course for experienced teachers which contained the academic study of the contributory disciplines of education. Second, there was a university-validated degree, designed specially for qualified teachers, taught on a regional basis, where half the study in the part-time degree was given to educational studies, under a choice of topics, and the other half was called a special subject study, offering applied main subject focus with the emphasis firmly on it as a curriculum subject within the school. The third, again validated by CNAA, was different again in that teachers could study either education or a main subject together with a professional course, or education with professional courses. A sixth case study was added as the most advanced in developing off-campus provision and this was a university-validated degree.

Taken together, these 6 case studies covered the various types of In-Service Degree Programme being offered and gave a satisfactory geographical distribution up and down the country.

I knew some of the tutors from the participating institutions, but none of the teacher-students. All the participating teacher-students were volunteers. Their tutors were asked to provide students to be interviewed, with as wide a range of interests as possible, attempting to cover all school age ranges and all subjects taught within the particular degree programme. They circulated a general invitation I wrote, which explained the purposes of the Preliminary Evaluation, quoting the abstract of the research, and asking for help in a piece of work which, it was hoped, would influence policy decisions which could affect their successors.

The revised set of categories was then sent to all the tutors and teacher-students who were to participate in each of the six institutions where evidence was to be sought. As I said in the Official Report (NFER 1981, p. 2) 'the first round of talks was intended to cover the revised categories, which were handed out to tutors and teacher-students before any conversations took place. Naturally. the coverage varied from place to place, according to the composition of the group and their interests'.

In all, the first round of conversations involved 63 tutors (51 men, 12 women), which included the 6 course leaders, and colleagues drawn from the various component parts of the degree programme. 164 teacher-students participated (93 men, 71 women). Some of the conversations were individual; some were in groups.

All those conversations were taped, using a small Sony tape recorder with a standard-sized cassette, and later transcribed. Each was searched for significant statements under each of the categories used in that first round of conversations.

Eventually, somewhat laboriously, I arrived at a set of 47 statements/hypotheses, grouped under 10 headings (see Appendix 3). To quote the report again,

> This list of 47 statements/hypotheses provided the framework for the second round of conversations. This meant that although the teacher-students and tutors in each of the six institutions all brought different interests, understandings, and perspectives to bear on the statements, and although only some of them were derived from what they themselves had said during the first round of visits, everything said in the second round occurred within the same framework. Some of the statements overlapped; by implication so did some of the headings. Moreover, the order of the headings and of the statements/hypotheses could have been varied in any one of a score of ways. None of this seemed to invalidate the list as an instrument. Whatever its composition, every contribution from either a tutor or a teacher-student was bound to be made under the immediate influence of current experience of the degree, either through teaching it or studying it.

For the second round of conversation, as for the first, the list of 47 statements/hypotheses was circulated in advance to all tutors and teacher-students who were going to take part in the second round. For the second round, there were 77 teacher-students (41 men and 36 women) and the same number of tutors (63).

In what was thus essentially a subjective as opposed to an objective inquiry, within the self-evident limitations, the one control mechanism which could be used to achieve consistency was to ensure that no one took part in the second round of talks within the case study institutions who had not been involved in the first round. How far that went towards the kind of reliability and validity which inquiries should achieve is another matter. It certainly argued for an authenticity which could not easily have been reached in other ways.

What all this amounted to was an attempt to get as close as possible to the evidence about In-Service B.Ed. programmes which seemed most important to those who were teaching it and studying it. Inevitably there must have been a continuing influence of those categories which I devised from the documentary evidence before they were put though the two-tier revision already described. But to a significant extent it seemed then, and seems now, as I re-read the story, that it was the tutors and teacher-students who identified what for them were the components of the course worth considering as material for evaluation.

Within the control mechanisms established – 47 hypotheses/statements as a common denominator for all conversations and the restriction for the second round to those who participated in the first round – there was room for proper variations and additions. The brief to each tutor and teacher-student was to respond to whichever hypotheses/statements seemed most interesting or pertinent or relevant to their own experience.

The internal brief I tried to work with was to get as comprehensive a coverage of the 47 statements/hypotheses as possible. Each conversation was allowed to range wherever it would, within the framework of the hypotheses/statements. Because the 10 sections overlapped in places, so that some of the statements/hypotheses overlapped as well, it was of no moment where any conversation began or ended. What mattered was the evidence which each and every conversation could yield. Moreover, a conversation has two contributors. So that a remark which interested me could just as well lead into other areas, as could the thinking of a tutor or teacher-student at any stage. Lateral thinking was ruled in, not out. Which takes us back to conversations as opposed to interviews. The idea of structured interviews is bound to have come from a recognition of the curious nature of unstructured interviews. It is the familiar problem. Those conducting interviews believe more or less implicitly in their capacity for extracting significant information from the interviewee as a basis for making whatever kind of decision lies beyond the interview. Reality is different. How often does an interviewee say afterwards, 'if only I'd had the opportunity to say ...'. And it has to be the case that the larger part of the responsibility for that lies with the interviewer. Considering the purpose of an interview, it is patently unsatisfactory for the resulting evidence not to include items which were significant for the interviewee. That evidence could well be of far greater importance than anything which was actually said, so providing a structure for an interview is a way of trying to reduce that deficiency.

Now it may well be that the difference between a structured interview and the conversations which were based on a set of statements/hypotheses is merely a question of semantics. I think not. The quality of the exchanges in those conversations reflected a lack of paramouncy between interviewer and interviewee, between the inquirer and the provider of information, which I do not think characterises the nature of the exchanges within an interview. In a conversation the two-way flow is axiomatic; in an interview that two-way flow may be intended but it is not the operating principle. All very subjective, of course, but then evaluation is a subjective business – like any other form of assessment for that matter – but that is another story. It will be obvious that the most subjective factor of all was the control, direction, pace and place of the interviews which I conducted. Sometimes, it was clear that interesting evidence was not forthcoming. Sometimes, teacher-students were weary and there was little point in extending an interview. Sometimes, teacher-students were rushed as they generously fitted in an interview to their heavy study-load, which in any case was an extra to heavy daytime teaching loads. In these circumstances, the only control factor was that I did all the interviewing and so at least I was able to attempt to guard against more blatant inconsistencies.

All the second-round conversations, again, were taped, transcribed, and searched for evidence which related to one or more of the hypotheses/statements. Any direct quotation which was selected for use in the final report was sent back to the teacher-student or tutor who had spoken the words, for clearance. Calling on all this evidence then, 6 case studies were written, offered to readers as evidence on which they could make up their own minds about those 6 accounts of the In-Service B.Ed. They had to make their own judgements on my professional judgement about the conversations I had had.

*Case Study 3: Appendix*

*Statements/hypotheses: second round case study conversations*

1     Institutional and professional context
1.1   Few teachers in schools are able and willing to contribute to the teaching of In-Service B.Ed. programmes as partners with tutors.
1.2   The teacher studying for the In-Service B.Ed. degree frequently experiences hostility and disdain from colleagues.
1.3   It is prestigious for a tutor to teach an In-Service B.Ed. course.
1.4   Where there are frequent changes in the tutorial staff teaching the course the In-Service B.Ed. has a low institutional priority.
1.5   A school-based provision of the In-Service B.Ed. for group registration from a single school limits the range of inquiry and discussion.

2     Rationale and content
2.1   The aims of the In-Service B.Ed., to reflect and re-value, are in conflict with the systems of assessment used on the course.

91

2.2 Teachers do not want the 'main course + education' kind of programme for their In-Service B.Ed. course.

2.3 'Professional' courses are either a waste of time or 'preaching to the converted'.

2.4 A part-time In-Service B.Ed. offers greater opportunities for further professional training than a full-time In-Service B.Ed.

2.5 The experience of attending classes with teachers from other schools is the most important contribution of the In-Service B.Ed. to further professional training.

3 Course structure
3.1 It is more helpful for teacher-students to study one course at a time than to study two or more simultaneously.

3.2 A part-time degree programme composed of numbers of modules or units to be completed each year is not appropriate for a post-experience course.

3.3 The course claims to offer a study programme based on a hierarchical sequence of conceptual development, but it does not provide this.

4 Use made of teachers' experience
4.1 The course draws its study materials from the teaching experience of the teacher-students.

4.2 School-focused courses enable teacher-students to systematise the knowledge which comes from experience.

4.3 Courses which include students' personal and teaching experience as study material are more demanding on teacher-students than those which do not.

4.4 Teacher-students do not want the In-Service B.Ed. programme to be school-focused.

5 Modes of study
5.1 The best attendance pattern for teacher-students is a varied programme of weekday evenings, periodic Saturday mornings, and weekends.

5.2 Attendance requirements prevent teacher-students from reflecting on their studies.

5.3 Teacher-students learn more from writing assignments with tutorials to follow than from attending lectures.

5.4 A part-time teacher-student needs more direction from tutors in his work than a full-time teacher-student.

5.5 The schedule of prescribed work for teacher-students forces tutors to set assignments at inappropriate stages in the course.

6 Workload
6.1 Teacher-students on part-time In-Service B.Ed. courses are seriously overloaded.

6.2 Disparities in work requirements between different but equally weighted parts of the course create difficulties for teacher-students.

6.3 Teacher-students on part-time In-Service B.Ed. courses find their school work suffers.

6.4 The volume of work demanded from teacher-students prevents them from attaining the standards of which they are capable.

7 Methods of assessment

7.1 An In-Service B.Ed. course in which results are based largely on continuous assessment appeals to teacher-students.

7.2 To be equitable, work handed in late should be penalised save in exceptional circumstances.

7.3 Written examinations at the end of a part of or the entire course are an inadequate means of discovering what links teacher-students can make between theory and practice.

7.4 Teacher-students' professional competence is valued, yet for assessment they are treated like undergraduates.

7.5 Teacher-students are over-assessed on their In-Service B.Ed. courses.

8 Teacher involvement

8.1 Being able to offer comments at the end of the course does not make teacher-students feel involved in their own In-Service B.Ed.

8.2 School-focused work ensures that a teacher-student can substantially determine content and methodology in the course he is following.

8.3 A teacher-student is fully involved when the work of the degree includes aspects of his work in school.

8.4 Teacher-students are insufficiently involved in planning the courses they study.

9 Tutorial staffing

9.1 The skills required by tutors for In-Service work are different from those required for initial training work.

9.2 Tutors are not innovators in schools so they are not in a position to teach new methods to teacher-students.

9.3 Tutors recognise that the professional experience of teacher-students is as important as their own.

9.4 Teacher-students find lectures/presentations by tutors inadequate.

9.5 The success of a course for a teacher-student depends on the tutor.

9.6 Tutors take personal affront if the content of their lectures is criticised.

10 Status of B.Ed./levels of attainment

10.1 Part-time students cannot produce the depth of study possible for full-time teacher-students.

10.2 The B.Ed. degree has an assured status within the education service.

10.3 Some teacher-students study for the In-Service B.Ed. because a BA or BSc is not available to them.

10.4 The In-Service B.Ed. requires more time than an M.Ed. and the same attainment level.

10.5 The performance of initial training and In-Service candidates for the

93

degree is different so it is difficult to justify the award of the same degree.

10.6   The award of an Honours or Ordinary degree should depend on a fully classified award system at the end of the course.

**Case Study 4**

**Interviewing in the context of non-verbal research**

*Di Bentley*

Expressions such as 'it's not what you do it's the way that you do it' give some inkling of the power of non-verbal communication in human interactions. My fascination with the hidden curriculum of communications came about in the context of teaching situations. I observed many conversations between youngsters and their teachers in which the youngsters were more powerfully persuaded by what the teacher didn't say than what they did. Frequently the youngster's assessment of teachers as 'strict', for example, seemed to be based upon the abilities of the teacher to exercise social control by means of non-verbal behaviour. One pupil compared her relationship with the head to that of a rabbit transfixed by headlights:

> when he looks at me, you know like he does in assembly, he kind of glares and doesn't say anything. Then you know it's time to sit down and be silent. He just has to stand there looking at me, and I feel like a rabbit in the headlights of a car. I'm kind of paralysed.

The whole notion of using a verbal medium such as interviewing to investigate non-verbal decoding skills is one that I find fascinating. Much of the information received by an interviewer is lost to a tape recorder, since, as Argyle (1969) states, in any interaction between two people, 60 per cent of the information received is non-verbal in nature, and only the paralanguage parts of this can be captured by the tape recorder, and hence only a part of the actual data. Much of the rest of the non-verbal cues from the interviewees can only be encapsulated in my memories of the scene. Further reduction, of course, occurs on transcription when parts of the paralanguage cues are lost as well. For a non-verbal researcher, these issues are very difficult ones with which to come to terms. To be aware that you are losing a large percentage of potential data in the methods of collection which you utilise and yet to know that if you want to investigate the ideas that people have, you need to talk to them, and only

94

to be able to record their conscious vocal behaviours, not the sum total of the interaction that you receive, when it is precisely those other parts of the interaction that are the subject of your research – that is hard indeed!

In the study reported here, I was investigating by means of an unstructured, informal interview what meanings youngsters attributed to non-verbal behaviour which they met from their teachers. All teachers have, for example, been in the situation of waiting for the class to be quiet, yet they choose a variety of non-verbal gestures to convey this. Youngsters seem to be able to decode these gestures with great rapidity, even when the teacher is a relative stranger whose non-verbal gestures they have not had time to learn. I took slide photographs of teachers posing various non-verbal behaviours which were commonly used in classrooms. The teacher behaviours were selected on the basis of being those that were common in all classrooms whatever the subject, and, where possible, were overtly non-verbal in their aspects, rather than just being an accompaniment to a verbal communication. Using the slides as a basis for an interview, I asked the youngsters what they thought the teacher meant when they displayed the facial expression or gesture in the slide. The youngsters were given a list of possible answers from which to choose, shown the slide for an exposure time of 30 seconds only and then asked to explain why they selected the answer they did. If their answer did not agree with the meaning that the teachers said they were trying to convey, the youngster was told what message the teachers thought they were conveying, and asked to examine the slide again in the light of such information. They were then asked whether they wanted to change their minds, and what particular clues had led them towards their original answer.

The interviews were conducted by myself, as the only interviewer, on a one-to-one basis, with youngsters ranging in age from 10 to 16, whose replies were tape recorded. There were 120 youngsters in the sample, 60 of each sex. Twenty teachers also took part. The selection of the youngsters was done by the class teachers who were asked for 10 youngsters from their class, 5 of each sex, with a spectrum across the ability range, since non-verbal decoding ability is not intelligence-linked. The interviews were informal in the sense that they were designed to be as relaxed as possible and there was a deliberate attempt to create atmospheres of informality in order to remove stress. The interviews focused around four major parts, which could really be described as the only attempt at structure within the process:

1  What aspects of the communication caused the interpretation selected by the youngster? e.g. stance, gaze, hand gesture?

2 Do all teachers do it that way?
3 How do they know that's what the teacher meant? i.e. what previous experience are they using as a basis for their judgements.
4 If they change their opinion in the light of being told what message the teachers thought they were trying to convey, what new aspects of the behaviour do they now focus on? e.g. do they now concentrate on mouth shape rather than frown?

## Setting the scene

Researching into non-verbal behaviour for any length of time, makes one acutely aware of one's own non-verbal behaviour, and its power to shape interactions. In the case of these interviews, I was a stranger to the youngsters, and I was putting them in a potentially uncomfortable situation, by sitting fairly close, and tape recording what they said. Moreover, I was questioning the behaviour of teachers, and even though the teachers in the slides were unknown to them, some youngsters found this difficult to deal with. They regarded me sometimes with extreme suspicion, as though I were a spy from the enemy camp wanting to know what they thought of the staff.

Being aware of the potential for uncomfortableness and suspicion, it was necessary to create conditions in the interview as quickly as possible which would allay such fears. I used precisely the behaviours I was investigating to create such conditions. It was not always possible to interview in comfortable surroundings, but before setting up the interview, I would visit the school and ask permission for a suitable place to be allocated. Often this would be the dining area during lesson time. Such rooms are large, acoustically poor, and it is difficult to create a closer, more intimate atmosphere in such places. My technique was to arrange two of the tables in a corner so that they partitioned off the rest of the room and the youngster and I could sit inside these, with the tape recorder on the table, complete with the slide projector and daylight screen. I would position the chairs at slight angles to each other so that the youngster was almost, but not quite, facing the screen, and my chair was at an angle of some 60 degrees to theirs with the tape recorder on the table at my right elbow, not quite out of sight, but almost so when the youngster sat down. Having 'set the scene', with the slide projector as the prominent feature, when the youngster arrived for the interview, I would walk out from behind my 'barrier of tables' before they reached me, and greeting them by name, with a smile which was careful to engage eye contact, I would either shake their hand, if they were an older person, or contrive to touch them as I invited them to sit down. This touch was usually just a light touch upon the shoulder as I showed them the seat. Mehrabian's (1969) research into social interaction has shown how such gestures of touching are powerful indicators of liking, and lead the recipient to construe that the toucher, even when a total stranger, is a pleasant person who likes them. Smiling and a positive approach to others, indicating that you have gone to the trouble of getting to know them in advance by learning their name also create feelings of 'positive affect' in dyadic interactions (Argyle, 1969).

Once the youngster is seated, I ask them if they are comfortably placed for seeing the screen, but ask them not to turn their chair round to face the screen entirely, as this may mean they are not positioned correctly for the microphone. This request has two purposes. Firstly, the question about the place of their chair is to enable them to assert the interpersonal space between us with which they feel most comfortable. The microphone statement is to disguise the fact that if they face the screen completely, they will deliberately put a barrier between us, in the form of the screen, and interact with that instead of me. When they have positioned their chair to their satisfaction, I then sit down, moving my chair slightly, if necessary, so that I can see the screen and maintain eye contact with the interviewee.

During this manoeuvre, I keep up a light inconsequential conversation, usually concerning the lesson they have just left, or are missing to work with me. This conversation is deliberately conducted using paralanguage (speed of speech, voice tone, volume etc.) which is designed to convey friendliness. The sentences are short, the speech speed slow, the words bright and at a low pitch. The paralanguage is accompanied by frequent smiling and head nods in agreement with their statements, to put them more at their ease and convey liking.

*The interview*

Once we are both seated, I explain carefully what I am going to ask them to do. I show them the tape recorder, ask their permission to use it, and offer to play the tape back to them at any point they wish, either during the interview or immediately after it. I tell them that it will be heard by no one else other than myself and a typist, and state that if I should want anyone else to hear a part of it, I would return first to play them the part and ask their permission. The youngsters

97

are often surprised by this level of care of their words, and I encourage a little discussion of the point if it seems they wish to do so, in order to continue the friendly scene setting.

I then ask them to read what is written on the pre-prepared card, having checked the details are correct, into the tape recorder. The card has their full name, age, school, and interview number written on it. I explain that the number is so that I can keep track of my recordings, and that I am asking them to read it into the recorder so that I can check the recording level and the typist can use it as a way of identifying their voice, and learning their name straight away.

I then give the interviewee the list of statements that explain what the teachers are trying to convey so that they can make their choices, switch on the recorder, and ask them to read their card. I tell the interviewee I am going to show the first slide, and ask them to look at the screen. The first slide, depending on the age of the interviewee, is a distractor, either one of my daughter and I fooling about in the garden, or one of the slides of the teachers, but upside down. This usually creates a little laugh, and reinforces the idea that I am a human person who has warm relationships with youngsters, or who makes mistakes. I laugh, apologise for the mistake, and then proceed to read from my list the number of the slide I have used. Since I have a bank of 80 slides, and I show only a maximum of 20 at any one interview, this is an essential part of the record-keeping procedure, which is repeated before every slide.

During the interview, I am careful to overtly display listening behaviours, nodding in agreement, smiling, maintaining eye contact whenever possible as they talk to me, and disengaging to indicate my turn for discourse. I sit in a relaxed, open position, being careful not to fold my arms as I listen and to lean forward from time to time, as if to catch what they say, but in fact to display liking. My verbal interview style is one of repeating what the interviewee said last but raising my voice at the end of the sentence to indicate that I am in fact turning their statement into a question to seek further clarification. This repetition also has the effect of increasing their belief that I am listening, and is known in social skill terms as mirroring. Where the youngster asks me a question about the slide or my opinion, my reply is 'I'm not really sure'.

The interview itself begins as the first slide is switched off. I ask the youngsters the same opening question:

What do you think was going on there in the slide? What might the teacher have been doing? Look at the list I've given you and try to choose one that fits best with what you saw.

When the youngster has selected a possible behaviour, I then ask:

What was it about the teacher that made you choose that one?

I try at this point to enable the youngster to make explicit the aspects of the teacher's expression that gave rise to their choice, without having the slide in front of us. If this is proving too difficult, I then ask:

Would you like to see the slide again? It might help you to pick out the things that made you choose ... (teacher behaviour).

If the response is yes, I then show the slide again. This part of the interview is the most difficult, since to impose structure here would be to lead the youngster. I am trying to elicit what features resulted in the youngster's choice, and sometimes it is necessary to say:

Was it the way they were frowning or the look in their eyes that gave you the clue?

Frequently, having done that on the first two or three slides, I do not need to draw out those sort of clues again because the youngsters quickly get the idea of what I am looking for. The rest of the interview then shapes itself in response to the youngsters' selection of clues for their interpretation of the slide. The only standard set of probe questions are those which ask:

Do all teachers do it that way?
How do you know that's what the teacher meant? (What previous experience are they using as a basis for their judgements?)
Now you know what the teacher thought he/she was trying to do, what bits of their action on the slide might make you pick that out? Anything? Or can't you pick up that message from this picture?

*Analysing the tapes*

The tapes were transcribed, and then listened to (usually ad nauseum!). From a continual listening and comparison, it became obvious that certain clues were ones the youngsters attended to most frequently. Other cues, such as body stance, for example, were less useful in conveying meaning than were eye direction. By continual listening, I allowed the categories of cues used by youngsters to select themselves. There were inevitably a whole range of paralanguage cues as youngsters sought to make explicit their judgements for non-verbal decisions, which came out on the tapes. I used the tapes to draw out the cues that youngsters use to interpret their teachers' non-verbal messages, and to attempt to elicit other messages that the youngsters construed from what they saw. Further analysis was then possible to make comparisons of consistency of such interpretations by age and culture. What I also gained was a whole new set of data which conveys the paralanguage cues people use when they struggle to make explicit judgements usually performed below the level of conscious awareness. However, as yet, that source lies untapped.

## Case Study 5

### Interviewing groups of students

*Dave Ebbutt*

This is a procedural and methodological account of a piece of small-scale research which my colleague Michael Watts and I undertook in the Autumn and Spring terms of 1984–85. We called the research our Autumn Term Project. The outcomes of the exercise are not yet complete. We have yet to tackle the task of cumulating/synthesising our analyses of the interviews from each school. The motivation for our engagement with the task was twofold. First we were conscious that the Secondary Science Curriculum Review, (our 'mother' project), although it had consulted a wide constituency (SSCR 1983) about its proposals for the reform of the science curriculum, had overlooked the idea of consulting school students. We saw our first and major task to remedy this omission. Our second, subsidiary task, was to explore the feasibility of deriving useful information by means of interviews with groups of students. It is the second of these two tasks which is addressed in this chapter. We both have had considerable experience of one-to-one interviewing. I had earlier done a little work interviewing groups of children as part of my teaching (Ebbutt 1981).

Between us we decided that we wished to elicit from students their retrospective views of, and current feelings about, their experiences of science education 11–16. Obviously we needed to talk to students for whom those experiences were still reasonably fresh. Consequently we decided that first-year sixth formers would form an ideal group for our purpose. In addition we felt that we wanted to conduct the interviews in an atmosphere which was as free from 'institutional' constraints, as possible. Therefore we selected sixth form colleges as ideal sites. This was because these tertiary colleges drew from many secondary schools, so the students with whom we wished to talk were no longer in the same school about which we were asking them to reflect.

*Negotiating entry*

I obtained permission, by telephone, from the Deputy Chief Education Officer to approach three Sixth Form Colleges in his authority. I then wrote as follows to the three colleges:

4 October 1984

Dear (Principal)

As you probably know —shire has given considerable support to the work of the Secondary Science Curriculum Review.

One aspect of the work to date has been to consult widely with various agencies about their views of science education, and our proposals about the future directions of science education. Unfortunately students themselves have been left out of this process. In order to redress this imbalance two of us on the Review Central Team would very much like to come to your school and talk (in a group interview situation) with first-year students, from a range of disciplines.

We envisage that this could be done in a double lesson, and so would make a minimum encroachment on teaching-learning time. We would like to do this soon after half term.

May I come and discuss with you more precisely the details of what we would like to do. Could I come and talk with you either on

Tuesday 16 Oct @ 10.00 or 2.00
Wed      17 Oct @ 10.00 or 2.00
Thur     18 Oct @ 10.00 or 2.00

I look forward to hearing from you shortly.

Yours sincerely,

All three colleges replied positively. I made a visit to each college, and met the principal. Subsequent to a chat with the principal, the details of suitable dates, of the sort of room I would require and of the sample of students with whom I wished to talk were dealt with, either by the head of science or by the director of studies.

What was very clear to me at this period was that having the cachet of a high-profile national project was very advantageous in terms of gaining smooth and rapid entry to schools. I had completed all three of my interviews by the Christmas vacation.

*Planning our role in the interviews*

Prior to this series of meetings, Watts and I drew up a loose schedule of questions which we felt would be useful in order to ensure that we covered similar issues in a more or less similar order. Nevertheless we both hoped that a fairly freewheeling discussion would ensue, where students would react to issues which others had raised. We also discussed the range of students whom we would like to see in our 'sample'. We felt that we wished to talk with students studying a full range of courses; scientists, artists and one-year sixth formers with an equal representation of boys and girls. We envisaged that between 9 and 15 students would attend each interview. Watts and I did not discuss in our planning session whether to issue our questions to the students before the interview. None of my three groups of interviewees had the questions prior to my arrival at the school. In retrospect I now wish that the students had been provided with an opportunity to consider our questions before the interview session. The loose schedule of questions which we used to frame the interviews was as follows:

- What do you feel is your clearest memory of your science experience 11–16?
- Did your science experiences 11–16 hang together for you as an unfolding story?
- What use do you feel your science experiences 11–16 have been to you?
- How important was it to you, or how useful was it to you to keep notes of what you did?
- What do you feel about the importance to you of practical work in science 11–16?
- Do you really believe the explanations which science 11–16 gives for various events?
- What is your view about the personality of science teachers?
- What is your opinion about the ways in which science teachers might differ from real practising scientists?
- What changes would you like to see in science 11–16 by the time your children face that particular stage?

Of course it was understood between us that these questions were 'starters'; we would be free to ask some follow up questions as well as attempting to elicit minority views and opinions.

Additionally we agreed that we would record the interviews on tape, subject to a token negotiation with the students. We decided, somewhat unsatisfactorily as it turned out, to have three battery-operated cassette recorders running simultaneously at three different positions in the interview room. This was the system I used throughout. However, Watts, who faced more bureaucratic obstacles in negotiating entry to his authority and his two chosen schools, on hearing the poor audio quality of my tapes, subsequently used a pair of good quality throat-mikes into a mains-driven stereo cassette recorder. The audio quality of his two interviews was greatly superior to that on my tapes.

## Interview day

I arrived at each school at least half an hour before the interview was due to begin and made my way to the designated room. I arranged the seating and the positions of the recorders to my satisfaction (basically a wide circle).

The students, whom I had never met and who, of course, had never met me, arrived in ones and twos and I gave them identification lapel labels on which to write their first name. When I thought they had all gathered I explained the task and its purpose, 'negotiated' the use of the recorders, switched them on and began with the first question. Of course the real world is a very messy place so inevitably there were students who arrived late and I needed to explain the procedural detail to each newcomer.

I was very conscious that I had been thinking deeply about the interviews for some time: I had a commitment to their 'success', whereas for the students I was just something that happened to interrupt, or perhaps enliven their routine. In fact I needed the students and their views, far more than they needed me. One often reads about the asymmetry of power said to exist between interviewer and interviewee(s); the balance is normally seen to reside with the interviewer. I am coming to the view that 'one-off' group interviews of the sort I am describing probably shift power back to the interviewees, although it is a power they probably do not know they have. It is a potential power held by virtue of numbers and differential commitment. Whatever it is, this interviewer felt a degree of tension as this extract illustrates:

> *Ebbutt*: Can I put something else to you – are you getting
> bored Nicola?
> *Nicola*: No.
> *Ebbutt*: Sure? If you are really getting bored just get up and
> go.
> *Nicola*: No I'm not getting bored, it's very interesting.

A further aspect of the 'one-offness' of the interviews was that I was not familiar with the students' names, hence the lapel badges. Yet I wanted to encourage a sharing of views between students and to be able to identify in the resultant transcripts who was saying what. Practically, this meant that from time to time during a fruitful discussion in the interview I had to interject a sotto voce 'voice-over' in order to identify a succession of speakers, a strategy which sometimes impeded the very flow I wished to encourage.

We decided at one site that it would be interesting if Mike Watts and I were both present at the same interview. Perhaps not surprisingly, this was the least satisfactory interview, both for the length of pauses before students responded (up to 46 seconds) and for the quality of the responses when they did eventually happen. Even now I cannot decide whether two interviewers were spooking each other or whether our combined presence daunted the students, I suspect both factors were in play. I really enjoyed two of the interviews; I have a less warm feeling for this one.

After each interview was complete I promised to send my preliminary analysis of the transcript back to the group for their comment. In each school one student agreed to receive the analysis and to ensure that each member of the group had sight of it. Further this student agreed to pass comments back to me. Here is a letter from the 'co-ordinating student' in one of the schools.

> Thank you for sending us the results of your analysis, we hope that we were of some help to you and we most certainly enjoyed the discussion. We have not added any comments to the interview as we feel it says all that is needed, but we all feel that the lack of time which is present in science lessons should be stressed. Good luck in completing your synthesis.
>
> Yours sincerely,
> M.A.

*Transcription of interviews*

Watts and I had decided to 'buy in' an audio typist. We knew from experience that this task is both time-consuming and tedious. I knew that the audio quality of my tapes was poor. However when I compared the typed transcript with what I could hear on the tape it was immediately apparent that the print was a very free and highly imaginative interpretation of the original. It took me three weeks of more or less solid work to remedy the infelicities using a professional transcription machine, the original cassette recorders and a hi-fi unit.

## Analysis of the transcripts

This is the stage I usually enjoy most and the Autumn Term Project was no exception. In the past this stage was characterised by a sea of paper littering the room. Partly because I now knew the transcripts almost by heart it was less messy than is usually the case. A word processor also contributed to a reduction in the amount of mess.

I took the first transcript and read it through several times. After some time I realised that most of the comments were about bad practice in science teaching. However, implied in all the comments was a vision of what the students saw to constitute good practice. This idea of good practice became my central organising concept. Then it was a case of teasing out from what had been said a set of categories under which I could classify different aspects of perceived good practice. At this point I think I asked Watts to look at the transcript and the analysis. He agreed that the approach was potentially fruitful and suggested further categories. Essentially I adopted a similar approach to the other two transcripts; of course these contained examples of categories not present in the first interview. These were the analyses which I eventually sent back to the interviewees. Watts has adopted a similar approach to his transcripts. As mentioned at the start we have not yet grappled with the issue of quite how we report the synthesis of the whole exercise. We are clear, however, (partly because the Review is a development project) that good practice in science teaching will be the major theme. Having recently looked through all 5 analyses I think that before we attempt a synthesis we may well have to look again at the categories as they are beginning to look a little crude, a little too inclusive, and they overlook some of the subtlety of the evidence which currently supports them. This scanning and refining process, moving backwards and forwards between the raw evidence of the transcript and the developing analyses, is the classic constant comparison method of qualitative analysis first put forward by Glaser and Strauss (1967).

*Examples of interviews in use*

*Group interview as a methodology*

All data gathering techniques have their limitations. Previously (Ebbutt op. cit.) I had used the group interview to obtain a feel about the extent that perceptions previously gleaned through individual interview were more generally applicable to a whole group. I found the group interview was useful to this end. As I see it the Autumn Term Project was more or less the reverse of this process. We used the technique to raise issues at a fairly high level of generality. Again it was a very fruitful method for this purpose. Group interview would I think be of little use in surfacing intensely personal issues, or issues where the interviewer has to probe an interviewee's perceptions with a succession of follow-up questions. I think that the dynamic of a group denies access to this sort of evidence. As a method it is roughly analogous to a limited sample questionnaire, but much more fun. Each time I look at the transcripts or the analyses I remember, with pleasure and amusement Marcus, Shona, Michael, Karen, Shani and Lup.

One great advantage of the group interview, it seems to me, is that it could be used by practising teachers with the minimum of disruption to their normal teaching procedures.

*References*

Ebbutt. D., (1981) 'Girls' science, boys' science revisited', in Kelly. A. (ed.) *The Missing Half*, Manchester, MUP.
Glaser. B. and Strauss. A., (1967) *The Discovery of Grounded Theory*, Chicago, Aldine.
SSCR (1983) *Science 11–16: Proposals for Action and Consultation*, London, SSCR.

**Case Study 6**

**How pupils read school assemblies**

*Steven Eales*

*Background*
The subject of my research was the daily assemblies of an East London junior school. The investigative work lasted approximately

9 months and was undertaken alongside my duties as a class teacher in the school.

My initial interest in the subject had been aroused by the negative attitude displayed towards the assemblies by many of the participants, staff and pupils alike. I was particularly concerned about how pupils viewed the event and the consequences of these perceptions for their attitude to school and learning generally.

The purpose of the study, then, was to examine the communication in the assemblies with particular emphasis on the pupils' perspective. Broadly speaking, the approach was ethnographic and sought to explain the perceptions of the participants in terms of their ideological and cultural viewpoints. Hall's televisual model[1] was modified to form the basis of the analytical framework. The signs[2] of the assemblies, in their many forms, were focused on; how they were encoded by the assembly leaders[3] and decoded by the pupils.[4] An evaluation of the assembly experience for pupils could then be made.

In brief, the findings were disturbing. The evidence suggested that much of the encoding was insensitive to the pupils' social and cultural position and to their academic skills. The encoding tended to

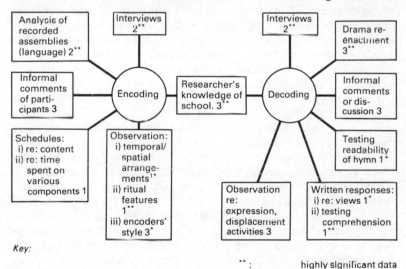

Key:

To indicate weight attached to method

\*\* : highly significant data
\* : significant data
no asterisk: supportive data

To indicate broadly the nature of the method

1: highly structured and/or formal
2: structured and flexible
2: less structured and/or piecemeal

*Figure 4.2*

107

reinforce the class-based divisions of the wider social structure rather than serve the working-class pupils for whom it was intended. Although pupils rejected some of the signs of the assemblies encoded in this way they nevertheless tended to accommodate themselves within the framework to which they were exposed. Any rejection remained covert and/or partial. Essentially, pupils accepted the subordinate role that the assembly encoding prescribed.

The data collection had to take account of the fact that all signs in the assemblies were conceived as message-bearers. A range of methods was therefore employed, varying in significance and style. The diagram (Figure 4.2) is a crude summary, with the codes attempting to loosely define the broad characteristics of the approach and the significance attached to each activity by the researcher. Paramount significance was attached to the interviews.

*Interviewing*

As a teacher-researcher conducting my own interviews, I was aware of the problems which may arise from a shift in my role; not least, that I and the research may not be taken seriously, that the novelty of the interviewing may undermine the consideration given to the responses (thwarting validity), that the authority of my teaching role may inhibit the responses of the pupils. In the event, these fears were unfounded. There may be a number of reasons why this was so.

I enjoyed good relations with the interviewees, both the assembly leaders and the pupils. This is not always the case. It may be that your chief source of data happens to be your worst enemy, in which case you are probably well-advised to forego the encounter in favour of alternative means of eliciting information. Good relations, however, can be encouraged: by ensuring interviews are arranged at a time convenient to the interviewee; by briefing the interviewee beforehand as to the reason for and nature of the interview and its context regarding the research (this also enables some preparation on the part of the interviewee and discourages rash responses); by asking if notemaking or taping is acceptable. It may be that your memory is a more reliable source than the perfunctory replies offered by a tense colleague who feels threatened by the presence of a cassette recorder.

Relationships are important. You have to give credence to your endeavour and this means convincing your interviewees that the interview is sufficiently important to warrant their devoting time to it. Colleagues may find they are more than willing but they have little time. It helps, therefore, to know your interviewees and the best way to approach them to gain co-operation. Setting a time limit may be a good strategy for encouraging full attention during an interview, rather than questioning someone with one eye perpetually on the clock. Fortunately, with the full co-operation of colleagues I was able to conduct my own interviews during the school working day. This helped not only to alleviate any anxieties about the time taken but also encouraged co-operation since the interviews gained a certain prestige by being allowed to be conducted during working hours.

However, just because someone is co-operative does not mean their suspicions are allayed. This may be so especially when an 'underling' interviews the 'boss', as in my own case. Suspicion can lead to the holding back or softening of important data which may confound your objectives, particularly if it is the interviewee's ideology which is sought. Relaxing the interviewee is important but, in my opinion, this is not achieved merely by conducting the interview amid carpets and upholstery. The interviewee agrees to participate and, in doing so, is vulnerable to whatever pressures are pertinent at that time. These may be personal (e.g. the relationship with the interviewer) or idiosyncratic (e.g. the dislike of being recorded on tape). More likely, however, the interviewee may be susceptible to pressures which arise from the position he or she holds. An individual in authority may be fearful of any consequences arising from the responses given. Fellow colleagues or an employer may take the interviewee to task regarding the responses. As well as such immediate local pressures there may be those brought to bear by the wider context of which the individual feels part. Interviewees may feel that they are representing not only themselves but the group to which they feel they belong. Some head teachers, for example, may feel their responses should reflect the views not only of themselves but of the school, the education authority, government policy or current educational theory. In this way we may posit that interviewees respond not merely as individuals but as representatives of a group. The extent and nature of this will depend upon the interviewee's ideology and how he or she perceives his or her own position in relation to the wider social influences which may appertain. In this way cultural and ideological factors become highly significant influences on the interviewee's responses and must be taken into account in the structuring of the questions and the subsequent analysis of the data elicited.

Interviewing the head teacher and deputy head teacher in the context of my own research led me to take steps to reduce the wariness that I was likely to encounter. I ensured that my colleagues were informed about the nature of the research, as well as the interview, and the reasons for it. Some colleagues in authority may be more forthcoming if they are aware that their opinions will be aired before an academic audience, rather than in a published article which may be read by their colleagues or employer. If it is opinions you are seeking it is worth making this explicit. It may seem obvious, but I found that by expressly indicating before an interview that the interviewee's opinions were important and the focus of attention, the subject was more forthcoming.

Most importantly, perhaps, I did not conduct an interview until I felt my research role had been accepted by the interviewees. I spent the first term of my data-collecting in assemblies in full view of the participants. With pen and paper in hand and, often, a tape recorder by my side, everyone was aware of my investigation. When pupils or colleagues asked what I was doing, I could explain. The questions were often accompanied by comments which began to assist my considerations. The participants became used to my notetaking and taping and to being observed. During that term I performed the highly structured tasks (marked '1' on the diagram above). The checklists were concrete and could be seen by the participants as evidence, albeit superficial, of serious endeavour. It was a period of intense observation in which the structure of the study was shifting and focusing. It allowed priorities to surface so that by the time the interviews were conducted in the second term, the questions could be more pointed and relevant than they might have been if they had been conducted earlier. Clarification could be sought regarding data from other sources. Moreover, having become accustomed to my role and to the research itself, the interviewees felt, in terms of the timing of the interviews that they were about to make an important contribution.

### The form of the interviews

### 1 The encoders

The first interview with the head teacher was of a general nature: attempting to discover her interpretation of the 1944 Education Act; her view of the role of assemblies in school; her views about the content; her personal convictions and the role of religion in assemblies; the problems (if any) of leading assemblies; her concept of the pupils; their attitudes, abilities and the value of assemblies for them; her expectations regarding pupil behaviour, and her role in the assemblies. A range of questions under these general headings formed the core of the interview. In this sense it was structured and formal. The interviewee, however, was free to digress and in doing so tended to dictate the order of questioning, amplifying the categories and illustrate her own priorities.

The second interview was in the style of a commentary. The interviewee was asked to guide the interviewer through a typical assembly. Comments and justifications for what took place were elicited. This was a highly detailed process focusing on as many elements of the assembly as possible. It allowed a comparison between the theoretical behaviour of the head teacher discussed in the interview and the behaviour exhibited and perceived by others (including the researcher) during the previous term. Similarly, the deputy head teacher was interviewed for both general views and in the 'commentary' style. However, the 'commentary' in this case was on a specific assembly led by the deputy head teacher earlier on that day. This permitted close scrutiny of the content of this assembly. Attention focused on the justifications for the various inclusions.

## 2 The decoders

Three sessions were conducted with a group of 5 children. The first session was not an interview. The group were set the task of devising a typical assembly to demonstrate to someone arriving from abroad what the assemblies entailed. The purpose of the exercise was to allow the pupils to reveal, through their decisions, some observations about the assemblies generally. It allowed the observing researcher to make notes of some of the pupils' perceptions before introducing his own categories and priorities in the following session. The drama also provided a concrete vehicle for discussion in the second session which was a commentary-style interview, similar to the one outlined above.

The third session was on the specific assembly which was also the subject of an interview with the deputy head. Unlike the deputy head the pupils were interviewed later than the day of the event for practical reasons. A recording of the assembly was played to the group to ensure the event was almost as fresh in their minds as it had been for the deputy on the day of his interview. This would hopefully enable a fair comparison to be made between responses as the questions posed remained fundamentally the same.

These interviews formed the core of the study and were taped with the participants' consent to allow further considerations, and for transcripts to be made. Other, more peripheral, interviews were conducted which were not taped. These included: testing the comprehension of the prayer from the specific assembly (mentioned previously) with a cross-section of pupils; follow-up discussions with my class after assemblies which raised points of interest; and informal discussions with pupils or colleagues. These were not usually taped, either because the responses were easy to classify by notation or because the interviewing was informal or spontaneous. In the latter case points of interest were noted mentally and recorded immediately afterwards or at the first available opportunity on the same day.

Interviewing pupils is potentially problematic as well as infinitely rewarding. The observations made earlier about the interviewer's relationship with the interviewee and the suspicion which may confound the task are a prime consideration here. Some children may be irrepressible and continually undermine the interviewer's purpose by steering the conversation away from the questioning. Many, though, may feel vulnerable and may find it difficult to be forthcoming unless steps are taken to provide the confidence necessary to be able to voice opinions. This circumstance may be all too evident in some school contexts. Many children are not used to offering their views freely in a classroom setting where the large group or the teacher is inhibiting. If the interviewer is not well-known, this too is likely to meet with wariness unless a relationship can be established quickly. The teacher-researcher must take account of how the pupils perceive his or her new role. The children may persist in their view of the teacher as an authority figure and, therefore, be reluctant to divulge certain sorts of information, not least perhaps if the topic under discussion is not usually discussed between teacher and pupil. Indeed, any adult may encounter the same problem if the child associates adulthood with authority and, therefore, suspects the motives of the interviewer. Clearly, the onus is on the interviewer to establish a relationship which encourages the child to respond freely and honestly, allaying any grounds for suspicion. To this end, the teacher-researcher is well-placed since the school setting is familiar and some understanding of the child and the child's school experience may assist in deciding the best way to approach the interview.

I chose my five main interviewees carefully. They were all fourth-year pupils, on the assumption that they were likely to be able to articulate their views more precisely than younger children. Our relationship was already well-established and on a sound footing as they were members of my own class. None regarded me as an awesome authority figure and none found the guise of researcher (at this stage) strange, although there had been questions in the previous term. Had we not been through this inquisitive period, one or two may have spent the interview bewildered and preoccupied with what it was all about. Those chosen were known to be constructive in a group situation (a group of twittering titterers can thwart the most earnest interviewer) and had previously demonstrated an ability to comment fairly and critically in discussion. They also had sufficient strength of character to consider their views carefully and express their own views. Teachers are only too familiar with the 'sheep instinct' displayed by many pupils in the wake of one original idea. All these factors seemed essential considerations with regard to reliability.

The interviews were conducted away from the classroom to reinforce the fact that the activity was indeed different from our normal classroom pursuits. In fact, we used the staffroom. Not, I hasten to add, to deliberately attempt to relax the pupils amid soft furnishings (see above) – leaving their peers behind in the classroom had done that – but to find peace and quiet. In retrospect it may be that the adult venue contributed to their approaching the sessions with due seriousness. It could, however, have proved counter-productive in different circumstances. These pupils had used the staffroom on previous occasions for lessons. Some pupils meeting a new venue such as a staffroom for the first time may have been distracted or overawed. Again, it is the teacher-researcher's knowledge of the children which determines the wisest course of action.

For me, there is one unequivocal factor about interviewing children. As a research tool it presides over all other methods of data collection since it requires no other ability on the part of the interviewee than to think and talk. In the written tasks I devised I found interesting comments but they were clumsily or vaguely expressed, or only half articulated. The children lacked the writing skills needed to express themselves at the level of sophistication I was after. In interview, the researcher can ask for an idea to be refined, approach an idea from a more fruitful angle, test the interviewee's statement with a similar question, challenge an assertion to test validity, discuss concepts so that meaning becomes more precise than it is likely to be on paper. In short, it is the best tool for the job. And there are incidental rewards for the teacher-researcher – discovering views and skills in the pupils which the classroom often leaves untapped.

All the interviews were structured. The timing of the interviews and the nature of the research made this essential. Clearly, many factors affected the structuring of the questions: the theoretical framework; the fact that I was a participant observer; the data already gathered which begged to be clarified or checked to see if it could be refuted. However, the commitment of the researcher to an examination of any element of the assembly which could signify meaning necessarily made for a broad inquiry. Comment on almost any aspect of the communication was potentially useful and could not be dismissed until the data was analysed. In this sense, the researcher must be aware of the dynamic aspect of the interview and be ready to develop any interesting comment which emerges. Failure to do so could be tantamount to losing an important cache of information. It is essential for the researcher to be fully conversant with the theoretical framework of the study so that any such avenues can be pursued creatively and to the purpose in hand. It is my contention, then, that specific and open-ended inquiry are not exclusive modes but may best serve the investigation by operating hand-in-hand.

## The analysis

At no point in the proceedings can an ethnographer, or any participant researcher, regard the research tool as distinct and immutable. Research becomes a process of continual interaction between the researcher and the researched. The methodology is subject to modification, re-assessment, progressive focusing. This holds true at each stage of the investigation but it is in the analysis that the researcher's judgements are critical. It is here that the match between theoretical perspective and data must be rigorously pursued. A convincing and representative account must be offered.

In my own case, the revelation of the ideology of the encoders and decoders was of prime importance. The main views and perceptions revealed in interview were noted and discussed in terms of the framework adapted from Hall's televisual model (see note). Cultural influences had to be assessed. Some of the comparison in the analysis was facilitated because, in some interviews, similar sets of questions had been put to both groups of interviewees. Clearly, the responses and preoccupations of the two groups had differed. This in itself was indicative of the priorities of their perspective and had to be reflected in the discussion.

In the interpretive paradigm it is the researcher's decisions regarding the inclusions and omissions of data and the explanations which accompany those decisions which are central to a valid presentation. It is likely, as in my own case, that the omissions will strongly outweigh the inclusions. Selectivity must convince the reader that the inclusions are indicative, indeed prime examples, of other findings. The reader must believe that the omitted evidence would lend support to the argument and not detract from it.

114

Transcripts of interviews, then, are essential to demonstrate the authenticity of the findings. Careful selection will be necessary, not least when one inclusion must represent similar findings from other data. Indeed, in accordance with the preceding argument, there may be a need for some protracted extracts to be included to prove to the reader that short quotations are demonstrative of views expressed in a wider context. It is, after all, easy to misrepresent a viewpoint out of context.

When transcribing, consideration needs to be given to the presentation of interjections, hesitancy and silences, since these may signify more than the words which follow. The alert researcher is likely to pursue such behaviour during the interview to seek clarification of meaning, but this does not solve the problem of written presentation should it be necessary. A case could be made for the development of a universal language for notating such behaviours but it would, in my estimation, miss the point. What matters is not the minutiae of transcription but the larger responsibility of critical appraisal. The researcher must resolve any contradictions in the data as overtly as possible and use as a basis for selectivity the data which best informs the theoretical framework.

It is a truism to say the outcomes of ethnographic research are speculative. The researcher's relationship to the investigation is complex but the findings have their own rigour. If the description is explicit, others may note the methods employed and attempt similar activities relevant to their own setting. If the description is convincing, generalisation may occur by implication and the body of knowledge is enhanced.

The teacher-researcher is well-placed to pursue an ethnographic approach. I have no doubt that this investigation was best served by using an eclectic range of methodologies, not merely because it permitted fairly comprehensive data collection but because it allowed mutually supportive data to emerge from different sources. What is clear to me, however, is that of all the tools at the teacher-researcher's disposal, none is more valuable than interviewing. Whether the interviewing is successful will depend on how well the researcher's planning takes account of the factors which may influence the undertaking.

*Case Study 6: Appendix: Notes*

1 Hall (1973) rejected the behavioural model of communication which conceived the televisual message as a linear progression, the message

passing from sender to receiver through the stage of transmission. It failed to take account of some of the more complex issues intrinsic in the concept of sign, on which Hall now focused, i.e. the role of television in assisting the establishment of hegemony. See Hall, S. (1973) *Encoding and Decoding in the Television Discourse*, Occasional Paper, CCCS; and Hall, S., Connell, I., Curti L. (1976) *The 'Unity' of Current Affairs Television*, in WCPS9, CCCS.

2 A sign is here crudely defined as any feature of the event which may communicate meaning for those participating. Any aspect, from the cleanliness of the floor to the ideology of the language, may be considered as a significant message-bearer. For a more detailed discussion of the concept of sign see: Barthes, R. (1973) *Mythologies*, Paladin.

3 Encoders: crudely defined as those formulating and transmitting the messages. In this case the chief encoders were the head teacher and the deputy head teacher.

4 Decoders: crudely defined as those for whom the messages are intended and on whom the onus is put to make sense of the communication. Any participant may be a decoder but the focus of the research was on the pupils. For more detailed discussion of codes and communication see: Hall, S. (1980) 'Encoding/Decoding', in *Culture, Media, Language*, ed. S. Hall, D. Hobson *et al.*, Hutchinson.

# Chapter 5

# Guidelines for practice

Having decided that information is going to be collected by interview, most researchers want to get on with it as soon as possible. In this chapter, we take a practical look at three stages of interviewing – preparation, making the first contact with the interviewees, and conducting the main interview.

The interview itself will take less time than both preparing for it and the subsequent analysis of the talk collected. In order to collect appropriate, valid data, the researcher needs to prepare meticulously. When the interview then takes place, the researcher is more likely to have an adequate basis for recording and be more alert to what is relevant to the inquiry.

*Stage 1: Preparation*

There are several elements to effective preparation:

(a)  Familiarity with the overall research plan;
(b)  Structuring (or not) the framework for the interviews;
(c)  Selection and briefing of interviewer(s);
(d)  Selecting and contacting the interviewees;
(e)  Planning recording and analysis;
(f)  Calculation of costs in time and money.

These are not listed in any strict sequence but each should have been considered before:

(g)  Piloting each of these stages and making appropriate modifications.

## (a) Familiarity with the research

All interviewers should be familiar with: the overall aims of the research project, the timetable, the relative importance of different parts of the inquiry and how information collected from interviews will relate to other sources such as observations, questionnaires and published documents. This is relatively easy in most educational research where the chances are that members of a research team are more likely to do the interviewing themselves, than employ professionals. Researcher-interviewers carry the well-known risk of interviewees fulfilling a researcher's expectations, but have the merit of being better informed about the project, and less expensive.

Constant reference to the overall research plan, and the major goals, is essential at all preparatory stages, since it gives the raison d'être to the interview structure – who will be interviewed, about what, and by whom. It also provides the framework for the recording and subsequent analysis of interviewees' statements. Keeping the project aims well to the fore, makes it less easy to slide into areas of little relevance to the inquiry.

Usually only one interview is possible – for reasons of time, the need for spontaneous reaction, the interviewees being busy. Very careful preparation in understanding the main issues and the context of the interviews means the interviewer is more likely to recognise the relative importance of informants' remarks and be able to construct or confirm hypotheses. Saran (1985) talks about this immersion in facts both before and during fieldwork being fundamental to the imaginative leaps researchers make in developing their explanations.

## (b) The structure of the interview

Talking to people can be fascinating and there is usually a tendency to be over-enthusiastic (if not overly curious), and ask more questions than are actually necessary to meet the researcher's specified line of inquiry. It requires considerable self-discipline not to slip in a few extra questions 'just in case ...' but all interviewers should develop this self control, if only as a survival tactic. For each hour of interviewing, a minimum of a further three hours should be allowed for preparation and summary. This is a modest estimate even for experienced interviewers and doesn't include full transcription, or detailed analysis. Every question needs to be carefully costed in interviewer and analyst's time and related to the overall purpose of the research. Furthermore, it is a basic courtesy to interviewees not to take advantage of their goodwill in participating, by asking irrelevant questions. Interviewers should fit into the limits of time and topics initially agreed with interviewees as compatible with meeting the needs of the research project. In deciding what to ask therefore, the prime question for the researcher is 'Why do I want to know this?'.

In Chapter 2, the processes involved in interviewing were considered in relation to more, or less, structured approaches. For a depth interview, which allows the widest possible exploration of views and behaviour patterns, the interview is adapted to the individual and no set questions may be asked, although the interviewer usually has an agenda to cover. The aim is to get informants to talk freely and openly about themselves, only initial stimuli being provided by the interviewer. In this case, it is more appropriate to have a list of possible topics. The discussion could range well beyond these, provided the interviewer feels it is relevant to the overall aims of the research.

Other interviews may be more closely directed, with the researcher controlling the order and even the wording of the questions. This may be especially important where several interviewers are working on a large-scale project. Examples of different interview structures are included in the case studies. We recommend that all interviewers prepare an outline of what they hope to achieve, even if it is undesirable to forecast detailed questions.

*(c)  Decide on the interviewers*
The convention in social science has been for the interviewer to be unknown to, or at least not a personal friend of the interviewee. With the advent of so much small-scale research and ethnographical inquiries, interviewer and interviewee may well be familiar to each other nowadays.

Accepting Goffman's point made in Chapter 3 that the management of the interviewer's identity is crucial, the choice of both informants and interviewers is important. Consider an example used elsewhere in this book. Data are collected in the same school based project, by a professor at the local university and by a research assistant. The former is white, male and of distinguished years and mien. The latter is a young black woman on a temporary contract and sister to one of the pupils. It is reasonable to assume that interviewees may well give different emphasis, if not different answers, according to who was asking the questions.

In Chapter 3, we examined in some depth how the dynamics generated in each interview will differ according to the people involved. In choosing the overall sample and in preparing for each interview, the researcher and/or interviewer should therefore at least

119

consider the relationships between interviewer(s) and interviewee(s) in terms of:

- relative status of the individuals and institutions concerned
- whether or not they are either professionally, or socially, known to each other
- race, age, sex.

Collaboration raises further issues here. Three collaborative situations are likely. In the first (see Jill Keegan's Case Study in Chapter 4), the researcher engages an interviewer and the two collaborate in arranging appropriate information to be collected by the interviewer. In the second (see Julia Field's Case Study, Chapter 4), there are several interviewers involved. Finally some researchers carry out their own interviews and, in this sense, are collaborating with themselves, in different roles – interviewer and researcher (see the case studies of Norman Evans, Di Bentley and Steven Eales). These categories overlap, as for example, where researchers collaborate with several others, and the whole team do some interviewing (as in Dave Ebbutt's case study). What is important, is that the researcher's intentions should be familiar and understood by each and every interviewer. Where several interviewers are involved, they should establish shared meanings and even, if necessary, a common wording of some questions. Agreement also needs to be reached on what, and how, data will be recorded and categorised. Even if only three interviewers are involved, as in the Rutter (1979) survey, it would be only too easy for one interviewer to ignore what another sees as being a gem of information. Multiply each difference of opinion over the detailed conduct of the interview, by the number of recordings and interviews and there lie data based on varied assumptions. There could even be sources of unreliability or lack of explicitness which draw into question the validity of analysis and conclusions of the research. Unfortunately, research reports usually give little or no indication of how several interviewers collaborated in the construction, recording and analysis of a series of interviews.

Essentially, if the project requires data to be compared, then interviewers need to be consistent. This applies equally to the third kind of collaboration – that within one person who is both interviewer and researcher. It is all too easy in this case for the interviewer-researcher to change questions unwittingly, to slide into practical changes as a result of the answers so far. Interviewers all do this to some extent but researchers have much more scope to modify their original ideas or emphasis and change the content or style of the interview. Fine, provided the changes are explicit in the research report and that information collected under different circumstances is not directly compared.

## (d) Selecting and contacting the interviewees

As the number of people to be interviewed has to be limited for practical reasons, it is as well to pay considerable attention to choosing informants. In some instances it may be possible and desirable to interview everyone directly concerned with a project e.g. the whole school staff. More frequently, it is necessary to take only a sample of people, chosen because they represent a wider group relevant to the researcher's interests. The case studies show different kinds of samples and there are many more complex methods of sampling necessary for large-scale quantitative survey work. Bearing in mind the costs in time and money, the sample should be as small as is consistent with obtaining valid data. The final list of interviewees should give appropriate representation of the range of views relevant to the purpose of the research. They should be accessible in terms of the interviewer's travelling time. They should be willing and have the time to participate.

Three other issues need thinking through carefully in contacting the sample: approvals, initial access and agreed explanations. In carrying out research within the formal educational system, it is common to need approval to conduct interviews from those protecting the interests of the teaching profession and pupils, or the reputation of the LEA and any of its schools. It is not just a question of strolling into a staffroom and asking the various teachers a few questions. For example, to interview a woodwork teacher, approval would probably have to be obtained from:

- the LEA – to conduct research in the authority
- the head teacher – to make inquiries which might affect the school
- the head of the woodworking department – to conduct research which might raise issues about the department
- the woodwork teacher – the interviewer would have to ascertain whether (s)he is willing and has the time to answer questions on the defined topic.

To interview pupils, parental consent may be necessary. In practice, the lower down the informant is in the hierarchy, the more approvals will have to be obtained. Julia Field's case study vividly illustrates the researcher's dependence on goodwill; some adolescents, who were part of her desired sample, were lost to the project because parents refused permission for their child to participate.

A useful rule of thumb is to consider who might be affected by the responses of the informant and to err on the safe side. Employers feel they have a right to control whether or not their employees should comment about their work. Similarly, parents feel they should control access to their children. The researcher has to balance the rights of interested parties, with those of the informant, whilst maintaining credibility and gaining valid data as final outcomes.

It is usually easier to get permission to interview a chief education officer, than a child, since it needs only a persuasive talk with him/her, once someone from the project has obtained access. Access can be tricky at any level. We recommend a formal letter, which is sent to each person, who has to agree that an interview may take place. This can be followed up with a phone call, or face to face initial chat. If the formal letter outlines the research project and includes information on the interviewer(s), it can be left with the interviewees in case subsequent queries arise. Examples of such letters are included in the case studies. Without such a formal letter, misunderstandings can easily occur, especially when the interviewee hears about the forthcoming interview from someone else, such as a senior colleague.

Imagine the difference it might make, at least initially, to the way you might respond to an interviewer, if you were asked directly, or through an intermediary, such as colleague, parent, head teacher? It might be the difference between volunteering and coercion. Although theoretically, everyone may refuse to co-operate, usually people agree to be interviewed if asked. Most would find it very difficult to refuse if the initial approach were sanctioned by an employer or someone in authority and probably pupils would not feel in a position to refuse at any time, nor would many teachers, if the request came from their head of department, head teacher or LEA adviser. Interviewees should be willing participants. If an informant gives information clandestinely, under coercion, or under a misunderstanding about the purpose of the inquiry (see e.g. Sharp and Green (1975)), the comments collected are of questionable validity. For Sharp and Green, the purpose of interviewing the head teacher (with whom incidentally the interviewer had been working for over a year) was the

> extent to which his perspective revealed any logical inconsistencies, internal contradictions or ambiguities ... because (the researchers') developing analysis of the situation had suggested that given certain pressure on him, some inner contradictions and ambiguities would be inevitable. (p. 49)

It would appear from this that the head teacher was not encouraged to discuss the inevitable contradictions and ambiguities. His role was to provide raw data from which the researchers could locate ambiguity. In this sense, the declared purpose of the interview did not correspond with the use the researchers intended to make of the ensuing data. Adelman (1985), as we quoted in Chapter 3, believes the participant observer has to be a competent member of the cultures (s)he is writing about. Should deceit be involved, then Adelman's (and our) sympathies are with the misrepresented community.

Interviewers should have a prepared explanation of the research and what they hope to gain from the interview. The same explanation should be given to all informants where data is going to be dealt with identically. There is probably more leeway in ethnographic approaches. In any case, the research report should make clear what the interviewees were told, and therefore what their expectancies might have been about the interview. We say 'might' since even when researchers say they will be recording informal conversations and situations, the results often come as a surprise to participants who react, 'I didn't realise you were noting that kind of thing'. Nevertheless, it is reasonable for the interviewer to expect to collect information based on the explanation given to the interviewee and agreed with the research team. Besides being morally questionable, information collected from misleading explanations, has limited meaning for the research community, unless the analysis has been subsequently discussed with the interviewee.

Sharp and Green draw attention, in their research report, to the widely differing styles of observation and staff interviews adopted by each of the fieldworkers. Green was virtually an observer, Lewis virtually a participant, with Sharp in between. The research team is very open about these differences and concerned that the data reflect the theoretical and substantive pre-occupations of the researchers themselves. Unfortunately, details of these critical reflections remained private and were not apparently part of the information given to the head teacher and staff being interviewed. One might ask how different the replies might have been, had the interviewees known the researchers' perspectives, and whether, or not, any differences would have been significant.

Part of the explanation to interviewees will include reassurances about confidentiality and anonymity. The interviewer should be careful only to give such guarantees as s(he) is confident can be met at different stages of the research – such as while interviewing other colleagues, and in the research report. In interviews, as presumably in the confessional, an individual admits to things (s)he would not, normally, declare publicly. Even if these are not germane to the situation, the interviewer, like the priest, has no right to embarrass the informant, who trustingly gave the information. Children also have their rights to privacy, confidentiality and anonymity. In many instances field workers, like Dave Ebbutt (Case Study 5 in Chapter 4), will check their final interpretation with the informants and negotiate the relevant sections of the final report. It is as well, to sort out these matters of confidentiality, and confirmation, as part of the planning process.

*(e) Method of recording and analysis*
Making a record of the interview involves careful preparation and monitoring of what is to be observed, how it is to be noted, and how material arising from the interview will be compared with data from other sources. We suggest this should be as thoroughly planned, as the conduct of the interview. The outcomes of pilot interviews could also be analysed, to see if the whole thing is going to work.

There is no substitute for a full tape recording of an interview. Even if a complete transcript is not made, there is, then, some record of what was said by interviewer and interviewee. Logan (1984) only realised the importance of his pupil interviewees' revelations after he checked through the transcription. It was then, that he found their responses were being tempered by the way in which they had cat-egorised him, the interviewer.

Once people have been assured of confidentiality and where poss-ible anonymity, few refuse to be taped. Tape recordings alone are usually insufficient for most researchers. Interviewers usually take notes of the circumstances in which the interview takes place as well as a condensed account of what is being said. Some researchers dislike using tape recorders.

> I feel that it is critical to maintain eye contact during interviews
> and not to miss facial expressions and other non-verbal cues.
> Tape recording would eliminate the need for note-taking but in
> my view, it inhibits most in-depth interviewing. (Spector 1980)

This may be true, but most people quickly become accustomed to the presence of tape recorders, which are overall less obtrusive than inefficient note takers. We would also argue that the effect of any obvious recording – by field notes, audio or video tapes – encourages those being observed to give their 'best' performance. That, itself, is interesting to the observer.

A small tape recorder should be used and introduced early in the discussion, certainly before the interview proper starts. The conversation with Jill Keegan (Case Study 2), illustrates how this might be done. Frequently it is the interviewer who finds the tape most distracting, in anxiety lest the tape run out, the machine jam or some other technical disaster. The nonchalant confidence of a well-prepared interviewer, will be contagious.

Ethnographers will want a fuller account of the episode. Note taking can be very distracting, so it needs to be unobtrusive and in some kind of reliable shorthand. With practice the ability to recall improves, making it easier to expand on field notes. The novice interviewer should not depend on this method for data collection, until practised. Our ability to recall events even immediately after their occurrence is notoriously unreliable. Usually there are other events intervening between the interview and writing up so here is yet another danger of loss and distortion of data.

The more open the interview, the more complicated the analysis. Even in small-scale research involving perhaps only up to 20 informants, the researcher should have a clear idea of the nature of the data being collected whether pre-coded multiple choice questions or meandering conversations and, just as importantly, how (s)he is going to handle responses. This should be as clear as possible before the main interviewing starts, and then constantly reviewed and adjusted, as necessary. Running a few pilot interviews focuses the mind wonderfully on potential data collection problems and gives the interviewer a chance to modify practices, before the investigation proper begins.

Analysis has to be linked to the questions asked, and to the informant's understanding of the purpose of the questioning and even of individual questions. Interviewees' comments will be affected by their assessment of the interviewer's intentions. If these are uncertain, where will that leave the interviewee? Here, again, Sharp and Green raise important issues:

> We found it difficult to adopt a clear-cut view of how the problem should be formulated once we had, in a sense, started collecting the 'data' ... There is a need to attempt to operate simultaneously at the epistemological, theoretical, and empirical levels with self-awareness given that there is no ready-made formula for producing knowledge, let alone the truth. (p. 234)

Even at this stage, the interviewer should be considering what notes and materials will be included in final report. The aim will be to give the reader sufficient background to make sense of the interviews. For structured interviews, it is simplest to include the full interview schedule in the research report.

What should be included for ethnographic studies is less easily defined. The case was made earlier for language being the key to culture and, therefore, it is essential to have verbatim statements from informants. It is insufficient to make a summary as this is translated into the interviewer's language, along with the interviewer's concepts and framework. Even partial verbatim comments are better than a summary.

Inclusion implies exclusion. If it is envisaged that it will not be possible, or desirable, to include full transcripts of interviews, the basis of selection should be made explicit. The reader will thus be reassured that, had all the material been included, the outcomes of the inquiry would have been the same.

A distinction should be made here between what is actually collected by the researcher and what is included in the report. For example, structured interviews might be taped and fully transcribed but the report might only include enlivening comments verbatim although the raw data would be available to the research community.

*(f)  Calculation of costs in time and money*
Most researchers are over-ambitious, in the number of interviews scheduled for a project. As we suggested earlier, a salutary exercise is to allow for each hour of interviewing, a further three hours for preparation, reporting and making initial analysis. This is only a modest estimate – accurate and full transcripts will take longer. In costing the initial stage of a small depth interview study of 20 respondents clustered in one part of an urban area, with an average interview length of $1\frac{1}{2}$ hours, a professional organisation, (Social and Community Planning Research) estimated a total of 304 hours, i.e. a minimum of 15 hours per interview, including travelling time. This included transcription. Without it, more time would be required at the initial stage of analysis, so it would still take a minimum of about 10 hours. Multiply this by the 10 or 20-plus interviews, and the researcher has a full-time job for several weeks.

Other items to take into account include travelling expenses, tapes, transcription and reprographic costs. A realistic budget is part of the essential preparation of interview projects. Even small-scale studies can turn out to be more expensive, than casually envisaged.

*Pilot interviews*
Once the interviewer is familiar with the general aims of the research, the appropriate order of topics and questions, and the overall strat-

egy for recording and analysis, there should be a pilot interview. There are rarely opportunities to interview the same person twice so it is crucial to get it right the first time. Since the purpose of piloting is to check that the proposed interviews will work, any trials should be as close as possible to the real thing. The interviewer can practise the whole exercise from making initial contact with the informant, conducting and recording the full interview and even an elementary attempt at analysis.

Pilot, or trial interviews have three major functions:

- a check that the structure, or organisation, of the interview meets the requirements of the research project
- a practical test of the logistics of the interview
- an opportunity to practise the social interactive skills necessary for the kind of interview chosen

Effective piloting usually results in changes related to each of these three functions.

In checking the structure of the interview, a trial helps to identify inappropriate wording or topics, ambiguities and gross mis-judgements in questioning, and if the order of questions and topics is suitable. A preliminary attempt at analysis will check that the right areas are being covered. It can also eliminate obvious errors in any coding system that might be used, or identify irrelevant data being collected.

The second function is to check the practical organisation. Most interviewers find it difficult to pace the first interviews in a series. They take longer than expected, partly because of unfamiliarity combined with enthusiasm for the project. The other main reason is because we usually underestimate the time needed for sheer prac-ticalities like getting to the appropriate location, setting up the equip-ment and making initial introductions and explanations. The trial interviews emphasise the importance of assembling the right equip-ment including spares. Tape recorders should be re-checked immedi-ately before meeting the interviewee. The interviewer should also have a spare tape long enough to *exceed* the expected duration of the interview. It is useful to index tapes to locate relevant topics later. Clipboards, notepads, spare pencils and erasers should also be to hand. In more structured interviews, it may be necessary to prepare, in order, cards with prompts or predetermined categories. Being well prepared, means that the interviewer can focus on the interviewee and is not anxious about what is coming next.

Pilot interviews offer splendid opportunities to monitor and practise skills of social interaction. Some of these have a slightly different emphasis to our normal conversations with other people.

An interviewer:
- listens more than speaks
- puts questions in a straightforward, unambiguous and non-threatening way
- tries to eliminate cues that will lead an interviewee to respond in a particular way
- will be diffident about putting forward personal experiences and opinions.

These are techniques, which may not be commonly used by interviewers in their other professional and domestic roles. Yet even inexperienced interviewers, can usually pick out their 'mistakes', by carefully listening to tapes of trial interviews. Sometimes interviews could provide our first sustained contact with a particular group of informants – such as severely handicapped people, headteachers, adolescents, senior administrators. The trials offer a chance to adapt to, and gain insights into the worlds of the interviewees we shall be working with subsequently.

A bonus resulting from pilot interviews can be the help obtained from the interviewees themselves to improve subsequent interviewing. They could be asked (after the interview), what they felt about being interviewed – if there were questions or technical terms which were difficult to understand; whether more information would have been helpful at the beginning; if they could have been made to feel more relaxed; in short any tips for making subsequent interviews more successful.

Where major modifications are made to the interview as a result of piloting, further trials should be undertaken before the collection of real data begins. To conduct a pilot interview is not a luxury; it means that even the first 'proper' interview will provide meaningful data.

*Stage 2: Initial contact*

To get the first interview, the interviewer needs to make an appointment, check that the necessary approvals have been obtained, and be prepared to explain the prospective interviewee's role in the research. Whether interviewing as an ethnographer, or more as a survey ıescarcher, the first contact by phone, letter, or face to face, is likely to colour all future links with that interviewee.

Basically the courtesies of interviewing are concerned with maintaining the dignity and privacy of the informant. Therefore plenty of time should be allowed to explain the purposes of the inquiry, how the informants can contribute and the length and kind of interview and outcome proposed. Informants should be reassured that the interviewer will preserve their anonymity throughout the inquiry and in any subsequent publications. Reassurances about confidentiality and anonymity may have to be given on several occasions, if the informant seems uncertain, or nervous about talking freely. The interviewer should only make such promises as can be kept.

Most informants like to have an indication of the kind of research report to be made. It is at this initial stage of the discussions that researchers clarify areas of negotiation that will be observed. For example, interviewees should know whether or not they will see any transcripts or reports of the interview in draft, or for that matter, when they are published. This initial phase is most important although the temptation is often to avoid raising issues that might hinder gaining co-operation. This is unethical and likely to be counter-productive in the long term. At the first meeting, the informants, should be told about the nature and purpose of the research. Interviewers should identify themselves, give proof of identity, if necessary, and details of how they might be reached. Informants are usually happier if they are left with some written information about the research, and details of the sponsoring body e.g.:

Research project: Inquiry into career aspirations of teachers in mid-career.
Research team: Dr Mary Bloggs (project leader)
             Dr Jim Smith
             Ms Jane Brown
             Mr Fred Black
Address: Haxford Polytechnic, Campus Green, Haxford (Tel: Haxford 291 extension 35)
Funding body: DES.

After all the explanations, and before proceeding with the interview, the interviewer should check that the interviewee is still willing to participate.

*Location*

The interviews should be in a place appropriate for the length and kind of interview. Where possible, this can be arranged at the same time as making the interview appointment. Survey researchers are used to conducting interviews in homes, cars, planes, corridors, offices, in the street and in many unusual places. However, conditions in which interviews take place, can bias informants' replies and distract the interviewer's attention. The kinds of locations that might adversely affect participants in educational interviews include:

- being within earshot or sight of other people significant to the interviewee – e.g. teachers, peer group, pupils, parents, headteacher, adviser
- rooms which have other connotations – e.g. the headteacher's room, the medical room
- spaces liable to constant interruptions – e.g. a corridor, hall, library, cloakroom, staffroom
- locations which are not conducive to the intimacy of an interview – e.g. large classrooms, hall, canteen
- anywhere that is so noisy that it is difficult to hear and difficult to tape the individuals in the interview without picking up other conversations and noises.

It would be unrealistic to assume that all interviews can take place in a small, cosy, quiet room, but it is worth thinking about the best location given the particular constraints operating in any set of interviews.

*Stage 3: Main interview*

We have gone into some detail about the preparation necessary for an interviewer to feel confident, and for the interviewees to understand and be willing to participate in the research. We shall assume that by the time it comes to the interview proper, interviewers are adequately prepared as outlined above. Now we move on to some hints on the actual conduct of the interview sequence – of initial exchanges, the main interview, and leaving the interview to write up immediate reactions prior to a fuller description of the interview, at a later stage.

*Initial exchange*

The relationship between interviewer and interviewee is based on the very first contact. Therefore, the interviewer needs to be alert to the signals being given by appearance, non-verbal behaviour and overall demeanour. The task for interviewers is not to demonstrate that they are devastatingly interesting people. It is to draw out the interviewees. Appearance should therefore not make a strong impact but be unremarkable to the respondents. What an interviewer wears should not signal messages likely to make interviewees uncomfortable or to distort the course of the interview. Clothes superficially indicate status, social class, attitudes or value systems and the interviewer should consider how these might affect the behaviour of the interviewee. Badges, newspapers, jewellery are indicators of ourselves. Either being clearly identified with the interviewee's subculture, or being in direct contrast, could limit the information obtained during the interview.

Through the door, and the interviewer needs to set the scene, confirming the purpose of the interview, confidentiality, indicating what is expected from the interviewee, checking the physical location of the interview, the proximity of the furniture and approval and location of the tape recorder. Opinions vary as to the best place to sit. Some researchers believe that people can be more forthcoming if they are side by side with interviewers, rather than facing them. It indicates less of a confrontation. We prefer the relative positions of people having a normal conversation, that is, either directly opposite or at least in such a position as to be able to make eye contact and pick up non-verbal signals. Interviewees should not sit close enough to read the interviewer's questions and notes.

Although the interviewer will probably have had some contact with the interviewee, it is advisable to confirm the approximate length of the interview, partly in order to discourage interruptions. The person being interviewed may be distracted by the activities normally expected to happen at the time of the interview or immediately afterwards such as playtime, a free period, a popular lesson, home time. The interviewer may also need to help the interviewee to detach him or herself from immediately preceding activities. By the time the interview starts, the interviewee should understand the purpose, format and length of the interview. (S)he should seem confident that the interviewer is organised, and that the whole event is not going to be stressful, or a waste of time. It is sometimes helpful to check before launching into the interview:'Is there anything else you wanted to know before we start?'

*Progress of the interview*
*Interpersonal factors*   Rapport between interview participants goes through different stages. To start with, both sides are probably

131

slightly nervous of each other. Spradley (1979) suggests that this early apprehension is succeeded, in ethnographic interviews, by exploration, then co-operation, and finally participation. The interviewer's task is to monitor and maintain appropriate rapport at different stages of the interview.

Eye contact helps to establish interest. If the interviewer looks at the interviewee, while asking a question – or just after – it is easier to see if the interviewee is experiencing difficulty, or anxiety, about the question. Too much eye contact can make the other person self-conscious.

The good interviewer can understand other people's problems without getting too involved with them. Interviewees are, for the most part, taking part in a strange new event in which they are expected to talk freely and frankly to someone, who is in charge of the interview and who often has a list of different topics to be covered. Interviewees are expected to discuss openly issues which may be sensitive, embarrassing or normally private. They may even have been coerced into participating in the interview, and need persuading that it is a worthwhile use of their time. Some concerns will have been met by reassurances at the beginning but people may still be worried about their ability to fulfil their role in the interview. As Saran (1985) says, it is the interviewers who must have the capacity for empathy. They need, as Saran says, 'the facility to enter into other people's feelings, to understand their purposes, aims and value assumptions.'

*Resistance and diversion by interviewees* However carefully the interview has been set up, some interviewees remain unhappy. The interviewer should be alert to problems and try to rectify them before the interview becomes unproductive. Uneasy interviewees resist questioning by various strategies. First of all, they may challenge the authority or credibility of the interviewer – perhaps by questioning the relevance or validity of the way the interview is going. Harriet Zuckerman (1972) said that her informants were constantly testing her competence and commitment as interviewer. Not many of us will be interviewing Nobel prize-winners, as she did, but each interview situation presents a comparable unique challenge for the interviewer, to gain and maintain credibility with the interviewee.

Some people resist a passive role as interviewee by asking questions, evading issues or diverting the interviewer. Interviewees may also give non-verbal signals of their lack of involvement, such as yawning or gazing around the room. Body movements, such as foot-tapping or slumping in the chair, or paralinguistic signals, like a bored tone of voice or off-hand intonation also indicate that the interview is not going smoothly. Sometimes this is the interviewer's fault: poor questioning, too long an interview, a focus on trivial issues (for the interviewee). Sometimes it is the interviewee's rejection of being involved in the interview at all.

It may therefore be necessary, from time to time, for the interviewer to reassure the interviewee about the nature, direction and duration of the interview, to confirm that things are going according to plan. As far as possible the interviewer should give the impression of talking, rather than quizzing.

*Interviewer's problems* Personal relationships are two-way. Interviewers' feelings towards their interviewees, may be ambivalent or even hostile, especially if the views being expressed, are contrary to the interviewer's own. However, an interview is the place for active listening, not debate.

Most of us have some doubts as our competence as interviewers. Will we cope? Will we lose control of the interview, or credibility in the eyes of the interviewee? Can we remain 'impartial'? Such frequent anxieties can tempt interviewers to retain control in ways injurious to the interview. For example, interviewers may assert superiority, by indicating they already know the answers. So why, the interviewee might think, is it necessary to ask the question? If interviewers believe that control is retained by the person speaking, they may be reluctant to let go – asking several questions at a time, or interrupting informants before they have finished answering.

An anxious interviewer is unlikely to be a good listener. The most obvious danger is hearing what one wants to hear, rather than what is actually said. Fortunately this can be picked up in listening to the tape afterwards, but the opportunity to follow up an interesting point may have been lost. Another more subtle danger is that instead of following up a point, an interviewer may make inferences about meanings and explanations, not explicitly stated by the interviewee. For example, an interviewer hears that the teacher concerned is unlikely to get promotion and assumes this is through lack of competence. She does not pursue the point to find out whether this is for reasons within the school, the authority, or even because of the teacher's own preference. Jill Keegan quotes an example of this in her case study. As we saw in Case Study 2, a less experienced interviewer, K, assumed that when the mother of a severely handicapped adult said that she loved her child too much to let her go to residential care, K assumed it was through anxiety about the child.

It turned out to be the mother's own dependence on looking after her daughter.

It is very tempting, as interviewers, to avoid awkward subjects or at least to keep their discussion to a minimum. Techniques vary, but inexperienced interviewers change the subject, offer advice, or share their own experiences, or emotions, with the person being interviewed, thus changing the roles of the participants in the interview. One of the most useful ways to combat this, is to go over video or audio tapes of interviews, preferably with another experienced interviewer. Rigorous self-evaluation soon leads to improved interviewing technique.

*Interviewer skills*

There are certain general skills which most successful interviewers develop.

*Logic* The logical order of obtaining information. In less structured interviews, this may focus on recognising the relevance and importance of different items of information and nudging the conversation on accordingly.

*Listening skills* Attentive and accurate listening is vital. It is a question of hearing what the interviewee actually said, and not what the interviewer thought (s)he said.

*Remembering* An interviewer may need to retain many ideas to follow up later in the interview, or even to save them for the subsequent write up.

*Perceptive skills* Visually, an interviewer needs to interpret non-verbal cues such as body movements, changes in an informant's position relative to interviewer, facial expressions – in short any indication of anxiety, boredom or frustration in the interviewee. Some cues might be picked up auditorily, such as change of voice, or hesitation.

*Sensitivity/empathy* This is usually conveyed mainly through non-verbal signals. Interviewees will probably become more involved if they feel that interviewers are interested and understand their points of view.

*Adaptability* It is not easy to adjust to different people, situations,

134

beliefs and opinions but it is essential for an interviewer to appear comfortable in whatever circumstances the interview takes place.

*Self-awareness*  Effective interviewers are constantly aware of how they present themselves, how they cope with the questions that need to be asked, and with the replies from interviewees. Such self-awareness can be critical and constructive, especially if interviewers review their 'performance' after an interview or series of interviews.

*Questions and layout*  Interviewers should feel comfortable with their own 'script'. Where this script involves direct questioning, this should be to the point and easy both for the interviewer to present and for the interviewee to understand. Whatever kind of cue the interviewer is using, whether it is in the form of topics for discussion, or carefully worded questions, the layout should be clear enough to act as a cue for the interviewer at very quick reading or a glance. Tongue-twisters should be avoided.

The layout of whatever structured guide an interviewer uses should promote the fluent progress of the interview and enable accurate and comprehensive recording of answers in a way that will facilitate subsequent analysis. Some interviewers use different lettering to indicate verbatim questions, prompts or instructions to themselves. There should be plenty of space for the questions, or topics, and for such notes the interviewer may wish to make during the interview.

*Awkward questions*  Hoinville, Jowell *et al.* (1977) list questions that are difficult for interviewers to ask including catch-all and long questions. An example they give of the latter demonstrates the risk of the interviewee only remembering part of the question and therefore not answering the whole:

> Do you think there are enough job opportunities for a person like you in this district, or do you think there are better jobs elsewhere for a person like you? (p. 41)

Besides being cumbersome, the question contains two parts, each of which should stand as a separate question rather than as apparent alternatives.

'Catch-all' questions are also trying to be economical in asking time, but offer only a single response to two (or more) different subjects:

Do you enjoy teaching third and fourth years?

or a more involved example, and making assumptions about the interviewee's current practice:

How effective is the reading scheme you use to teach phonics compared with the other schemes you use?

The first question should have been either:

Do you teach phonics?

or

Do you use a reading scheme?

The other questions contained in the example would have followed a 'yes' to the first question.

It is difficult to answer questions which contain unfamiliar words and phrases. This includes specialised vocabulary, or even questions which involve unnecessary generalisation and abstraction. Education is full of jargon and technical terms. Even as professionals, we may each have difficulty in giving the precise meaning of some words in common educational usage: 'model', 'conceptual development', 'action research', 'intervention', 'ideology', 'personal construct', 'curriculum', 'therapeutic'.

It is in interviewers' own best interests and a reasonable courtesy to interviewees, to keep questions as simple as possible.

Hoinville and Jowell suggest other kinds of questions to avoid. These include negatives, which require mental agility to answer. Their example requires interviewees to state whether they agree or disagree that:

Children, who steal, should not be punished.

Try to answer. It is much more difficult than responding to the positive statement:

Children, who steal, should be let off with a caution.

Hypothetical questions may give unreliable results, with responses based on different assumptions. Some interviewees might respond in terms of their ideal, others in more realistic terms. Some people are unwilling or find it difficult to react to a situation they know will never exist.

Often unwittingly, interviewers ask leading questions. For example, they may assume that interviewees hold a particular point

136

of view, and fail to provide for the contrary view. Examples from Hoinville and Jowell again:

What makes you like your job?

or

Do you agree your hours of work are unsatisfactory?

To avoid such leading questions, the interviewer would have to ask 'whether or not' people like their job, or agree about their hours of work. Questions should not be phrased in such a way, as to suggest there is only one socially acceptable answer, especially where certain biased words or phrases are used.

*Bias*   As Hoinville and Jowell point out,

> in normal conversation, people often bias what they tell another person towards what they think he or she wants or expects to hear. Such responses do much to smooth ordinary social relationships, but have great dangers in an interview. (p. 100)

If the interviewer is not trying to lead the interviewee, questions should be asked, and answers received, in a neutral, straightforward way. Any verbal, or non-verbal, feedback should be as non-committal as possible. Even expressions such as 'Good', 'Oh, really!', 'I do agree' will inform the interviewee about the questioner's own position.

The interviewee may also exhibit bias in the sense that Saran (1985) suggests:

> recollections of past feelings are often selected to fit into their current points of view. The well-informed researcher can test answers for implausibility, unreliability, and by grasp of what Whyte calls the informant's mental set and how this influences any interpretation of events. But ultimately *the researcher arrives only at approximations of reality in terms of what happened, and only at insightful awareness of the ambivalence of human motive and behaviour.* (Our emphases)

*Prompts and probes*   Survey researchers normally set out clear guidelines on the uses of prompts and probes. A *prompt* suggests possible answers to a respondent, offering the kind of answer the researcher expects. In projects where consistency is important, interviewers should have clear guidelines including actual wording for their prompts. Sometimes these are in the form of cards, listing relevant alternatives. This is helpful to both participants if the list is long, or difficult to remember. For example,

Which of these schools would you prefer to send your child to?

1 Single sex grammar school
2 Mixed sex grammar school
3 Single sex comprehensive school
4 Mixed comprehensive school
5 Single sex independent school
6 Mixed sex independent school
7 Other kind of school (please specify)

There must be easier ways of getting this information. However, if this is the preferred way of asking, the interviewer would have the alternatives typed on a separate card. The interviewee could have the card as the interviewer reads through the choices. It is always useful to have a category 'other'. Responses in this last category, should be specified both to ensure that they do not fit into an existing category, and to help with subsequent analysis. A response in category 7 above, might be 'boy's public school' which, when clarified, would fit into category 5. Only complex prompts need to be presented on separate cards – usually a simple prompt is read out or spoken. The most important thing to remember, is that a note of the actual prompt used is part of the interview record. In informal situations, an interviewer may unconsciously prompt and thereby affect the nature of the reply.

A *probe* is a neutral verbal, or non-verbal, way of encouraging the interviewee to answer, or to clarify or extend, an answer. Probing is more non-committal than prompting. It needs no detailed recording beyond a note, perhaps, of where probing was necessary. Even this information is not always pertinent. For example, if a researcher is trying to identify which topics cause interviewees to hesitate, then it is helpful to know where the interviewer had to encourage further reply or information. Probing is extensively used in informant interviews, where the initiative is largely with the informant. Interviewers can make use of a repertoire of verbal, and non-verbal, techniques to elicit more information from the interviewee:

Eye contact, especially an inquiring glance.
'Could you tell me some more about that please?'
An expectant silence.
Repeating back the interviewee's own words,
'Mmmm ...', 'Uh-huh ...'

'I'm not quite sure if I understand what you are getting at.'
'How do you mean it's because of the system?'
'Exactly why do you think it is too often?'

Some of this kind of probing is to clarify what interviewees have said, particularly when they have used relative terms, such as 'important', 'often', or, of course, ambiguous words. Probing should not harass interviewees but give them sufficient time and opportunity to answer fully.

Both prompts and probes need to be used carefully as not only may they lead interviewees into a particular line of answering. They also reduce consistency in presentation between interviews, unless used in the same way in each interview.

*Silence* Experienced interviewers can use silence most effectively. It gives the impression of being unhurried and enables interviewees to expand their answers in their own way. Some people find it quite hard to tolerate silence. They jump in too quickly, interrupting the interviewee's thoughts, thereby disrupting the informality of the interview. New interviewers might find it helpful to incorporate silence deliberately in trial interviews, if only to see the maximum period which is both useful and tolerable.

*Recording what the interviewees say* All the information should be recorded as accurately as possible during the interview. This is easier with a tape recorder, than with note taking but if either the tape recorder or notebook is causing the interviewee to 'freeze up', the interviewer should put it away and depend on ability to remember as much as possible. An interviewer may think (s)he can remember answers accurately but in practice this is not possible. Therefore, even with the use of a tape recorder, it is sensible to check through immediately after the interview.

*Ending the interview* One of the basic laws of interviewing is that the most interesting material emerges when the recorder is switched off. An informant is chatty and forthcoming until the formal interview starts. The converse is also true: an interviewee has given monosyllabic answers, until the interviewer prepares to wind up the session and leave. This releases a flood of ideas and comments and puts the interviewer in a dilemma about whether or not: to switch back on, get out the notebook again, try to remember what is being said and note it down as soon as possible after the interview – or just forget it happened. Whatever choice the interviewer makes, this must be made explicit in the write-up of the interviews.

*Getting away*   On the practical side, interviewers need to check that they have covered all the necessary topics and questions. It is worthwhile to ask the interviewees, if they have any questions, or if they wish to add to the information and comments, they have already made. This may not only provide the interviewer with some unexpected gems of insight, but also leave the interviewees with the feeling that they have been appreciated and the whole exercise was worthwhile.

Even in interviews about education it is possible that interviewees become upset. This might be expected when the subject touches upon obviously sensitive areas, such as asking parents about the education and future of their severely handicapped children. Sometimes, an individual may react to the interview in a very emotional way. For example, researchers often find that they are being used as a confessor figure. The interviewer should aim to safeguard sufficient distance to be able to leave the interview without distressing the interviewee. At any event, the interviewer should not leave an interviewee until (s)he is in an apparently calm state. All interviewees should be left feeling positive about the interview.

Certain difficulties may occur after the interview because the participants already know each other, or are at least going to meet again in a different context. Teachers' or pupils' behaviour, or publicly expressed attitudes may contradict the information their teacher-researcher colleague collected in previous interviews. The latter may then find it difficult to remain silent or may feel that interview was of questionable usefulness. Professional interviewers are seldom faced with this dilemma since there is usually no further contact with the informant after the interview.

### Conclusion

In this chapter we have tried to give practical hints on how to prepare for an interview, make the initial contacts and actually carry it out. Our suggestions are limited and deliberately biased towards structured or respondent interviews. This is based on the assumption that it is easier to become less formal than the other way round. Ethnographers may be all the more subtle in presenting and reporting their interviews, if they are keenly aware of such potential hazards as prompts and probes. In the end, we are not advocating any single style We do urge clear reporting of whatever does occur in an interview, as we outline in the next chapter.

*Appendix: Preparation checklist*

## Familiarity with research plan

- Aims of research project.
- Aims of interviews and their place in project.

## Structuring (or not) the framework for the interviews

- List questions/topics. Construct interview schedule.
- Check if all included questions, or topics, are necessary.
- Check if all necessary questions, or topics, are included.

## Selection of interviewer(s)

- Who?
- What skills do they need?
- Agreement on collaborative methods.

## Selection of and contacting the sample to be interviewed

Selection:
- Who?
- How many?
- Why those?
- Links between interviewers and sample?

Contact:
- Obtain necessary approvals
- Who tells what and to whom?
- Arrangements for confidentiality, anonymity.

## Preparation of method of recording and analysis

- How does interview data relate to other sources of information?
- What is to be noted?
- What is the best method?
- Mechanics of recording?
- Equipment?
- How are responses or collected information to be analysed?

## Calculation of costs in time and money

- Length, travelling time, writing up and analysis of each interview?
- Travelling and other costs × total number of interviews?

## Piloting

- Try, or consider each stage.
- Make necessary modifications.
- Run further pilot as necessary.

# Chapter 6

# The transcription, logging, and analysis of data

*Introduction*

In this chapter we are concerned with the development and detailed scrutiny of the interviewing database. Analysis is a process of gains and losses, and it is important that researchers report both aspects as fully as possibly. As Davies (1985) says:

> All we ask is that readers are aware of where they (researchers) win and where they lose.

Before we explore these issues further, let us focus on the notion of analysis itself. We take analysis to be *the detailed examination of the database that ensues from single or multiple interviews*. That is, analysis can be about the detail of what occurs within a single interview or across several. For us, however, analysis must go beyond a simple description of the data. Analysis is every bit as much an act of constructing interpretations as is the interview session itself, and the analyst will bring to it some interpretation of the data, if only by a process of selection. As in other chapters, too, we consider first some general issues involved with analysis before considering specific examples and the fine-grain detail of actually undertaking it.

The development part of the chapter is the transcribing of the interviews and the logging of all other relevant data involved in the research. The detailed scrutiny is the analysis of what accrues. The term 'database' needs some explaining. We intend it to mean the entire recorded data of the interview *and* those parts that are relevant of the *un*recorded data. The recorded data is probably self-explanatory, although we would include a fairly comprehensive sweep of data within that. For example, it would include:

• the research design

- descriptions of the initial approaches made to interviewees
- details of any institutional organisations involved
- the research questions
- instructions given to participants
- any stimulus or focus used
- the audio, or video recording of the interview sessions themselves, or the field notes taken
- details of leaving the interview
- all the biographical detail of the interviewees
- any feedback to interviewees.

The unrecorded data is less obvious. Stenhouse (1979) calls this kind of data the researcher's 'second record'. It is what Hull (1984) calls a 'black market' of records of events and on-the-spot interpretations, the accumulated knowledge of participants' meaning systems – only some of which appears on the written record. As soon as one walks into a school, for instance, impressions are gathered about the kind of place it is, its ethos, the staff and pupils, the noise level, the state of cleanliness or otherwise, all of which go towards colouring perceptions. In an interview, similar impressions concerning the interviewee are an inevitable part of the proceedings. The person's attitudes towards the interview, or the subject-matter, can show themselves in a number of small ways which are not always clear from the words they use. Posture, tone of voice, eye contact, gestures and so on are aspects of the session available only to the participants in many cases. As Johnson (1975) says:

> When I listened to the cassette recordings of home visits, on several occasions I realised that I knew certain things about the actions that had not been stated in so many words. This is not to imply I had to read between the lines of the transcripts or review them in an ironic or metaphorical manner to understand them. It is to say some of the crucial features of the action were not expressed verbally.

There are two concerns with this kind of data. Where the analyst is also the interviewer then the data is probably invaluable in making sense of what is being said and done in the interview. It is therefore a resource that the interviewer/analyst calls upon when selecting and describing points of note within the data. But how can all the perceptions that are accrued in the course of conducting the research be made open and available to others who have an interest in what is being said. And how can the interpretations arrived at in this way be authenticated? The answers to both questions are not easy to provide and are discussed somewhat more fully later in the chapter. Where the tasks of interviewing and analysis fall to different people the 'second record' may not be called upon (with all the loss of rich data that that implies) and, where it is, would need special provision for it to be made available. Again, ways of tackling this are discussed a little later.

There is a sense in which it is possible to collect both too much and too little data. Not all data is relevant to the task in hand. There is often a strong temptation on the part of beginning researchers to note anything and everything on the basis that it may prove useful later. That is, the research design is not entirely clear and the door is being left open so that other contingencies can be catered for as the interview evolves. Discarding irrelevant or unusable data is throwing away time and personal commitment – both of which are a most precious resource. The researcher may or may not have time to spare. But, more importantly, interviewees are asked to make a substantial investment in the process of interviewing and whether it is in the initial approaches, the interview itself, any follow-up activities or the provision of personal biographical detail, their investment is not something to be squandered. Too little data is, of course, equally if not more debilitating for good research.

In a paper we have already mentioned in earlier chapters, McDonald and Sanger (1982) argue that the means used for recording what takes place in an interview actually generates different kinds of encounters, with different kinds of outcome products. Using a tape recorder frees the interviewer to concentrate upon the task at hand – exploring the interviewee's account. Some of its drawbacks have already been noted: a tape recording under-represents the communication by providing only the sound component – a component that is reduced even further at the transcript stage; tape-based interviews are often skewed in favour of the most articulate – at the end of the day there is little you can do with an empty tape; tapes take a lot of listening to and are difficult to scan, and, importantly, transcription is very slow and expensive of resources. Field notes by themselves can mitigate some of these weaknesses (there is no delayed and costly transcription) whilst introducing obvious drawbacks of their own. Scott (1985) offers some interesting thoughts. Tape recordings, she suggests, lead to a reification of data. This can amount to as much as three-quarters of the data so that there is a sense in which the interviewer becomes an extension of the tape recorder – rather than the other way round. 'Truth' lies on the tape, it becomes objective fact through transcription, whilst the researcher's own understandings of what was happening and being said in the interview are relegated to 'unreliable data'.

The chapter falls into three main parts: the transcription of the interviews; the logging of other data; and the task of analysis itself. Throughout, we stress two main points. Firstly, the database is best seen as a cumulative bank of data that has to be tapped for the information it can bring to bear upon what is being said. Not only does it have a bearing on the analysis, it is also highly pertinent to what is said about the interviews at the reporting stage – an issue we take up in the next chapter. Secondly, we return to our theme that much of interviewing can best be treated as a co-operative venture – much use can be made of friends and colleagues in the process of analysing data.

## Transcribing interviews

Differing kinds of interviews require different kinds of transcription. A 'verbal questionnaire', for example, would probably be completed during the course of the actual interview and would not require extensive or elaborate transcription after the event. Interviews concerned with linguistic features have, on the other hand, often been subjected to very detailed and intricate transcription. Many projects, however, consider it essential to be as accurate as possible as far as the content of the speech is concerned, but relegate the representation of intonation and pitch range to relative unimportance.

The process of transcription will vary depending upon the aims and needs of the research design, and whether or not the transcription is undertaken by the interviewer, analyst, or both. It will make a difference, for example, if all the interview dialogue is seen simply as a pilot study where a few quotes will suffice to make a point, whether it must be typed, kept on computer file, made amenable to numerical coding and analysis, fed back to the interviewee for appraisal and so on. It is very difficult to suggest particular ways of working for a multitude of purposes and so in what follows a few examples, some from our case studies in Chapter 4, have been chosen in order to illustrate some points at issue.

The role of transcriber is to provide a record as accurate as possible of the discourse, and preparing a transcript is undoubtedly an acquired skill. Full transcription is immensely time consuming; ratios of between 6:1 and 10:1 are not uncommon – that is, 6 minutes of transcribing time to 1 minute of 'talk time'. Writing out discourse in longhand obviously takes longer. Figures like these mean that an hour's conversation will take between 6 and 10 hours to transcribe – it is often time that is not considered or built into research programmes at the outset. Moreover, in the kind of transcript shown in example 1 below, 1 minute of discourse occupies about 2 pages of typescript; 1 hour's would produce a document about 100 pages long. The sheer bulk, transport and storage of interview transcript is also a feature of interviewing that is seldom considered and planned for at the outset of research projects. One of the very first decisions that has to be made in the planning of a research project, therefore, is whether or not the whole interview is to be transcribed. Woods (1985), for example, recommends transcription in two stages. The first occurs as soon as possible after the interview, when the researcher listens to the tape and makes an index of its contents, picking out particular points. Some telling points may be transcribed there and then. The index remains as a record of the conversation during the period between the interview and any resulting transcription, which may be transcribed only in part depending upon the selection of relevant parts.

Before engaging more fully with the examples below, two further points need to be made. Firstly, the form of the spoken word is very different from the written and this generates a feeling that the page looks unruly as the conversation develops. In contrast to normal written material, dialogue seems disorganised. Speakers may not seem to have clear ideas, talk is discontinuous, frequently occurs in rapid bursts, and distinguishing some words is often made the more difficult by intrusive background noises. It is extremely difficult to note everything that is being transmitted by speakers. Even where only one person is speaking and enunciating clearly, there is always the problem of how to convey emphasis. Gestures, faltering, pauses, voice quality, facial expressions, postures and the proximity of speakers all give that additional layer of meaning to the words spoken. It can happen that a speaker can convey exactly the opposite of what is being said, and much of this extra meaning will not appear on the manuscript. Initially, there may be the temptation to 'correct' written talk full of inconsequence and pauses, contradictions and confusions, and at points where the dialogue seems disorganised. However, in preparing a transcript, it is necessary to withhold the expectation one would have of the written word.

Given that a transcription cannot represent everything featured in the original spoken language, it follows that any transcription is an *interpretation* by the transcriber of what is being said. What is written down is inevitably selective. As such it is just one of the many acts of selection that the researcher has to undertake within the research –

but nonetheless it needs to be recognised as such. Where transcripts form part of the database it is important to remember that they are not 'raw' data, but represent a transcriber's eye-view of the event. Part of proposing a style and notation for transcribing is to draw attention to the possibility of 'tunnel vision', the prejudging of the intention of a speaker. Full transcription is best tackled in at least two distinct stages. The first is to represent the whole interview verbatim as far as possible, including hesitations, pauses, laughs, sighs, coughs and so on. The second is to replay the conversation whilst entering emphasis, annotation and comment. Needless to say, these two stages need not be done by the same person, though – in order to make explicit some of the 'black market' – the second is most realistically done by the interviewer, as the person present at the time of the interchange.

Two examples below have been chosen to illustrate some of the points to be made. The first shows a level of detail that focuses on the substance of what is being said, without too great a regard for extremely fine detail. Many researchers will, of course, operate with far less transcription detail than this and for very good reasons. It does, however, represent a fairly standard and often used level of interview transcription. The second shows a different layout that includes a greater emphasis on paralinguistic considerations. This is a more sophisticated and specialist level of transcription and it is consequently much more informative, and difficult to produce.

*Example 1*
This first example is taken from a study within science education (Bentley and Watts, 1986), concerning the perceptions of both teachers and youngsters of the function and effectiveness of science education television. Youngsters were shown extracts from recent programmes and then asked to comment on such issues as the visual impact, clarity of commentary, relevance and usefulness of what they'd seen. They watched the extracts in groups and were interviewed individually. Brigitte is a 15-year-old, fourth-year student at a school in Suffolk.

In this case the interview was conducted by an independent interviewer recruited for the task. It was audio recorded, the interviewer making a series of field notes to accompany the tape. The transcript was prepared by an accomplished audio-typist, using a fairly standard typist's playback machine that takes normal audio tape cassettes rather than the small business dictaphone size. The machine had foot-controls for stop, rewind and forward, and the material was typed directly to computer disc on a BBC using a Wordwise

Plus word processing package. This information is only relevant for the process of transcription (and later analysis) and bears only slightly on the actual finished transcript. Printed transcript copy was passed to the interviewer for amendment and annotation, and then to the others for analysis. The actual transcript has been tailored slightly here to exemplify certain points:

*041*. **I:**   In what ways would you like to change that programme to fit in with what you're doing in with your lessons?

*042*. **Brigitte:**   Well we've only just started learning about electricity, how it works and that, so I, maybe if they started off by saying what electricity was made up of and that and explained what it was used for and things like that, it might be a bit more helpful to understand what it really is, so I might be able to understand it a bit more.

*043*. **I:**   How would you change, urmh, if you could change the programme then would you change the commentary at all?

*044*. **Brigitte:**   Yes, I'd get a more enthusiastic commentator because I thought his voice was a bit monotonous, and it sort of made you feel as though you were a little bit sleepy (laughs). The pictures held your attention but the commentary was a bit dubious. (Counter number 169.) And I think I'd change the order. I think the principle of the electricity, as I've said before, is really important, having that at the beginning, and then going on to the larger-scale thing, and how it's made and that. I think the order could be better.

*045*. **I:**   Which parts of the programme – if any – do you feel are relevant to your everyday life?

*046*. **Brigitte:**   Well everybody uses electricity, so I thought it was all relevant because you've got to know where it comes from, because everybody uses it and you've got to have some basic knowledge of it really. I thought most of it was relevant – yes.

*047*. **I:**   In what way were the ideas about how electricity is generated that were put over in that programme, different from the ideas that you had about it before?

*048*. **Brigitte:**   ... (15) ... Umh. Well I didn't really appreciate that it was done on such a large scale, I mean it's obvious now that it has to be because so much is produced, but seeing the actual pictures of the stations makes you realise how big how much electricity is needed and how much fuel is used, so it helps you appreciate the scale of it, of the production, so that was helpful, for me anyway. I suppose I really appreciated how it was transmitted before, but it wasn't such a large gap between the

two things, how it's transmitted for me than it was for the other two things and there's a large gap between these two, er ?????
*049.* **I:**   What two things do you mean, sorry I'm ...?
*050.* **Brigitte:**   The previous ones about how big the station is – those two.
*051.* **I:**   Ah I see – yes. (Counter number 201.)
*052.* **Brigitte:**   Urmh, but I think, I appreciated the transmission more than I appreciated the scale anyway so ...
*053.* **I:**   Thank you. Does it generally matter if there's a difference between your ideas of something in science and the ideas that are put over on a television programme?
*054.* **Brigitte:**   Well no, as long as it doesn't patronise you and make out that you're really thick, or you're really brainy, it's got to be sort of suitable for your age group. Different people have different ideas, I mean nobody's got the same ideas so you can't have it exactly the same, its sort of coinciding with what you think, sometimes it's good to see somebody else's point of view, then you can realise what else is sort of happening, if you know what I mean. No it doesn't really matter as long as they don't treat you like you're really stupid.

The style adopted here is to represent speech reasonably closely to written dialogue. Capital letters, quotation marks, full stops, commas, semi-colons and the like are features of written language and correspond in only a very crude way to features of speech. In this example the speech has been divided into approximate sentences and normal punctuation used to indicate sentence beginning and end. That is, the transcriber has interpreted when a sentence has begun and ended and signalled this. It is not always clear how that decision has been made and why a full stop and capital letter have been used instead of a pause or a comma. However, the general structure of the text allows for the dialogue to be read in a fairly direct way. The level of punctuation detail is not always important. Here, for example, where Brigitte is in full flow about the monotony of the commentator, her words can be understood clearly. Where there is some confusion, however (utterance 048), and it is unclear what 'two gaps' she is referring to, then the punctuation and layout do become important.

Clearly, the transcript is laid out with wide margins on both sides for comments and additions to be made. The notation used is that of 'I' for the interviewer, and the interviewee's full first name. These appear in emboldened type, a facility that a word processor allows quite easily. Each new piece of speech is numbered as an 'utterance number' at the start. Transcriber's doubt is indicated by a series of question marks (as at the end of utterance 048) with as much of the sound included as possible. Where the transcriber is doubtful about a word or phrase this is given in brackets with question marks. Pauses are shown as dots or a hyphen, except for long pauses which are timed roughly and shown as a figure in brackets (as in utterance 048).

'Urmh's' and 'er's' are included and serve slightly different functions. 'Urmh' suggests a non-verbal response by a listener that accepts a comment by the other person, an indication of agreement or contemplation that does not break the flow, so that the speaker will continue with what is being said. 'Er' suggests that the speaker is searching for a word or phrase, or is in the act of breaking into another's speech, as in 'Er, before you go any further ...'. The audio tape revolution counter number is included at various intervals to aid the process of returning to the tape for clarification. The annotation of the transcript includes a complete revision by the interviewer using field notes, drawings etc. The early part of the discussion with Brigitte, for example, was obscured by youngsters outside the room moving from one room to another, at the change of lessons during the school day. The interviewer notes:

> (At this point a teacher passing through the room comments that there is a lot of noise going on outside, saying 'I think the door's still open'.)
> *005.* **I:** I don't think it is I just think everybody's going to their lessons. (To Brigitte) I shall turn off and we'll hang on a minute. (Approximately 3 minutes later.) Right that's better, fine then. Don't be nervous.
> *006.* **Brigitte:** No I'm not nervous (laughs).
> *007.* **Interviewer:** No. Good, well you can see things go wrong, don't they, they go wrong for me as well. Now the first few questions are about....

In some cases the paralinguistic effects are noted on the transcript in abbreviation or code. Coxon (1979), for example, uses (tg) where two people speak together, (l) laughs, (c) coughs, (t) voice trails off, (?) inaudible or possible mis-hearing, and ( + ) for pause.

*Example 2*
This example is taken from the work of Wells (1981) which concerns the linguistic development of young children. It is clearly important that the data is transcribed to include considerable information about interaction with others, intonation, tonic stress, pitch, the intention

151

of utterances (interrogative, declarative) and so on. The conventions and layout that accompany these transcripts are detailed in the study and are not reproduced in full here, save to provide a short example extract and to make some comments.

The speech is separated into columns, the child's on the left, other participants in the centre and contextual information enclosed in square brackets on the right. The underlining in utterance 5 indicates where the two speakers talk at once, the arrows indicate shift of voice pitch relative to the speakers' normal range, the numbers between words show changes in pitch as the person is speaking. Pitch is numbered 1 to 5 from high to low. For example, 243 in utterance 10 is a falling then rising tone that does not return to the same pitch as it began. Normal punctuation use is suspended, each of the usual symbols taking on particular roles in the transcript.

· The level of detail of the transcript is clearly shaped by the needs of the research. In this case the purpose is to chart and monitor children's linguistic and communicative competence and to relate this to pre-school and early school experiences. Consequently the level of detail is fine, with all the attendant problems of encoding and decoding that this entails. In Case Study 2, Chapter 4, though, where long extracts are included of the conversation between Janet and Jill, we have deliberately opted for a more 'grammatical' transcription for the sake of readability.

### Logging interview data

This section deals with all the non-transcript data that is included in the database. To return to our distinction above, we deal with the 'first' and 'second record', and in that order.

We suggested earlier that the recorded data would be fairly comprehensive, and that it might include:

- the research design
- descriptions of the initial approaches made to interviewees
- details of any institutional organisations involved
- the research questions
- instructions given to participants
- any stimulus or focus used
- the audio, or video recording of the interview sessions themselves, or the field notes taken
- details of leaving the interview

- all the biographical detail of the interviewees
- any feedback to interviewees.

Undoubtedly some of this data, for example the research design, would be logged in traditional ways in terms of a submission to a funding organisation, a proposal to a research supervisor or higher awards committee, recommendations or a brief from a working party, or an in-house or departmental proposal for research. It is the sort of document that is often requested by local education authorities when permission is required to conduct research in their schools or institutions. It is important to recall that research projects do not always follow the linear sequence of, for example, a traditional qualitative research design. Many ethnographic studies may have a theme or a focus but do not have a clear pre-ordained beginning or end. Nor is it always clear to the researcher how everything might turn out. That is, some methodologies may be cumulative – but then so may be some of the research goals. There may well be occasions where the research design is not documented and it then becomes important to write down the goals and purpose of the research in a structured format. Inevitably, it will be these goals and intentions that both shape the research and the report that ensues, and more importantly, shape the analysis of data. Within this there should be some indication of the point of the research, the background against which it might be viewed, the methodologies to be adopted, some schedule of activities, the likely resource implications involved and the sort of outcomes that might evolve.

Describing the initial approaches to interviewees is important because it allows an interested observer or reader of the research to contextualise the main interview sessions. It gives an indication, for example, of the ethical stance of the research. What was the 'research contract' that was established at the outset between interviewer and interviewee? How were the interviewees recruited? Personally? Through some hierarchical management arrangement? Anonymously? Were pupils or students invited or 'volunteered'? Were letters sent home to parents for permission to interview? There are many questions like these that can legitimately be raised about any piece of educational research and it is important that answers can, at some stage, be furnished. Novak and Gowin (1984), for instance, provide an example 'home letter' they used in their study. Dave Ebbutt, in Case Study 5, gives an example of the letter used to approach the sixth-form colleges he used. In the same sense it is also important to record the normal procedure for ending the interview. Whether it is simply thanking individuals for their involvement,

*Example 2*

| | |
|---|---|
| 34 | M: 31 Pardon? |
| 35 24 Linda wa –/ 324 wash them | |
| 36 | M: 23 No |
| 37 | M: 23 Mummy's going to / 35 wash them |
| 38 15 Linda wash them | |
| 39 | M: 24 'No / Linda's 34 'not going to / 45 'wash them |
| 40 24 Linda not going to / 54 wash them | |
| 41 | M: 35 No |
| 42 | M: 35 Mummy wash them |
| 43 2 This is 13 Daddy's socks / 43 Mum(v) | |
| 44 | M: 32 Pardon? |
| 45 This is 24 Daddy's sock | |

*Appendix 2*

*Name:* Jane      *Record Number:* 7
*Date of Birth:* 8.4.1970      *Date of Recording:* 10.1.1975

*Sample number:* 8      *Participants:* Mother, Jane
     *Time:* 11.57 a.m.
     *Location:* Kitchen
     *Activity:* Mother preparing lunch, Jane watching

[Radio on]

| | |
|---|---|
| 1 Ma(v) | |
| 2 I've got a * cos I didn't – I – that make me sick that do | |
| 3 Ma(v) can I go out? | |
| 4 | M: No |
| 5 | M: It's cold out now |
| 6 | M: One two three four five six seven eight nine ten (sings) |
| | [Mother counts before lighting the gas stove] |
| 7 Mum(v) what we got? | |
| 8 Mum(v) let me have a look what's burning | |
| 9 Mum(v) that egg's burning in'it? | |
| 10 | M: What? |

154

11 That egg's burning

12 Oh Mum(v)!(with consternation)
13 Which – where my egg?
14 Mum(v) we both got to have eggs
15                                    M: I'll be a bag of nerves if
                                        you don't shut up (shouts)
16 Mum(v)                           . . .
17 Lift your bag up (command)
18 Oh! what's that?
19 " * * * * * <all the food>"
20 * *
21 Mum(v) we both –                              [Mother beating eggs]

---

| | |
|---|---|
| *Sample number:* 9 | *Participants:* Jane, Mother |
| | *Time:* 12.07 p.m. |
| | *Location:* Kitchen |
| | *Activity:* Mother preparing lunch, Jane watching |

1 "Oh"                              . .
                                    . . 4 . .
2                                   M: What you doing?
                                    . .
3                                   M: You do it the hard way don't you?
                                    . . 4 . .
4 "Don't fall out"                             [Jane doesn't seem to
                                                expect any answers]
5 Ah! baked potato!
6 * * * *                           . . 6 . .
7                                   M: Oh God!
                                    , , 7 . .
8 That egg and chips

 9 That egg is dirty Mummy(v)       M: NR
                                    . . 6 . .
10 Oh! bacon!
11 Now what's this?                            [Jane mistakes chops for
                                                                bacon]
12                                  M: What! (exclamation)
13                                  M: You got bacon on the mind
                                        or summat?
                                    . . .

(From Gordon Wells, *Describing Children's Linguistic Development
at Home and at School*, pp. 160 1.)

answering questions, establishing future contacts or negotiating the reviewing or release of interview data, the interview end is an integral part of the proceedings and needs to be noted. What happens when the tape recorder is switched off can be as important as what happens before it is switched on.

Details of institutions involved, as with the approaches to interviewees, are the kind of data often collected almost as a matter of course as the research takes place. Institutions, being what they are, commonly produce descriptive material which details their activities and functions and are usually more than happy to provide that level of information easily. In some cases it will form the main thrust of the analysis – in that, for instance, interview responses might be noted against type of school, geographical location, or policy as stated in a school's brochure. There will inevitably be particular research requirements that need much fuller details than those provided in public brochures, a need that will probably give rise to a questionnaire or researchers' proforma.

Given all that we have said so far about the shape of interviews and the form of questions that may, or may not be developed in advance of the interview, there will certainly come a time when, if only for the purposes of the researcher or analyst, a note is made of the questions asked. Again, in the context of schools and education authorities, it is often the kind of information that is requested in advance of permission being granted for research to take place at all and, in social survey studies, developing the questions is one of the major tasks to be accomplished in preparation for the interviews. Similarly, the instructions given to the interviewee at the start of the interview are also worth noting.

The stimulus to the interview, or the interview task has already been discussed in Chapter 2 and some interesting examples have been highlighted in the case studies. Whether it be slides of non-verbal behaviour (as in Di Bentley's case study, Case Study 4), science television programmes (Bentley and Watts 1986), pictures or photographs, laboratory equipment or whatever, the details need to be logged.

The biographical details and notes on the interviewee need recording. Any information about the interviewees which has direct relevance to the interview situation should be noted. Pertinent comments, too, should be included – any auditory deficiencies or manipulatory problems, for example, that might affect the way the interview is conducted or analysed. Dates and names, or interview codes, should be written on tapes, tape boxes, interview schedules or questionnaire sheets before the interview takes place. Again, the level of detail will depend on the research design and on what is required. The order of events can also be important. Did the interviewees see all the photographs *before* commenting, for instance, or one at a time? Were they asked for biographical details at the beginning or at the end? When (as in Jill Keegan's study) were they paid for their attendance?

It is common to find interviewees indexed on a card filing system similar to that shown below (Watts, 1983b).

```
┌─────────────────────────────────────────────────────┐
│                                                       │
│                                                       │
│   Name               Class:          No:              │
│   ─────────          ──────────      ──────────       │
│   M/F     Age:       Tape 1/2        Date:            │
│   ────    ─────      ──────────      ──────────       │
│   Background notes:                                   │
│       (school; lesson; biographical notes etc)        │
│                                                       │
│                                                       │
│   Interview notes:                                    │
│   ──────────────────────────────────────             │
│                                                       │
│                                                       │
└─────────────────────────────────────────────────────┘
```

Finally, a description of any triangulation mechanism, inter-judge reliability exercise, or simple feedback from researcher to researcher, or researcher to interviewee is a necessary adjunct to the database. The point and purpose of such activities are taken up in the final chapters and are not discussed here beyond noting that, like all the other integral aspects of the interviewing process, they will require some description at some stage.

These are not all the data that can be logged, and therein lies a major problem with interviewing as with any other kind of research. The interviewer carries with him or her a wealth of impressions that may or may not bear directly on the outcomes of the research. One approach to logging this data is to have the interviewer write up the 'context' of the interview, perhaps, as Jill Keegan notes, taking as much time to do that as the duration of the actual interview. Another is for the researchers to spend time de-briefing the interviewer. This is the approach adopted in the first of the examples described above (Bentley and Watts, 1986). The interviewer was asked to revisit recent interviews and to recall and recollect impressions, to talk through the contexts in which they had taken place. In this case she was also asked to draft these impressions in general terms so that these could be included in the final research report. A third approach is that this data is not presented separately from the main body of interview outcomes but that the research results are written through, are embedded within the interview contexts as fully as possible. The skills required here are those of the story teller so that the prose can be brought alive in the atmosphere in which the research took place.

## Analysing interviews

We begin this section as we have others, by saying that there are many different kinds of analysis and many different terms used to describe them. The analysis that follows from having conducted interviews is likely to depend upon a number of factors:

- the purpose of the research
- the purpose of the interview within the research
- the particular interview approach that has been adopted
- the data collection methods
- the quality of the interview sessions
- the reporting procedure envisaged.

Before we explore these constraints further, we return to the notion of analysis itself. We earlier took analysis to be *the detailed examination of the database that ensues from single or multiple interviews*. We suggested, too, that analysis is an act of constructive interpretation. We look a little further at this here before considering the detail of analysis of a single interview – or across several.

### Approaches to analysis

We begin by stressing the notion of congruence, in particular 'methodological congruence' (Watts and Bentley, 1985). Congruence in general means consistency, or compatibility, and here we use it to suggest that the analysis of data should be consistent or compatible with the general underlying philosophy of the research. To unpick this a little we need to consider different kinds of research philosophy, different approaches to analysis and then see how well or not these can be matched together. If some analyses can be seen to match with particular kinds of philosophy then we have methodological congruency. Where this does not occur then the general assumptions that underwrite the research, and the methodologies being used to fulfil it would be incommensurate. There would be a distinct clash between the message and the medium – a position, in our view, to be avoided.

It is possible to glean some idea of underlying philosophy if, as an example, we consider Marton's (1981) distinction between first-order and second-order perspectives. Research questions that belong to the first order, he suggests, are those that have a matter-of-fact quality about them, and commonly concern issues such as the performance of students, the evaluation of one teaching programme over another, and so on. An example might be that of the Assessment of Performance Unit (DES 1981; 1982). Examples of second-order research questions might be those found in Marton, Hounsell and Entwistle (1984) where the focus of research is upon the experience of learning as it appears to participants. That is, it is learners' own accounts of, and reactions to, learning that is important.

Some research, then, can be seen to be about the context of education, about institutions, resources, provision, attendance, performance – the establishment and comparison of norms and features in the educational system. Other research is about the perceptions and values of the participants. In broad and general terms both would need different kinds of analysis when researched by interview. The first is more amenable to a move from content analysis to statistical analysis, the 'what', 'how much' or 'how many' of education. Such data is more directly researched, for example, by respondent interviews and the responses coded, or fitted into pre-code categories of response. The second is less amenable to this sort of approach, is about the 'hows' and 'whys' of education as people see them. It is about 'insider stories', experiences and accounts. In this kind of approach it is more common that informant interviews are used and that analysts set out to construct distinctive descriptors of major elements of what is being said. The categories may well have been established in advance and be coded, but in general terms the categories would more commonly be shaped in the analyst's interpretive constructions. Sometimes this lends itself to statistical analysis but, on the whole, more descriptive methods are chosen in order to be consistent with the form of the research. The existence of numbers in an analysis does not of itself guarantee – or even indicate – rigour. Nor is the converse true – the absence of numbers does not denote lack of rigour or quality. Returning to work described by Marton, Hounsell and Entwistle (1984), Entwistle says:

> ... the method of qualitative analysis is distinctive and exceptionally rigorous. It sets out to identify concepts which describe important differences in the ways in which students learn and study. The specific differences give rise to distinct categories and each category is defined, or delimited, in terms of those extracts from the interview which together constitute its meaning.

In this way other researchers are able to follow similar procedures and then make detailed comparisons between concepts and categories identified in the various studies. This procedure thus carries the 'hallmark' of scientific research, while not following the methods of the natural science.

One major problem comes, for example, when statistical methods are used to describe or explain issues that do not lend themselves to such an approach. That is, when the phenomenology of a person's account of their own experiences is fed into a statistical package of some sort. It is at this point we might have methodological *incon*-gruity. We need to note, however, that as Pines and Leith (1981) have said, we

> have nothing against quantitative research and tight experimental design when and where they are appropriate. However, when such research methodology becomes like the proverbial child who given a hammer and learns to use it then proceeds to hit everything in sight with it, (we) become alarmed.

There are some similarities in Marton's distinction – between first- and second-order perspectives – to what has been called traditional and 'new paradigm' research (Reason and Rowan, 1981), traditional and ethnogenic research (Cohen and Manion, 1981), or paradigm 1 and paradigm 2 research (Gilbert and Watts, 1983). There is no sharp divide between the two and many studies might place themselves, or be assigned, to some third ground between these kinds of poles. The traditional approach to educational research is well established and needs little introduction or description. Our own disposition, however, tends more towards the non-traditional, which is less well-referenced, and we consider this in a little more detail.

## Reduction, abstraction and interpretation

We suggested earlier that analysis must, for us, be something more than a direct description of the data. That is, it is a creative, con-structive affair and is not simply an act of isolating and describing something that might be considered self-evident. The traditional ethos of educational research has, in the past, been based on the notion that if a sufficient number of relevant facts are assembled the laws governing these facts will then be revealed (Pope, Watts and Gilbert, 1983). It is a tradition which places emphasis on the conduct of research according to the common picture of 'scientific principles'. When applied to studies of human enterprise the tendency is to succumb to a mechanistic model of people, a model which lends support to the reductionism inherent in that form of scientific research where clearly defined components (dependent and independent variables) are essential units. Reductionism is a tendency towards analysing complex arrangements into simple constituents or, more insidiously, that complex systems can be fully understood in terms of such simple components. For Reason and Rowan (1981), reductionism means reducing *people* to sets of 'dependent and independent variables' which are somehow equivalent across persons and across situations. And, they say:

> Studying variables rather than persons or groups or communities is a flight from understanding in depth, a flight from knowing human phenomena as wholes. It means that the person, group or community *as such* is never known. (Emphasis in the original.)

Educational research in general, and interviewing as a particular methodology, are inseparable from people and are very often exclusively about people. We share this reservation about reductionism where it leads to a gross over-simplification of a very complex area of inquiry. But that is not to throw the baby out with the bathwater. In many respects, analysis is the reduction of data to some manageable amount or into a 'handleable form'. The very task of the analyst is to work through the data and to re-present it in a form that can be appreciated by the intended audience. Outside of case study work, there should not be as many categories of description of data as there are individuals interviewed – otherwise the researcher might just as well present raw data as analysis. As Bliss, Monk and Ogborn (1983) says:

> Data is one thing and descriptions of it, however complex or subtle, are another. The description cannot, and should not try to, capture everything. Furthermore, the description has some ulterior motive which the data does not share: in a word, an analysis is a limited view chosen for a purpose.

Sometimes a 'seven-plus-or-minus-two' rule of thumb has been used (Watts 1983b) to indicate the number of categories that might most suitably arise from data. This is based on the notion that if there are much more than ten categories, then the analysis is becoming cumbersome; if there are fewer than four then it raises questions of how close to the data the categories are, such a rule is more heuristic than principle, and should be treated only in that light.

The literal meaning of 'abstract' is 'to draw away from'. Abstraction usually implies some act of generalising, generalisations that are 'drawn away' from a number of particular instances. As Bolton (1977) points out, abstraction in itself is not a hindrance, except where there is a tendency to imagine that somehow data is self-evident and simply 'there' to be abstracted. An analyst of interviews does not merely recognise facts and phenomena present in the responses of the interviewee. Rather, on the basis that we perceive things from a point of view, our intentions inform our attention. That is, analysis is a reconstructive and not a reproductive process. Hull (1984), for example, describes analysis as an 'exact art' and likens it to literary criticism. In support of this argument he quotes Leavis (1943) as saying that

> analysis is not a dissection of something that is already and passively there. What we call analysis is, of course, a constructive or creative process.

Analysis is a combination of forming hypotheses, testing them and then interpreting the outcomes. Inevitably, whether the interview is a respondent research interview or an informant unstructured one, the responses made must be interpreted. These can be coded, possibly for counting and then subjected to a statistical operation, or models constructed and subsequently described.

To summarise this section is to return to the notion of methodological congruity. It is, in effect, counsel *against* eclecticism and *for* care and attention to the methodologies to be used. Care that is, as Coxon (1979) says,

> in matching data with appropriate and sensitive models for their analysis, whilst recognising that no single representation can capture all the relevant aspects of the phenomenon.

### Analysis between and within interviews

Firstly, analysis can be between (inter-) and/or within (intra-) interviews. As a simple (and by no means general) rule it might be said that informant interviews are commonly analysed between interviews, and respondent ones analysed by reference to what is being said within the interview – 'intra' analysis. It is worth illustrating this distinction with two examples. Following on from our example transcripts, they are numbered 3 and 4.

*Example 3*
This example is taken from the work of Bennett *et al.* (1984). The authors use different types of interviews in order to study the nature and content of classroom tasks and what they call the 'mediating factors' which influence their choice, delivery, performance and diagnosis. In short, quite how well teachers are able to match particular tasks to individual pupils within the classroom situation. The research questions centre on the teacher's intentions in setting a specific classroom task, how those intentions are manifested in the task, the instructions given to the pupils and the pupils' own perceptions of what they are asked to do. The research design incorporates a pre-task interview with the teacher, classroom observation to describe the task set and performed, a diagnostic interview with the pupil and then a post-task interview with the teacher. A small part of the analysis focuses upon the teachers' perceptions of their success at matching task to pupil. The research team use the responses to questions in the post-task interview, where teachers are asked to evaluate the child's work, comment on whether the task had been well matched to the child or not and to identify what the child's next step would be. The authors say

Teachers responded to the above questions in their own terms. These were idiosyncratic. In imposing patterns on the responses across 16 teachers it was necessary to look for expressions which would be taken as synonymous ... In this way teachers were perceived to identify three levels of children's capacity to cope with an assigned task. These were:

1 The child was in difficulty.
2 The child was getting by.
3 The child was doing well.

The key term here is 'synonymous'. The onus on the researchers is to decide what are the intended meanings of the teachers concerned, to sift their comments for expressions that could be equated and then collate them. As with the other interviews in this particular research, the interviewee responses are often coded onto a 3- or 5-point scale and then tabulated in numerical form. Often, but not always. In one instance the researchers make a fairly detailed analysis of a youngster's activities and subsequent interview, an analysis that forces them to 're-appraise radically' their initial view of one particular youngster's 'limitations'. They go on to say:

The problem for anyone attempting to understand how these processes actually do operate to the benefit or detriment of children's learning is that a task is embedded in the more general life of a classroom containing a large number of other children ... The social scientist is faced with the problem of interpreting an ever-moving scene from a series of snapshots.

*Example 4*

A contrasting example is taken from the work of Denicolo (1984). In this instance the interview is treated as a single case (no matter how many interviews have actually been conducted) and analysed as such. Denicolo uses interviews in conjunction with repertory grids to explore chemistry teachers' perceptions of the way they teach, and in particular the way they see the use of metaphor in their teaching. Her research questions address not only whether (and how) teachers use metaphors, but also why. Important parameters in her inquiry are individual teacher differences, background experiences and ambitions, and individual philosophies of science, teaching, learning and communication. Her fieldwork consists of classroom lesson observations, semi-structured interviews and two repertory grids. She describes her analysis as a reflective method, a 'form of tri-angulation process ... to illuminate the various foci of attention from different perspectives'. Her main interest is to unravel the motives of individual teachers, rather than look for comparisons or differences between teachers. She presents her analysis as a series of case studies to demonstrate the 'chemistry' of interaction generated between the teacher and particular groups of students. She says:

Teachers, it seems, are much more complex animals than earlier educational research has given them credit for being. Simple interaction analysis, such as Bales's, may result in neat classifications leading to quantifiable results. An in-depth multi-perspective analysis reveals that teachers insist on climbing out of every box into which any attempt to insert them is made.

Not for her, then, a simple direct classification, rather a detailed search for consistency of philosophy and approach through different forms of data.

As with interviews themselves, we are going to suggest that each of the many different types of analysis have their advantages and disadvantages. Both the 'within' and 'between' types described here have their value and flaws. Rather than attempt to cover all types we settle for describing below three approaches that have been used.

We have suggested in earlier chapters that interviewing is a complete process, one that includes all the planning and pre-organisation, along with some scheme for analysis. We suspect that it is commonly the case that interviewing is often set up as part of an inquiry without great thought given over to detailed planning of the stage of analysis. Somehow facts, figures or features will emerge from the ensuing data and piece themselves together nicely in preparation for the final stage of reporting. We are in no doubt that the quality of the overall research will depend upon the thought that has been invested in planning it.

Our advice in this section would be the very obvious strictures to be aware of the quality of data that is required from the interview, aware of the purposes it is required to serve and to plan in detail the form that the analysis will take. Will, for example, the analysis be undertaken by the same person who conducted the interviews? Will there be one or more than one analyst? How will the outcomes of the interviewing be presented?

Any analysis is constrained by a series of factors. In considering those constraints here, we have also included some 'do's and dont's' by way of advice and guidance, for those inexperienced in undertaking analysis. We have illustrated on a number of occasions the major or sometimes peripheral role that interviewing can play within an overall research plan. Its place in the scheme of things will also affect the type of analysis that takes place. If the interview, for example, is seen as a pilot study for a questionnaire then it may be that a detailed analysis is not needed. The responses will not themselves be coded or reported, but used to help shape the next stage of research. If the interviews are one of a number of complementary research methodologies then the outcomes from the sessions might be combined with the outcomes of other data to produce compilations of results.

*Example 5: Content analysis*

An example of content analysis from interview data can be seen in a work already referred to in other chapters. It is a study of sixth-form students' retrospective recollections of their science education from 11 to 16 (Ebbutt and Watts 1986). The problem, as in many other studies, is to separate out what are considered to be the major themes that run through the interview responses. In this example, as described in Dave Ebbutt's Case Study 5, it was a case of trying to unpick themes through five group interviews. The analysis was undertaken from five fairly full transcripts. One usual procedure is, as reading through what is said, to mark significant passages or comments on the page. Another technique is to use coloured 'text highlighter' pens that mark passages in various colours without obscuring the print. There is also the common approach of making photocopies of the transcripts, cutting out the significant parts and physically sorting these into relevant piles. The word processor is beginning to replace some of these techniques. Ebbutt and Watts (1986) refer to material in our Case Study 5.

> Analysis is the stage we have enjoyed most in the past and this project was no exception. Previously this stage has been characterised for both of us by a sea of paper littering the room. Partly because we now knew the transcripts almost by heart it was less messy than is usually the case. A word processor also contributed significantly to the ease of our preliminary analysis. Instead of physically cutting, sorting and pasting sections of transcript, we were able to use the text-handling facilities of the computer to reduce the labour.

The themes emerge as the analyst's hypotheses about what is being said. They sometimes emerge directly from the questions that have been asked. Sometimes, in an extended or unstructured situation, they are an answer to the analyst's question: 'What exactly is it that I think is being said here?' In some cases the analyst turns that answer into a series of propositional statements – *this* is what is being said. As Ebbutt and Watts say:

> Our method of analysis was an iterative process of reading, discussion, reflection and examination of each of the transcripts in turn. The first transcript was considered very closely and the tentative hypotheses drawn from it were discussed and described between us. These hypotheses were then visited upon the second transcript – with varying degrees of success. Those that seemed to be substantiated to some extent were strengthened, those that were not were shelved. Any further hypotheses from the second transcript were then visited back upon the first. This iterative process was continued as each new transcript became available and was drawn into the pool of data. This scanning and refining process, moving backwards and forwards between the raw evidence of the transcript and the developing analyses, is a classic example of the constant comparison method of qualitative analysis first put forward by Glaser and Strauss (1967).
> A close reading of the first transcript indicated that most of the

comments were about bad practice in science teaching. Implied in all the comments, however, was a vision of what these students saw to be good practice. This idea of good practice became our central organising concept. Then it became a a case of teasing out from what was said a set of categories under which we could classify different aspects of perceived good practice. Each of the interviews was analysed individually and it was these separate analyses which we eventually sent back to the interviewees.

This is just one example of this kind of approach and there are many variations on how the mechanics of analysis can be undertaken. In some cases a section of transcript might be marked and coded as a group activity and perceptions pooled (Watts, 1983b). Often it is a very solitary exercise where the researcher, or analyst, spends long periods of time agonising over the import of parts of the transcripts. From our experience, exchanges of views about data have proved invaluable. Living with and through some one else's data has probably stretched many a friendship, but there are few better ways of shaping and sharpening ideas and hypotheses than to talk them through with a colleague. Clearly, an obvious, sometimes complicating, source of advice and counsel is the person(s) who were originally interviewed.

*Example 6: Networks*
Although we feature networks in this example, we are really focusing upon it as a method of coding responses in a fairly clear and economical way. The system of network analysis has been developed for educational research largely by Bliss, Monk and Ogborn (1983). They say:

> To categorise is to attach a label to things; in effect to place them in boxes. A network can be seen as a map of the set of boxes one has chosen to use, which shows how they relate to one another ... To categorise is to draw distinctions and to name them, recognising that distinctions may need to be drawn along several independent dimensions, and that any distinction may need to be further divided into subsidiary divisions. Networks offer a uniform notation to express such schemes at any required level of complexity, and a terminology intended to clarify and assist communication of the issues involved. At this level all they do is formalise the obvious.

The relationships that are drawn between categories are based upon inclusion and exclusion – 'and'/'or' distinctions. The notation is simple in that the broadest, most encompassing, categories are

167

placed on the left, the tighter more detailed ones on the right. As one passes down any branch of the network tree from left to right the distinctions become finer and finer – what the authors call an increase in delicacy. This movement from left to right can also be seen as a movement towards the data away from more generalised descriptors. The reader is referred to Bliss *et al.* for fuller details and examples of networks, and to Cohen and Manion (1985) for a view of networks within other research methodologies.

*Example 7: Dilemma analysis*
A final, brief but interesting example is worth noting before passing. Elliott (1985) considers something he calls 'dilemma analysis'. A dilemma, he says, is

> a situation which appears to require two equally desirable but mutually exclusive courses of action. The equal desirability stems from the perception that each course of action would fulfil certain ethical requirements in the situation, and the inconsistency stems from the perception that each requirement can only be met by denying the other. Dilemmas are essentially moral problems and as such can be confronted with technical problems.

His procedure for presenting analysis of a dilemma is to

(a) describe dilemmas in what has been said (or has taken place) and cite evidence in support of them;
(b) describe and explain the responses made to the dilemmas and, again, cite evidence which supports the account;
(c) examine implications of the response for the practice of the research (in Elliott's case, educational action research).

*Summary*

In this chapter we have attempted to look at various facets of logging and analysing interview data and to give some examples of how others have tackled the problems inherent in this. The examples are just that – they are not meant as models of research work. Each researcher will adopt and adapt particular methods to suit his or her own purpose – and it is important for each person to do so. For that is the way that educational research will develop and grow. Our only caution is that the adaptations that take place retain some consistency with the philosophy of the research itself.

# Chapter 7

# Reporting interviews

## Introduction

This chapter is about good practice in the reporting of interviews. Each of the previous chapters has been about types of interview; the characteristics of interviews, interviewees and their relationship; the conduct of interviews and their analysis. Now it is time to explain each of these elements – and explain them to a public who can then appraise the conclusions and implications of the research from a clear understanding of what occurred. The need to spend time on such issues stems from the worrisome problems we have experienced in reading about interviews and in turn reporting some of our own. In part, too, it stems from the general problem that readers of interview reports are faced with in wanting to both understand and believe the story that the researcher is trying to tell. Our worries arise from a disquiet that often comes from being provided with (or being able to provide) too little information rather than too much. Within any interview it is the responsibility of the interviewer, or the researcher to report the substance of what is said. Clearly, the provision of quality information depends both on the sensitive observations and willingness of the reporters – and on the kinds of limitations imposed upon researchers, not least of which is the task of tailoring reports to the needs of specific audiences.

The reporting of interviews could be seen as the construction of a 'story' around the events that have taken place and around the perceived outcomes of the interaction between interviewer and interviewee. Readers, however, are often provided with so little detail that they can only make assumptions about the methods and procedure from the overall context of the research and from the reputation of the researcher. In reading a research report and wanting to believe the researcher's story, we should feel confident that the results obtained are reasonable in the circumstances and that, therefore, the conclusions and implications that have been drawn can be justified as a basis for debate.

This means that there should be no part of the interview process where it is uncertain what has been done. Such strictures apply to data collected as part of the process of verification of theory generated by logical deductions from 'prior assumptions. They apply equally forcibly to 'data generated by the research act' which provides the basis for theory. For us, the 'grounded theory' of Glaser and Strauss (1967) should not have to depend on unspecified sources of information. Whatever the style of research, elegance and good experimental design alone cannot compensate for a full description of the researchers' request for meaningful verbal relationships and their consequences for action.

## The kind and context of the interview

The interview is sensitive to many variables and it is difficult to believe the researchers' story when such sensitive variables have been ignored, or at least not reported. Our 'do's and don'ts' in this chapter are in part a list and in part a definition of the most sensitive variables involved in the act of interviewing. When it comes to reporting outcomes, both our main interview types (informant and respondent) have their own kinds of problems which is hardly surprisingly given the variety of theoretical origins.

In any research report, a description of the interview itself is clearly of fundamental importance – as is some rationale for the interview method. The report should say whether the interview takes place with an individual or a group; whether the interviewer/interviewee relationship is formal or informal; if closely structured or very conversational; what the main issues concern; the length, location and occasion of the interview. If these variables seem to be self-evident it has been pointed out that, in our short appraisal of recent large-scale research reports (Powney 1982), such information is not often made easily available.

Arguably, the more unstructured the interview, the more difficult and lengthy a process it is to describe. Unstructured interviews offer the interviewer considerable flexibility and with it more responsibility. The content and direction of the interview may, for instance, be largely determined by the interviewee's responses (see e.g. Watts 1983a, 1983b). Successive interviews can be very dissimilar and therefore the description of the sessions and the responses becomes

170

increasingly complex. Moreover, alongside issues of flexibility, it is the researcher's responsibility to make clear the status of the interview – whether or not, for instance, it is seen to be: an exploratory device, preparatory to data collection – possibly in another form; the main instrument of research and data collection; or as a supplement to other methods being used (such as follow-up to a self-completion questionnaire or as confirmation of classroom observations).

## The characteristics of the participants and their relationship

The sensitive variables in this section concern the participants in the interview session. It is important to know, for example, the number of participants (whether they are individual, small-group or large-group interviews); the basis for selection and the method of selection of the interviewees for the interviews. And similarly of the interviewer(s), what experience they have, their status and relationship to the interviewees.

This may be seen to be a sensitive issue. Educational research interviews suggest particular hazards which are likely to occur more frequently than others as various models of teacher-as-researcher proliferate. Most teachers and most academic researchers are inexperienced interviewers. They often use self-taught techniques for preparing, carrying out and reporting interviews. In many cases the people being interviewed are already known to the interviewer either personally or in status terms. The need to report their own experience – however short – is an act of exposure that requires a degree of courage. However, all interviewers have to begin somewhere, and have to report the outcomes that accrue. If the interviewer's prowess is limited as yet, then the results need to be written – as seen – as more tentative and exploratory than might otherwise be the case.

Teachers on in-service courses and/or engaged in curriculum development in their own schools may sometimes be interviewing junior and senior colleagues, or well-known or relatively unknown pupils. We consider some of the complexities of both in the next chapter where we pick up on some of the theoretical issues involved with interviewing. Simons (1981), for example, has focused on some of the problems associated with adults interviewing pupils. These include, for instance, talking too much or listening too little – an issue we raised in Chapter 3.

Information about the interviewer gives the reader some indication of the possible expectations and perceptions of the participants. A

171

mismatch between interviewer and interviewee may well occur for other reasons than interviewing experience. It might happen, for example, as a result of differences in culture, age, language or sex. Whilst these may be unavoidable, they can and should be reported in detail. It is important for the researcher to note, too, such points as who exercises control over the progress of the interview and who has access to the records of the session afterwards. Anonymity and confidentiality are two normal guarantees of social survey work which may not pertain to small-scale inquiries by teacher researchers. If informants cannot remain anonymous, however (since any pub-lication of data is likely to make then easily identifiable), they may feel justified in checking or even negotiating the report of the interview.

It is important, too, to describe the physical situation where interviewing takes place. As Jill Keegan suggests in her case study (Case Study 2) there is sometimes a need to spend as long describing the interview context as there is the interview itself. In Jill's case the interviewees met at a person's house, someone closely connected with the research, and were paid a small attendance fee for being there. She says she likes to get the business of paying the interviewee over and done with before the interview takes place. The whole notion of making payment to interviewees and the how and where of it happening add a particular flavour to the story and, as with any similar set of circumstances, need to be reported. Di Bentley, too, describes her interview set-up quite closely because, for her, it is important for the reader to appreciate the significance of the physical proximity and relative positioning between interviewer and inter-viewee.

## The purposes of the interview

Research reports using interview data should indicate not just the context and structure of the data from each interview, but also a clear statement of the researcher's purpose(s) in conducting the interview in the first place. These purposes need to be given in relation to the initial introduction and instructions given to the interviewees. What were they told it was all about? Again, returning to Jill Kee-gan's study, she makes a point of saying that she records the intro-duction to the interview so that she can check later that successive interviewees were given the same context and instructions for the interviews. That is, what the *interviewees* are told about the session, about the interviewer, the purpose of the discussion and so on. For instance, it has been common practice in experimental psychology to mislead 'subjects' in order that behavioural observations will not be contaminated by subjects directing their behaviour positively or negatively in relation to the experimenter's purpose. Sharp and Green (1975) and Rosenthal and Jacobsen (1968) provide educational examples of this practice. This obviously forms part of the research design and needs to be included and defended.

For us, newer directions in educational research benefit from attempts to dissolve the traditional researcher-subject approach so that genuine two-way interactions between participants can occur. That is, the interviewees are fully informed from the start of what the researchers and the interviewers are trying to establish. Whatever the case, it is necessary contextual information to know the purpose of the interview, the expectations of both researcher and researched, and about the outcome(s) (including action) predicted and expected as a result of the interview.

Research methods cannot be neutral – they act as filters through which the environment is selectively experienced. Young (1980) makes this point in his criticisms of the Rutter team (1979) who, he says, ignore factors which their implicit model does not regard as important, 'questions of power, conflict, boundary maintenance, categorisation, etc.' These might be considered to be the essential contributions of interview material but, as Young points out, no schedules are presented in the report and it might, therefore, be assumed that the schedules used were precoded and the interviews tightly structured. Not to give this kind of data is to treat it as unproblematic, as unimportant, when it can make considerable significant difference to what is being concluded or claimed as outcomes of the research.

## The method(s) of data collection

Experienced interviewers (like Julia Field and Jill Keegan, for example, trained in survey research, and Di Bentley in non-verbal communication) are aware of many of the pitfalls, especially in semi-structured or depth interviews, where the information outcome of the interaction depends not only on the language, content and order of the interview but also on subtle non-verbal cues, silences and practical organisation. The use of 'probes', 'prompts', and 'cues' may change the direction of the interview. This presents an immense challenge for 'the softer methodology (which) involves representation of reality for purposes of comparison and analysis is of language and meaning' (Cohen and Manion 1981). Here, the sensitive variables that need to be noted include any use of written notes, tape recordings, full transcripts, recalled information etc. It helps to know the scope the interviewer has to probe responses, his or her maximum tolerance of silence and the legitimate areas for questions by the interviewee. People are likely to respond differently when their comments are tape recorded (as opposed to noted down on paper) so this aspect of method should be reported. It helps also to know what range (and order) of issues are covered – even if all of these are not subsequently included in the analysis.

Where an interview is only one of several data collecting strategies some indication ought to be given of the relative importance or weight attached to the interviews.

## Analysis of data

In quantitative analysis the statistical methods employed are usually discussed and developed in specialist texts and articles. The methods are commonly well-documented and seldom need even referencing in a report. In qualitative research, little is ever usually written about the process of analysis at all. Few writers make explicit the sequence of activities involved in what they do. Moreover, little is said of who the analysts are, whether or not they were also the original interviewers and which particular perspectives they adopt. If there are several analysts, then how are disagreements resolved, what measure of interpreter reliability is used? Other questions, such as whether full transcripts are always used, how much is reported, what level of uncodable or unsortable data is tolerable, what basis is used for filtering the data, are also pertinent and need to be reported.

Included here there should also be some indication of how the data is to be represented. Interview data lends itself very easily to being reported as individuals' quotes, by extracts from transcripts. Using quotes is a useful way of bringing the text alive, of allowing the participants to make cogent points, and to make the 'story' more believable. What is then problematic is how to justify the inclusion of some quotes and not others. In a recent report on school children's learning of science from television programmes, Bentley and Watts (1986) suggest the inclusion of transcript extracts as follows:

> We have chosen to exemplify both the pupil and teacher categories we have derived by discussing some of the comments made, and have used extract quotes from the transcripts. We have chosen

each of the transcript extracts with particular purposes in mind. First they neatly exemplify the particular point we are making. Second, they are substantive of the point being made by the respondent – it is a major point in their transcript. We are not suggesting that any one youngster, or teacher, would necessarily subscribe entirely to the categories we have devised. Nor are the categories exhaustive, they do not attempt to fully encapsulate everything that the respondents are saying. Needless to say, we do not think the categories capture the essence of what was being said. As there are numerous extracts that make the same point the particular extracts chosen are balanced so as to be representative of the geographical areas visited, and the sex of the respondent – where possible. Where this is not the case, where there are many more responses of a particular kind by girls, for instance, we raise this in discussion and look for some possible reason. One obvious example concerns the image of women portrayed by the programmes, when the girls and the boys tend to respond in different ways.

Whilst this is not offered as a model of research reporting, it is an acknowledgement that such detail does need to be included.

## The scrutiny of results

This final section concerns information that is made available about the other persons involved in the scrutiny of the outcomes of analysis. Whoever (if anyone) is deemed to be the most suitable judge(s) of the research outcomes requires some description, along with the procedures that are used, the methods of incorporating the fruits of the scrutiny into the analysis process and, again, how any disagreements are resolved. Whether or not one argues that the terms 'validity' and 'reliability' have a meaning within newer paradigms of research, it is still necessary to attempt to be systematic and rigorous about the evaluation of the outcome of interviews. Whatever the processes are that are chosen, they need to be outlined and included within a description of research. The academic community needs to pay as much attention to the association between interviewing and data collected as critics usually apply to statistical arguments. Of six critiques of the work of Rutter *et al.*'s report (1979) only Young (1980) makes reference to data generated by interviews.

One theme throughout this book is that many research studies underestimate and under-report 'the interview'. Simons (1981) suggests that the practice of interviewing 'is not discussed on the grounds that interviewing is an idiosyncratic, interpersonal process that is not susceptible to systematic analysis'. She continues '... we must begin to discuss the problems we experience in practice however self-evident, situation-specific or limited when restricted to the written work they may seem'.

In fact, reports commonly contain the idiosyncratic choices of the researcher rather than what might be required by the research community at large. Whereas it is common practice to include statistical tests, questionnaires and even observation schedules, it is rare to find either interview schedules or *full* accounts of the progress of interviews. For example Southgate *et al.* (1981) are exceptional in providing a full list of questions asked and a fairly full discussion of the responses. Indeed most of the 'sensitive variables' we have listed were met in that study.

Though we seem to have asked for a lot, much could be broached in the body of a report without necessarily diluting or detracting from the story line. Other pertinent information could well be made clear in an appendix. Along with others (for instance, Wragg 1981) we have hoped to provide a checklist for those about to embark on, or report on, a research project with interviews. Whatever the case, the variables listed above seem to us to provide the very minimum of information for a research report to be properly evaluated.

We feel (Powney and Watts 1984) that the checklist that follows is a quick and useful guide to what might be included in a report.

*Checklist for reporting interviews in educational research*

1   Kind and context of interview

- What is the rationale for using interviews?
- What kind of interview is it?
- How is the interview structured?
- How much flexibility does the interviewer have?
- What is the length, location and occasion of the interview?

2 Characteristics of the interview participants

(a)  Interviewees

- Who and how many people are involved?
- What is the basis for their selection and how was the selection made?

(b) Interviewers

- Who and how many people are involved
- What experience of interviewing do they have?
- What is their relationship to the main research?
- What is their status and relationship to the interviewees?

3 The purpose of the interview

- What are interviewees told about the purpose of the interview?
- Is this understanding shared with the interviewer?
- Who will have access to the data collected and is it negotiable?

4 The method(s) of data collection

- How strictly controlled is the method of asking questions?
- How are responses recorded?
- What other methods of data collection are being used?
- What is the relative weighing between the methods?

5 Analysis and reporting of data

- Who analyses what?
- How are the interviewers concerned with the analysis?
- How many analysts are there and how are disagreements resolved?
- Are full transcripts used?
- What basis is used for filtering the data?
- What level of uncodable or unsortable data is tolerated?

6 Sorting of results

- How are the outcomes of the interviews being evaluated?
- What access may the academic community have to raw data?

# Chapter 8

# Some theoretical issues

*Introduction*

A chapter that is entitled 'theoretical issues' does rather presuppose that interviews are somehow underwritten by theory. There is always a temptation to treat any methodology as rootless, simply a method for undertaking a particular task. We have already hinted at some of these issues in Chapter 6, where we argued for a sense of coherence, or continuity between theory and practice.

There are a number of ways of approaching the sorts of issues we want to tackle here. There is a sense that interviews *are* underwritten by particular kinds of theories, and this deserves being drawn out further for examination. Arguably only certain kinds of theories place value on, and are therefore congruent with collecting personal responses by face-to-face (or voice-to-voice) interaction. There is a sense, too, that any data gathering methodology is 'theory laden' and interviewing can be no exception. The notion that observation, for example, is theory-laden is now no longer a controversial issue within either the human or the physical sciences. Thirdly, there are issues which, whilst not the sole domain of interviewing, are not matters of research pragmatism and therefore can be seen to be matters of theory, not practice.

Many of these issues arise from the use of interviewing in social science research but here, as in the book as a whole, we are concerned with issues of especial relevance for educational research. Some of these problems may even be more likely to occur in educational research than in other forms of social research. We begin at the beginning and revisit an issue which in Chapter 6 we called 'methodological congruity' (Swift, Watts and Pope 1983; Watts and Bentley 1985).

*On being congruent*

In interviewing, the researcher has to convince any participant or eventual reader that the complicated practical management of the actual interview sessions has been conducted properly. But what is proper and what is improper? Our argument is that the interview process used needs to be conducted in accordance with a set of principles, or philosophical perspective. That is, the participant or reader has also to be convinced that the conduct of the interviews is compatible with the researcher's own stated assumption – in other words, a compatibility of theory and practice. It is a real concern for the interaction of philosophy and methodology. At the very least, interviewing as a method must be formally consistent with the philosophical assumptions which form the basis for the research being planned. Although this might seem blatantly obvious, most of us can think of research projects where the actual style of the interviewing belied the explicit theoretical position of the researcher.

*Consistency and pluralism*

First, we do not see interviewing as compelling any researcher to adopt a single theoretical perspective. There is a wide variety of theories that use interviews and a wide variety of interview methods to service any one theoretical framework. So what of consistency? We would want first to draw a distinction between being pluralist and being eclectic, and then illustrate this with an example.

For us, many researchers verge on what Boring (1950) calls 'sheer eclectic laziness'. To be eclectic means to choose freely with little concern for particular principles underlying the choices. In research it means the use of a variety of methods without regard for their origins or their philosophical assumptions. By pluralism, on the other hand, we mean the use of a variety of methods which are all intentionally congruent with a set of principles or philosophical assumptions.

For an example we turn again to aspects of the work based on George Kelly's 'Personal construct psychology'. Over time a large number of people have explored features of his theories and have used its philosophical basis, constructive alternativism, as a framework by which to shape their work. Underlying Kelly's philosophy is a strongly humanistic stance that sees, for example, the researched and the researcher very much on an equal footing. As Kelly (1969) says

179

research, as I see it, is a co-operative enterprise in which the subject joins the (researcher) in making an inquiry.

Even in research directly within the ambit of personal construct psychology this kind of approach is often notable by its absence. Where people breach this stance they become inconsistent with its underlying philosophy.

Over time, too, a number of research methods have been developed out of Kelly's work. Some of these have strayed a long way from the spirit of Kelly's work and are used in ways that bear little relation to his humanistic stance. When this happens, too, these developments are no longer methodologically congruent with the underlying philosophy which gave birth to them. His own methodology, the repertory grid technique, has been used in a variety of ways well out of sympathy with the original philosophy. Kelly said (1969) that he was

> very sceptical of any piece of human research in which the
> subject's questions and contributions have not been elicited or
> have been ignored in the final analysis of results.

The subject's questions, note, not just the researchers'. As Pope and Keen (1981) point out, Kelly's methodologies have frequently been used with little or no recognition of this stance.

So what does all this mean in more general terms? In many ways it is simply a plea for consistency. Interviewers need to be aware of the kind of research in which they are engaged, its philosophical basis and the kinds of outcomes it is attempting to reach. They then need to select the kind of interview method that sits most easily within that framework, one they can then justify when pressed to account. This is not an attempt to stifle creativity – there are many more interview techniques possible than those mentioned in this book, many yet to be invented and amended. They need to be chosen or designed, though, with care and attention. That is methodological pluralism – the thoughtful selection of methods matched to articulated principles.

At a very pragmatic level, the researcher has to be aware of what (s)he wants from an interview and how different kinds of interviews work in practice. A crude example would be the incongruity of attempting to derive a clear statistical analysis from an in-depth ethnographic interview. Some particular theories look for certain kinds of outcomes in order to verify or disconfirm derived hypotheses. And on the whole, interviewing as a method might well be seen to be consistent with those theories that value human response in its actuality.

## *Theory laden data*

We suggested earlier that the notion of data being 'theory laden' was no longer a controversial issue. That said, it does not make it any the less problematic. The problem concerns the level at which a theory can be said to determine the very nature of the data collection and its interpretation. Is the data 'hard' or 'soft', valid, reliable, can it refute theoretical conjectures, to use Popperian terms? Our position is not dissimilar to that described by Bliss, Monk and Ogborn (1983) when they say

> any analysis of data is the analyst's responsibility, being unavoidably his or her own perception of data. And every perception of data is a perception through some idea about the data, some previous 'theory' of it. The 'theory' is not necessarily very good, deep, profound or clear: it may be little more than common sense (and for that reason the harder to notice). Even what counts as 'data' depends on one's theory, point of view or perspective.

The main point behind this is that data is not something that is just 'there' to be analysed, not neutral and self-evident simply waiting to be discovered. It is generated for a particular purpose, derived from particular methodologies, looked at from particular perspectives and reported from particular points of view. Social processes, issues and conditions are never just 'there', as Harris (1979) says

> their existence in the present is the result of at least two factors – the historical process that brought them about, and the ongoing practical and theoretical conditions that maintain and reproduce them in the present. . . . Investigations, and methodologies for investigation, are necessarily theory laden. Put crudely, theory determines what counts, and how to count it: there is no such thing as non-theoretical knowledge.

For us, one consequence of this means that the underlying theories and philosophies, the details of the methodologies and the direction

181

of the reporting need all to be included in the eventual accounts of the interviews so that they may be considered in their proper light.

During the earlier chapters a number of issues came to light that we might now revisit to do them greater justice than was allowed before. These issues are not self-contained and will be seen to run the one into the other. They are not the only theoretical issues that might be developed a little further, though they do – given what we have just said – signal some we think to be important. They are:

- qualitative v. quantitative paradigms
- anonymity and confidentiality
- peer group research
- the language of interviews
- inclusion and exclusion in analysis
- inclusion and exclusion in reporting
- invasion of personal space
- generalisability
- judgemental and non-judgemental positions.

## Qualitative v. quantitative paradigms

The debate about qualitative and quantitative research has been around for some long while. There are few signs yet that it is abating. We have only modest intentions here of adding to the arguments and do so only in the context of interviewing.

There have been repeated attempts to bridge the chasm between the two paradigms (Gilbert and Watts 1983), and suggestions that a rapprochement in some areas is possible (Pope, Watts and Gilbert 1983). Here, we see the two as complementary. There are many occasions when the traditional survey research interview – with its emphasis on counting and statistical patterns – is inappropriate. Equally so, the ethnographic interview, with its own emphasis on rich data from a limited number of participants, cannot cope with producing answers to all questions.

## Anonymity and confidentiality

It is commonly the case that, before asking any questions, an interviewer reassures the interviewees that replies and comments will be treated as anonymous and where practical confidential. Interviewing has always to be accompanied by assurances about anonymity and practical confidentiality. In fact, as Platt (1981) points out, in most research reports it is usually assumed about interviews that:

    (a) the relationship between the interviewer and interviewee is an anonymous one;

    (b) the research roles are separated from all other roles and are context free;

    (c) at the close the interviewer leaves the interview behind and has no wider responsibility associated with it; and

    (d) the interviewer can manipulate the situation safely as the respondent is usually of relatively low status.

Interviewing gives access to information that is potentially powerful. For example, from a school-based research project, the interviewer could find out colleagues' mutual attitudes; the head teacher's distribution of resources between departments; knowledge of personal circumstances and ambitions of colleagues; knowledge of families of pupils. Researchers have to be aware of potential uses of findings. Spradley, the American ethnographer, pointed out that the information given him by local drunks would make them more vulnerable to arrest if his report was made public:

> Cultural descriptions can be used to oppress people or set them free. (Spradley 1979.)

*Peer group problems*

The problems of anonymity and confidentiality pose problems enough even when professional interviewers are used. Much field work in education, however, is carried out not by professional interviewers but by researchers themselves, possibly with the help of research assistants. Much of this kind of research often uses what we have been calling ethnographic interviews, often by people close to the informants' own situation. They may, in fact, be close colleagues – or at least previously aware of each other's career history and current function. Although we would not suggest that researchers would betray confidences, the fact that the inquiry is almost a family affair with people who are known personally or by reputation to the respondents, is highly likely to affect both the data and the data gathering process.

Moreover it is not a state of affairs openly acknowledged in textbooks on interviewing. Platt (op. cit.) in her paper, focuses discussion on the interviewing of one's peers and shows how the normal assumptions about the relationship between interviewer and interviewee listed above are inappropriate for peer group interviewing. Not only might informant and interviewer be close colleagues, they might both have a history and a future of colleagueship and collaboration. That is, their roles cannot be distinct and separate after the interview has taken place. Moreover, neither participant will be the same again. As she says, after the interview successful interviewers should be left:

in possession of information normally only available under conditions of greater intimacy.

Yet this information cannot be used publicly without betraying the contract of confidentiality established at the beginning. On the other hand perhaps it cannot be publicly ignored either. One way for an interviewer to deal with potential ambiguity or difficulty with a colleague who had been interviewed is to pretend the interview had never taken place. The intimacy established in the privacy of an interview might be offensive if continued afterwards. Platt suggests, though, that it could also be offensive to pretend it never happened – this would be ungracious to the contributor or might even define the interviewer as being embarrassed by the confidences. It is worth remembering Platt's stricture that, in this and other interviewing contexts, the ordinary respondents who are not sophisticated in these matters, often feel much less anonymous than in practice they are to the interviewer. To the latter the informant is only one of a crowd whose identity it is seemingly a professional obligation to forget. However, the profession is relatively small and it is difficult, even in fairly large-scale surveys, to disguise the identity of unique schools, colleges or even distinctive styles of educational management. Therefore it is possible that even individuals can be tracked down.

Concealing the identity of informants becomes still more problematic in small-scale educational research. Nor can it be assumed that they are not going to discuss the interviews among themselves. Think for example, of the speed a new skill, game or joke, travels through a children's playground, being picked up by all the participants. Similarly details behind a researcher's interviews will fly around the staffroom or classroom of school informants, be they pupils or staff. An interviewer who is part of the normal scene is both more likely to be biased and to pick up discrepancies between the information given during the formal interview and that collected or observed before and after. These observations would not provide part of the interview record and therefore remain unofficial.

This assumption certainly does not apply when interviewing colleagues, some of whom may be further up in the hierarchy. As we suggested of Kelly's work earlier, implicit in some research are assumptions about equality between the interviewer and the respondent. For others, notions of reciprocity and symmetry in the relationship are a myth perpetuated by would-be democratic interviewers. That is, even in unstructured interviews the interviewer is seen as determining the direction. This question comes alive when considering the problems interviewers have with their peer group or, in particular, interviewing a more elite informant. For example, Harriet Zuckerman (1972) prepared meticulously for interviews with Nobel prize-winners, finding out substantial biographical detail, including present and past associates. She considered this time well-invested as each interview began with the Nobel laureate testing out the interviewer's competence and commitment:

> In all cases, the difference in rank between the laureate and the interviewer impressed itself on the situation.... The prize-winners were not much interested in impressing the interviewer or gaining her good opinion.

In most research, respondents do not normally feel entitled to question the credentials of the interviewer but are more likely to feel in a privileged position having been 'chosen' for interview. For those respondents who do not immediately adopt an acquiescent set, it is necessary to gain credibility and appear to have clear hypotheses. Yet, full explanations which might gain one status, or at least confidence among one's peer group, might be seen to be too revealing and bias the subsequent information given to the interviewer. In any case one's peers do not always obey the rules. They will not normally remain at simple respondent level.

One's peers are not very happy merely to respond to a fixed list of questions. They insist on referring to shared knowledge and understandings; they offer interpretations and syntheses more in line with being informants than respondents; they criticise the methodology; they refuse to change from their normal social role with the interviewer and simulate an unknown respondent.

Moreover, there is some justification for accepting this and engaging with it. It is arguable that research may be just as legitimate within an existing peer context than when trying to isolate respondents artificially from each other, from the interviewer and from their common history and future. One danger in using a common framework between interviewer and interviewee is that the data becomes 'thinner'. If colleagues know that the interviewer is familiar with an event or experience which is the subject of the interview, they will be somewhat puzzled if the interviewer simulates ignorance for research purposes. It would be too pedantic and stilted then for the interviewer to require a detailed explanation of an experience which is well known to all participants through their common membership. For example, if a teacher-researcher is inquiring about attitudes to curriculum change in the school, it may be desirable to identify colleagues' interpretations of how such change was implemented but at the same time difficult to pretend ignorance on the topic. Not to accept a point quickly on the order of events in the curriculum change would be careless interviewing but would maintain social ease.

To ask for explanation is to define oneself as not a member of the same community and could distort a personal relationship. (Platt 1981).

It is important to remember that researchers conducting their own interviews among their peers will have to continue that personal relationship after the research project is finished. They cannot walk away afterwards as professional interviewers can. Remaining with the point about status – our rule of thumb is that it is easier to use less structured approaches with people of higher status and to make them 'informants', than it is to adopt a respondent approach. As Platt notes, however, unstructured interviews do not offer an unequivocal advantage; if one loses control of the direction of conversation it may cease to be useful or relevant for the research. She adds that there were indeed occasions when there were lengthy conversations of low value for her project which she could see no way to redirect without defining her role.

A further point about peer group interviewing concerns the negotiation of release of data. We have already suggested that the interviewer may be in the position of having both personal and sensitive information. Their eventual report may be one where he or she 'writes through' the broad issues involved without revealing the identities of informants, or allowing their identity to be revealed by implication. There may be cases, though, where the urge – or the need – to refer directly to interview data, or to use quotations becomes very strong. And here negotiation needs to take place. The ownership, release and use of data is something that needs to be negotiated at each stage of the interview process. Most commonly it takes place at the beginning of the first encounter between interviewer and interviewee. The point, purpose, practice and procedure of the research in general and the interview in particular are normally made known and agreed at this time. It is always possible that the interviewee might want to be much more cautious and circumspect *after* the interview than before it has taken place. This simply means that the negotiations and assurances given must be more carefully managed.

It is worth pointing out that negotiation and consultation are very different. As we see it, negotiation requires that the ultimate resolution of a set of discussions is a compromise, or some jointly agreed course of action. This is not the case in consultation when once having consulted, there is no obligation on the researcher to necessarily accommodate to the interviewee's point of view, or requests. It is not always a nit-picking exercise. The eventual 'owner-ship' of data rests upon the agreements that are made before, during and after the interview has taken place. Some interviewers may assume that having consulted their respondents or informants about a particular course of action, that then encompasses negotiation – and therefore agreement. It is always left to the interviewee to with-draw permission to use material. Webster's dictionary definition (1983) of 'negotiate' is

> to confer with another so as to arrive at the settlement of some matter ... to deal with (some matter or affair that requires ability for its successful handling): MANAGE ... to arrange for or bring about through conference, discussion, and compromise. ...

*Invasion of personal space*

Interviews invade privacy and where the method encourages a one-way flow of information, it is sometimes difficult to see what gains there are for the interviewee. It is a problem that may be exacerbated in interviewing children. For example, having gained parental approval, does the interviewer need to accord children the same rights to privacy and confidentiality as adults? What of the infor-mation children innocently give about family circumstances? – it may convert them into being members of a 'problem family' with all the concomitant expectations of teachers and members of the 'caring professions'. Interviews with children underline the points we have made in relation to inequality of status and the power of knowledge held by the interviewer.

Ethnographic methods also invade privacy in pervasive but inexplicit ways. Participants may not always be aware of the detailed level of observation and analysis being adopted by the participant-interviewer. Should this approach, therefore, need more discretion in reporting? Or is there no need for anxiety since it is axiomatic that reports and data will be negotiated with the participants before wider publication? Should secretive invasions, of discreet non-negotiated observations take place at all? It is our belief that the educational research community has an obligation to see that the trust of research informants is not abused.

Some researchers may see good pragmatic and methodological reasons for deception as a necessary part of the interviewer's role. For example, Hammersley (1979) says

> If we tell participants what we are studying, consciously or unconsciously they may change the pattern of their activities whether to defend their presentation of self or to help us ... such motives cannot be used to justify anything and everything, the crucial issue for me is the consequences of the research rather than the presence of deception itself.

Interviewers may also be deliberately provocative either by their own questioning or, for example, by inviting several informants on the same topic in order to provoke a reticent individual into giving more accurate information. As Hammersley points out, confronting informants with counter-evidence was one of the more directive ways of ethnographers used by Nadel as long ago as 1939.

## Judgemental and non-judgemental positions

Interviewers who take a more active participant role in the community they are studying can often be put in a moral dilemma. It would be a violation of research ethics for them to manipulate people in the community or to take sides in strong debate unless they had established their social position on that basis. In practice it may be very hard for interviewers to maintain a non-judgemental role. In past chapters we have referred often to Whyte's (1981) seminal research *Streetcorner Society*, an analysis of observations carried out in the Italian slum area of North Boston, USA, in 1937–40. He reported this kind of difficulty in his work. Although not normally judgemental or argumentative, Whyte could not help joining in arguments on street corners. In fact it would have looked strange if – as an accepted member of the group – he had not participated.

This approach may pose problems when an interviewer considers the topic for investigation immoral or illegal, or as evidence of taking sides. Whyte, for example, was so absorbed by his participant role that he even voted illegally on more than one occasion in a local election.

Educational research is unlikely to pose such extreme risks for interviewers. Consistently identifying with one group of informants, however, could lead the interviewer into some difficult situations. A contemporary example might be a long-lasting teacher–management dispute for salary increases which creates rifts both among school staff and between many head teachers and their staff. An unsuspecting interviewer might be caught in the cross-fire, to the detriment of her or his research.

*Generalisability*

Jill Keegan, in her Case Study in Chapter 4, raised an important issue in terms of generalisability. This is a problem for all kinds of research work and not just for interviewing, though it does raise its head here too. An interviewee is at one and the same time an individual and a member of many different groups. Age, sex, class, schooling, occupation, parent, pupil, teacher, governor etc. are just some of the many familiar groupings possible. To what extent can any one individual be said to be representative of a group? Some individuals, if asked, may well enjoy being classed in a certain way whilst others would deny and resent it. In many respects the choice of sample is always problematic and is also, in some respects, self-selecting. Telephone interviews, for example, are clearly selective of those people – whatever other group is sought – who have (and answer!) telephones.

Group interviews, Jill Keegan's original point, offer further dangers. Some groups will be well established, often chosen because they already are a group and are used to working together in a common context. Others will be convened especially for the occasion as was the case in Jill Keegan's study. A few might lie between these two – individuals who are known to each other but who would not commonly meet for such a purpose. The problem of generalisability occurs for each. For the interview to be of value, then, the outcomes are the product of the dynamic of that group. As Walker (1985) notes, ideas may be generated which would not have occurred to any one individual. Successive discussion can both accelerate and retard the advance of participants' thinking in unanticipated ways. Some may find it necessary to defend ideas, others to attack ones they hold themselves. How generalisable, then, are the outcomes? There is a strong sense in which the outcomes of an individual interview can be more readily generalised than can those of a group interview. For the individual it is possible to keep more factors – sensitive variables – constant and therefore generalise to other similar cases. Because the dynamic of the group is unpredictable it is not always possible to generalise even to other similarly constituted groups. Group views cannot be quantified – unless the level of transcription is highly detailed it may not be possible (as Hedges (1985) points out) to determine if the same viewpoint is put forward by several people or by one person several times. All these problems simply mean that the researcher must be very careful in interpreting interview data and in particular in the kind of general statement they make as they summarise interview outcomes.

### Doing and thinking

One basic and well-known hazard in interviewing is the discrepancy which can often appear between what people say and what people actually do and think. The problem is that what interviewees say they believe, prefer, or do, may not correspond with 'actuality'. This is not to say there is necessary deliberate deception of an interviewer. Cockburn (1980) suggests there is a distinction between respondents who wilfully distort and respondents who are genuinely unaware that what they say they do, is not in fact what they do. Researchers have to make the assumption that people are knowledgeable and logical in their self-awareness. In order to give some kind of answer, people will even make up a story which they will maintain consistently. Powney (reported in Watts and Powney, 1985), for instance, compares the responses an interviewee gives to an interviewer on video tape, with those she gives to a second interviewer when watching a playback. When the informant was asked on video tape a personal and sensitive question which she did not wish to answer (partly because a colleague was directing the camera), she lied. Having deliberately made that choice, she then had to maintain her changed story in face of each new question. By concealing sensitive personal information at the start of the interview she is then in the position of having to continue lying so as to 'make her story consistent'. She could have refused to answer altogether but she wanted to gain the approval of the interviewer who appeared from

190

his posture and non-verbal signals to be rather diffident. 'I wanted him to like me,' she said.

Such discrepancies might not normally be seen to be a problem. A survey research interviewer seldom has the opportunity to re-question a respondent, or to see the ways they conduct their affairs. If there is a discrepancy between word and deed then the chances are that the researcher will not know about it. In some cases attempts are made to substantiate respondents' answers, though this is not common. It is an interesting point. Normally, priority is given to objective reality rather than informants' expressed subjective reality. In other words, where statements can be corroborated or con-tradicted by observed events, it is the observation which has recog-nised validity. Though they are usually seen to be the more 'tra-ditional' and scientific, survey interviews rely almost exclusively on uncorroborated verbal statements. For ethnographers or cultural analysts, on the other hand, subjective reality is pre-eminent. The interview has greater saliency for them than for positivists and behaviourists. However, in ethnographic cases the researcher is able to explore and examine a much wider context, the situation around the informant, and is more able to see and report any discrepancies.

Aside from these convoluted theoretical problems, small-scale educational researchers may be much more troubled by the fact that they cannot walk away after an interview. Consequently, they have to lie with the mis-match between a colleague's verbal comments and actual or subsequent behaviour.

## Problems of analysis and reporting

We have left till the end probably the most interesting points for discussion, some of which stem from points made in Chapter 6. If any methodological problem about recording interviews is identified at all, it is usually the constraints of taping, note taking etc. Problems of analysis usually concentrate on filtered versions of these records. Selecting some items for analysis means that other items and responses are left out. The reader is usually not aware of what has been omitted, or of the criteria for inclusion and omission. The reader trusts the integrity of the researcher to include all relevant data whether or not it supports the researcher's main hypotheses or argument.

We would argue that many interviewers ignore this area of responsibility and provide inadequate data for criticism and debate. Hull (1984) suggests that even where the full transcript of an interview

191

is available, this is an incomplete record of what occurred. What was said does not necessarily give access to the participants' perceptions as they had voiced them at interview.

> Data analysis and presentation became a matter of finding passages in the transcript which accurately conveyed (in print) what the participant/analyst interpreted as having been the interviewees' intended meanings at the time of the event.

From this argument it becomes necessary for the interviewer to *add* his/her view of the interview to explain more fully what actually occurred. These additions must come from what Hull refers to as the interviewer's own 'black market' of understandings. It is 'black market' or illegal because there is no public access to the data as there is access to transcripts, photographs, videos and field notes. The interviewer makes on-the-spot interpretations, in the light of his/her 'accumulated knowledge of the participants' meaning systems'.

We have already suggested that some of this can be made available for analysis through a 'second record', writing the context of the interview or by de-briefing. Much of the information, though, must remain private, and cannot be substantiated. Such a record can seldom give the impressions of the interviewer gained from the non-verbal gestures, intonation and emphasis, changes in posture and so on. Zuckerman (1972) notes that one of her elite informants started 4 feet away from her and ended the interview 10 feet away. What is not clear is how the analyst should use such information. How should they use off-guard comments, including those made outside the 'official' interview? If the 'black market' record is used the interviewer is in an unusually powerful position since the interpretations

> are not accountable to what is available to others as 'project data' but contingent on understandings unique to him as a participant in the live situation from which the data is distilled. (Hull, 1984)

In particular the interviewer will inevitably use his second record 'black market' in making the selections for analysis in order to convey interviewees' intended meanings. But there are few ways of authenticating such interpretations. As Hull suggests

> Such approaches increase the dependence of reported interpretations on the special understandings of participants and therefore put those interpretations still further beyond accountability to the data as they are inaccessible to a public readership.

192

Wolcott, a cultural analyst, makes a similar point, quoted in Cockburn (1980):

> Well, I guess my suspicion is that people can't tell you their own meanings so that to me you can only go so far even by interviewing. And I don't know what it's like in other people's heads but I spend enough time figuring out my own meanings. And I am inside the system looking out....

In one sense, therefore, the positivists are right: interview data is unreliable compared with observation. But it depends what one is after. The research report is the interviewer's story of the interviewee's story. The choice for both between lie or story is an important reality. Eventually it depends on what the reader wants to believe, what the researcher wants to know, what respondents do or what respondents would like to think they do. In the end, the best an interviewer can hope for is insight into the respondent's favourite self-image.

# Bibliography

Adelman, C. (1985) 'Who Are You? Some Problems of Ethnographer Culture Shock', in Burgess, R. G., *Field Methods in the Study of Education,* Falmer Press.

Adelman, C. and Walker, R. (1975) *A Guide to Classroom Observation,* Methuen, London.

Argyle, M. (1969) *Social Interaction,* Methuen, London.

Bassey, M. (1981) 'Pedagogic Research: On the Relative Merits of Search for Generalisation and Study of Single Events', *Oxford Review of Education,* 7, 1.

Bell, B. and Osborne, R. (1981) 'Interviewing Children' a check list for the I.A.I. interviewer, mineograph, Science Education Research Unit, University of Waikato, New Zealand.

Bennett N., Desforge, C., Cockburn, A. and Wilkinson, B. (1984) *The Quality of Pupil Learning Experiences,* Lawrence Erlbaum Associates, London.

Bentley, D. and Watts, D. M. (1986) 'Looking for Learning: Perspectives of Science Education Television'. Independent Broadcasting Authority/Secondary Science Curriculum Review, London.

Berreman, G. D. (1962) 'Behind Many Masks: Ethnography and Impression Management in a Himalayan Village', Monograph No. 4, Society for Applied Anthropology, Ithaca, NY, Cornell University.

Bliss, J., Monk, M. and Ogborn, J. (1983) *Qualitative Data Analysis for Educational Research,* Croom Helm, London.

Bloom, B. S. (1953) 'Thought Processes in Lectures and Discussions', *Journal of General Education,* 3, 3, pp. 160–7.

Bolton, N. (1977) *Concept Formation,* Pergamon Press, Oxford.

Boring, E. G. (1950) *History of Experimental Psychology,* 2nd edition, Appleton-Century-Crofts, New York.

Brenner, M. (1981a) 'Patterns of Social Structure in the Research Interview' in Brenner, M. (1981b).

Brenner, M. (1981b) (ed.) *Social Method and Social Life,* Academic Press, London.

Brown, J. and Sime, J. (1981) 'A Methodology for Accounts', in Brenner, M. (1981b).

194

Burgess, R. G. (ed.) (1983) *Experiencing Comprehensive Education: A Study of Bishop McGregor School*, London, Methuen.

Burgess, R. G. (ed.) (1985a) *Field Methods in the Study of Education*, Falmer Press.

Burgess, R. G. (1985b) 'Conversations with a Purpose?'. Paper presented to British Educational Research Association Symposium on 'Interviewing', Annual Conference, Sheffield

Carr, W. (1985) 'Action-research: Science and Professional Development', Paper presented to British Educational Research Association, Annual Conference, Sheffield.

Cockburn, J. (1980) 'Some Uses of Interview in Contemporary Educational Research'. Seminar Paper. Centre for Applied Research in Education. University of East Anglia.

Cohen, L. and Manion, L. (1981) *Perspectives on Classrooms and Schools*, Holt, Rinehart & Winston, London.

Cohen, L. and Manion, L. (1985) *Research Methods in Educational Research*, 2nd edition, Croom Helm, London.

Cortazzi, D. and Roote, S. (1975) *Illuminative Incident Missing Half*, Manchester University Press.

Coxon, A. P. M. (1984) 'Bringing Accounts Back In: Formal Data and Subjects' Accounts'. Paper presented to British Psychological Society Conference, City University.

Davies, L. (1985) 'Ethnography and Status: Focusing on Gender in Educational Research', in Burgess, R. G. (1985a).

Davies, M. and Kelly, E. (1976) 'The Social Worker, the Client and the Social Anthropologist', *British Journal of Social Work*, vol. 6, no. 2, pp. 213–31.

Denicolo, P. (1984) 'A Metacommentary on Metaphor and its Research'. Paper presented to the Annual Conference for Postgraduate Psychology, Nottingham University, April.

DES (1981) 'The School Curriculum', HMSO, London.

DES (1982) 'Science Education in Schools – A Consultative Document', HMSO, London.

DES (1984) 'Science in Schools, Age 15: Report No 2: Report to the DES, DENI and WOED on the 1981 survey of 15-year-olds', HMSO, London.

Donaldson, M (1980) *Children's Minds*, Fontana.

Durant, H. (1946) 'The Cheater Problem', *Public Opinion Quarterly*, vol. 10 pp. 288–91.

Ebbutt, D. (1981) 'Girls' Science, Boys' Science Revisited', in Kelly, A. (ed.) *The Missing Half*, Manchester University Press.

Ebbutt, D. and Watts, D.M. (1986) 'Science is like a Spider's Web? Sixth Formers' Perceptions of their Science Education 11–16', *Secondary Science Curriculum Review*, London.

Elliott, J. (1985) 'Facilitating Action Research: Some Dilemmas' in Burgess R. G. (ed.) (1983) *Experiencing Comprehensive Education: A Study of Bishop McGregor School*, Methuen, London.

Engle-Clough, M. E. (1984) 'The Development of Understanding of Selected

Aspects of Pressure, Heat and Evolution in Pupils Aged between 12 and 16 Years'. Unpublished PhD. Thesis, University of Leeds.

Flavell, J. H. (1963) *The Developmental Psychology of Jean Piaget*, Van Nostrand, New York.

Gilbert, J. K. and Pope, M. L. (1983) 'Children Discussing Energy', Mimeograph, Department of Educational Studies, University of Surrey, Guildford.

Gilbert, J. K. and Watts, D. M. (1983) 'Concepts, Misconceptions and Alternative Conceptions', *Studies in Science Education*, 10, pp. 67–98.

Gilbert, J. K., Watts, D. M. and Osborne, R. J. (1985) 'Eliciting Student Views Using an Interview-About-Instances Technique,' in West, L. H. T. and Pines, A. L. (1985) (eds), *Cognitive Structure and Conceptual Change*, Academic Press, London.

Glaser, B. and Strauss, A. (1967) *The Discovery of Grounded Theory*, Weidenfeld & Nicolson.

Goffman, E. (1971) *Presentation of Self in Everyday Life*, Penguin, Harmondsworth. First published 1959, Doubleday, New York.

Hammersley, M. (1979) 'Data Collection Procedures', Open University DE304 Block 4, Part 3 p. 168 ff.

Harris, K. (1979) *Education and Knowledge*, Routledge & Kegan Paul, London.

Hedges, A. (1985) 'Group Interviewing', in R. Walter (ed.) *Applied Qualitative Research*, Gower, Aldershot.

Hodgson, V. (1984) 'Learning from Lectures', in F. Marton, D. Hounsell and N. Entwistle (1984) (eds) *The Experience of Learning*, Scottish Academic Press, Edinburgh.

Hoinville, G. (1983) 'Methodological Research on Sample Surveys – A Review of Developments in Britain'. Paper prepared as Part of Survey Methods Centre's work at Social and Community Planning Research funded by SSRC.

Hoinville, G., Jowell, R. *et al.* (1977) *Survey Research Practice*, Heinemann Educational Books, London.

Holland, J. (1981) 'Social Class and Changes in Orientation to Meaning', *Sociology*, 15, 1, February.

Hull, C. (1984) 'Between the Lines: Data Analysis as an Exact Art, Research Intelligence', *British Educational Research Association*, No. 15. January.

Hull, C. (1985) 'Between the Lines: The Analysis of Interview Data as an Exact Art', *British Educational Research Journal*, 11, 1, pp. 27–33.

Johnson, J. M. (1982) 2nd edition *Doing Fieldwork*, Collier-Macmillan, The Free Press, London.

Johnson, N. (1983) 'Using Networks to Represent Karen's Knowledge of Maths in Bliss, J. et al. op. cit.

Kelly, G. A. (1955) *The Psychology of Personal Constructs*, vols 1 and 2, Norton, New York.

Kelly, G. A. (1969) 'Ontological Acceleration', in B. Maher (ed.) *Clinical Psychology and Personality: The Collected Papers of George Kelly*, John Wiley, New York.

196

Kitwood, T. M. (1977) 'Values in Adolescent Life: Towards a Critical Description', unpublished Ph.D thesis, School of Research in Education, University of Bradford

Leavis, F. R. (1943) *Education and the University*, Chatto & Windus, London.

LITRIP (1985) 'A Collaborative Survey of Teachers' Perceived Needs in Their Language Teaching', Sheffield Polytechnic

Logan, T. (1984) 'Learning Through Interviewing' in Schoslak, J. and Logan, T., *Pupil Perspectives* by Croom Helm, London.

McDonald, B. and Sanger, J. (1982) 'Just for the record? Notes towards a theory of interviewing in evaluation'. Paper presented to the Annual Meeting of the American Educational Research Association, 19–23 March 1982, New York, in a symposium entitled 'Evaluation Methodology'.

Madge, J. (1953) *The Tools of Social Science*, Longmans, Green and Co., London.

Malinowski, B. (1922) *Argonauts of the Western Pacific*, Routledge & Kegan Paul, London.

Marketing Direction Limited (1984), 'Results of Stage 1 (Qualitative) Research to Evaluate the "Understanding Electricity" service for schools', The Electricity Council.

Marsh, C. (1982) *The Survey Method: The Contribution of Surveys to Sociological Explanation*, Contemporary Social Research Series No. 6, Allen & Unwin.

Marton, F. (1981) 'Phenomenography – describing conceptions of the world around us', *Instructional Science*, 10, pp. 177–200.

Marton, F., Hounsell, D. and Entwistle, N. (1984) (eds) *The Experience of Learning*, Scottish Academic Press, Edinburgh.

Massarik, F. (1981) 'The Interviewing Process Re-examined', in Reason, P. and Rowan, J. (eds) *Human Inquiry: A Sourcebook of New Paradigm Research*, John Wiley, Chichester.

Mehrabian, A. (1969) *Silent Messages*, Belmont, California.

Nixon, J. (1981) *A Teacher's Guide to Action Research*, Grant-McIntyre.

Novak, J. D. and Gowin, D. B. (1984) *Learning How to Learn*, Cambridge University Press.

Open University (1979) 'Data Collection Procedures', Block 4, DE304, *Research Methods in Education and the Social Sciences*, Open University Press.

Opie, I. and Opie, P. (1969) *Children's Games in Street and Playground*, Clarendon Press, Oxford.

Osborne, R. and Freyberg, P. (1985) *Learning in Science. The Implications of Childrens Science*, Heinemann, London.

Piaget, J. (1929) *The Child's Conception of the World*, Harcourt Brace, New York.

Piaget, J. (1930) *The Child's Conception of Physical Causality*, Routledge & Kegan Paul, London.

Pines, A. L. and Leith, S. (1981) 'What is Concept Learning in Science? Theory, Recent Research and Some Teaching Suggestions', *Australian Science Teachers Journal*, 27, 3.

197

Platt, J. (1981) 'On Interviewing One's Peers', *British Journal of Sociology*, 32, 1, March.

Pollard, A. (1985) 'Opportunities and Difficulties of a Teacher Ethnographer: A Personal Account', in Burgess, R., 1985a.

Pope, M. L. and Keen, T. R. (1981) *Personal Construct Psychology and Education*, Academic Press, London.

Pope, M., Watts, D. M. and Gilbert, J. K. (1983) 'Constructive Educational Research'. Paper presented at the 9th Annual Conference of B.E.R.A., London University Institute of Education, September.

Posner, G. J. (1979) 'Tools for Curriculum Research and Development: Potential Contributions from Cognitive Science', *Curriculum Inquiry*, 8, 4, pp. 311–40.

Powney, J. (1982) 'The Interview – An Underestimated Technique'. Paper presented at the 8th Annual Conference of B.E.R.A. at the University of St Andrews, September.

Powney, J. and Watts, M. D. (1984) 'Reporting Interviews – A Code of Good Practice', *Research Intelligence*, September.

Reason, P. and Rowan, J. (1981) (eds) *Human Inquiry: A Sourcebook of New Paradigm Research*, John Wiley, Chichester.

Rosenthal, R. and Jacobsen, L. (1968) *Pygmalion in the Classroom: Teacher Expectation and Pupils' Intellectual Development*, London, Holt, Rinehart and Winston.

Rutter, M., Maughan, B., Mortimore, P. and Ouston, J. (1979) *15000 Hours: Secondary Schools and Their Effects on Children*, Open Books, London.

Ryder, N. (1978) *Science, Television and the Adolescent*, Independent Broadcasting Authority, London.

Saljo, R. (1982) 'Learning and Understanding: A Study of Differences in Constructing Meaning from Text', *Goteborg Studies in Educational Sciences*, 41, University of Goteborg, Sweden.

Saran, R. (1985) 'The Use of Archives and Interviews in Research on Educational Policy', in Burgess, R. G. (ed.) *Strategies of Educational Research: Qualitative Methods*, Falmer Press, Sussex.

Scott, S., (1985) 'Working Through the Contradictions in Researching Postgraduate Education' in Burgess, R. G. (1985a).

Secondary Sciences Curriculum Review (1983) Science Education 11–16: 'Proposals for Action and Consultation', SSCR, London.

Shaffir, B., Stebbins, R. A., Turowetz, A. (1980) *Fieldwork Experience*, St Martin's Press, New York.

Sharp, R. and Green, A. (1975) *Education and Social Control – A Study in Progressive Primary Education*, Routledge & Kegan Paul, London.

Sheatsley, P. B. (1949) 'The Influence of Sub-Questions on Interviewers' Performance', *Public Opinion Quarterly*, vol. 13, pp. 310–13.

Simons, H. (1981) 'Conversation Piece', in Adelman, C. (ed.) *Uttering, Muttering: Collecting, Using and Reporting Talk for Social and Educational Research*, Grant McIntyre, London.

Southgate, V., Arnold, H. and Johnson, S. (1981) *Extending Beginning Reading*, Heinemann Educational for the Schools Council.

Spector, M. (1980) 'Learning to Study Public Figures' in Shaffir, W. et al. (Eds), op. cit.

Spradley, J. P. (1979) *The Ethnographic Interview*, Holt, Rinehart & Winston, New York.

Stenhouse, L. (1979) 'The Problems of Standards in Illuminative Research'. Lecture given at the Annual General Meeting of the Scottish Educational Research Association. University of Glasgow, mimeo

Swift, D. J., Watts, D. M. and Pope, M. L. (1983) 'Methodological Pluralism and Personal Construct Psychology: A Case for Pictorial Methods of Eliciting Personal Constructions.' Paper presented to the 5th International Congress on Personal Construct Psychology, Boston, Massachusetts, July.

Sykes, W. and Hoinville, G. (1985) 'Telephone Interviewing on a Survey of Social Attitudes: A Comparison with Face-to-Face Procedures', Social and Community Planning Research, London.

Thomas Fox Jr., G. (1981) 'Pictures of a Thousand Words: Using Graphics in Classroom Interviews', in Adelman, C. (1981) (ed.) *Uttering, Muttering: Collecting, Using and Reporting Talk for Social and Educational Research*, Grant McIntyre, London.

Tizard, B. *et al.* (1980) *15000 Hours: A Discussion*. University of London, Institute of Education.

Walker, R. (1985) *Doing Research: A Handbook for Teachers*, Methuen, London.

Watts, D. M. (1983a) 'Some Alternative Views of Energy', *Physics Education* 18, pp. 213–17.

Watts, D. M. (1983b) 'A Study of Alternative Frameworks in School Science'. Unpublished Ph.D.Thesis, University of Surrey, Guildford.

Watts, D. M. (1984) 'Alternative Framework – An Alternative to Piaget?'. Paper presented to the British Educational Research Association Conference, Lancaster, August 1984.

Watts, D. M. and Bentley, D. (1985) 'Methodological Congruity in Principle and Practice: A Dilemma in Science Education', *Journal of Curriculum Studies* (in press).

Watts, D. M. and Powney, J. (1985) 'Levels of Truth'. Paper presented to the British Educational Research Association Symposium 'Interviewing', University of Sheffield, September.

*Webster's Dictionary* (1983).

Wells, G. (1981) 'Describing Children's Linguistic Development at Home and at School', in Adelman, C. (ed.) *Uttering, Muttering: Collecting, Using and Reporting Talk for Social and Educational Research*, Grant McIntyre, London.

Whitehurst, G. J. (1979) 'Meaning and Semantics', in Whitehurst, G. J. and Zimmerman, B. J. (eds) *The Functions of Language and Cognition*. Academic Press, New York.

Whyte, W. F. (1981) *Street Corner Society*, 3rd edn, University of Chicago Press.

Woods, P. (1979) *The Divided School*, Routledge & Kegan Paul, London.

199

Woods, P. (1985) 'Conversations with Teachers: Some Aspects of Life-history Method', *British Educational Research Journal*, 11, 1, pp. 13–26.

Wragg, E. (ed.) (1979) *15000 hours, Perspectives*, School of Education, University of Exeter.

Wragg, E. C. (1981) *Conducting and Analysing Interviews*, Rediguide 11, Nottingham University.

Young, M. (1980) 'A Case Study of the Limitations of Policy Research', in Tizard, B., Burgess, T., Francis, H., Young, M. and Hewison, J., *15000 Hours: A Discussion*. University of London, Institute of Education.

Zuckerman, H. (1972) 'Interviewing an Ultra Elite', *Public Opinion Quarterly*. vol. 36, pp. 159–75.

# Author index

# Subject index